FOAL

# THE BUS ON JAFFA ROAD

*A Story of Middle East Terrorism
and the Search for Justice*

## MIKE KELLY

LYONS PRESS
Guilford, Connecticut
Helena, Montana

*An imprint of Rowman & Littlefield*

*For my mother, Patricia, and my father, Edwin,*
*who always encouraged me to read and to be curious*

An imprint of Rowman & Littlefield

Distributed by NATIONAL BOOK NETWORK

British Library Cataloguing in Publication Information available

Library of Congress Cataloging-in-Publication Data available

ISBN 978-0-7627-8037-2

∞™ The paper used in this publication meets the minimum requirements of American National Standard for Information Sciences—Permanence of Paper for Printed Library Materials, ANSI/NISO Z39.48-1992.

# Contents

*Put me as a seal upon your heart . . . for love is as strong as death.*

—SONG OF SONGS, 8:6

# PROLOGUE

# Ten Years Later ...

HE DIDN'T LOOK LIKE A KILLER.

No. Not this squat, stocky man with the hook nose, the nervous smile, and the brown eyes that darted across the prison meeting room, sizing up the metal chairs, the wooden table, the prison guards, and, finally, me.

But killer he was. And, as I would soon discover, Hassan Salameh was proud of the deaths he had caused.

I had traveled all morning to this maximum-security detention center in the Negev desert of southern Israel, leaving my Jerusalem hotel at dawn in a cramped Toyota with a driver, a translator, and a photographer. It was Sunday, the first day of the workweek in Israel, and we wanted to embark before the morning traffic clogged the city's roads and highways.

As the sun peeked over the Mount of Olives, we drove along the stone walls of Jerusalem's Old City and rolled by a row of palm trees near the Damascus Gate. We crossed Jaffa Road, then cut through the western hills and passed the patches of sleek cedars and the craggy limestone outcroppings that take on a soft, rose-colored glow in the early morning sun. After several miles, the land sloped downward to a grassy plain that stretched like a lush, green blanket all the way to the Mediterranean Sea. For centuries, these flatlands were considered a convenient, all-too-inviting pathway for invading armies who saw Jerusalem as a prize to capture. On this day, the only invaders were a line of tired-looking trucks carting crates of vegetables from Israeli farms and commuters rushing to their city jobs.

"So you want to talk to Salameh?" the Israeli prison officer asked when he called my Jerusalem hotel a day earlier.

"Yes," I said.

"We're talking about a high-profile terrorist with a lot of blood on his hands," the officer said.

"I know," I answered. "Several of his victims were Americans. That's why I want to speak to him."

The officer paused.

"But I don't know if he'll talk to you."

⌒⌒

My journey to the prison in the desert did not start in Jerusalem or even with that brief phone call. In ways I never could have expected at the time, it began several years earlier and thousands of miles away—on a Hudson River pier in Jersey City, New Jersey.

On the morning of September 11, 2001, I stepped from that pier to the deck of a tugboat and crossed the Hudson to reach the sixteen-acre landscape of national pain that came to be known as "Ground Zero." Standing on the deck with me that morning was a team of Jersey City firefighters who volunteered to rescue survivors from the rubble and several Roman Catholic priests who pledged to pray over the dead—all of us heading into a landscape and, indeed, a nation that had become suddenly surreal.

The seemingly impregnable twin towers of the World Trade Center, which had gleamed like a glass and steel tuning fork above New York City and the surrounding suburbs for three decades, had collapsed an hour earlier in a massive cloud of gray-brown dust. As the tug cut through the choppy Hudson and US Air Force fighter jets ripped across the cloudless sky, no one talked. Or, if they spoke, the tone was hushed, almost a whisper. Drawing nearer to the Manhattan shoreline, we clustered on one side of the tug, gazing at the billowing smoke. As a journalist, I had covered my share of disturbing stories—stories that did not seem to have a logical beginning, middle, and ending. But the scene I looked at from the side of the tugboat was deeply unsettling. Two giant skyscrapers. Gone. I assumed thousands had died. And with the news already choked with reports of a terrorist attack, I wondered where this story would end—if it would end at all.

I stepped onto the Manhattan side of the river with a pragmatic mission. I was a journalist in search of context, with a deadline rapidly approaching to file a column for my newspaper, *The (Bergen) Record*. In those early moments, I could think only of this day—what had to be written and when I had to finish. But as I walked quickly down sidewalks and streets covered with white ash and made my way to the pile of smoking rubble that rose more than seven stories above me, I found myself wrestling with a question that seemed to defy easy answers or deadlines: What should I make of all this?

As the months and years wore on and I followed the discordant ripples of this story to victims' funerals; to hearings with the 9/11 Commission in Washington, DC; to detention centers at the US Naval Base in Guantanamo Bay, Cuba; and to Iraq as my newspaper's correspondent at the side of National Guard soldiers from New Jersey who had left their families and jobs behind for a war few understood, I continually returned to that question and its ever-elusive answers.

As expected, the 9/11 attacks left America with deep and painful wounds. The robust economy of the 1990s soon sputtered. Now otherwise confident and capable politicians seemed baffled about how to handle basic concepts of personal liberty, civil rights, and even methods of waging war in a world transformed by international terrorism. But for all the wide-ranging political, economic, military, and constitutional questions in the aftermath of 9/11, I found that some of the most painful were being voiced by ordinary people who lost sons and daughters that day, mothers and fathers, husbands and wives, friends. Why did their loved ones die? What should they make of all this?

For them, terrorism was personal. An emotional hole had suddenly been ripped into their lives, impossible to understand yet impossible to forget. As one father told me as he reflected on the daughter he lost: "It will always be eleven o'clock in the morning. That's when I knew she was gone."

Some relatives of victims sank into the understandable quicksand of bitterness. Some tried to pour their heated cauldrons of anger into charitable projects. Some enlisted in the military. Some showed up at "Ground Zero" and pleaded with rescue teams for a chance to help dig through the rubble. A few became political activists, testifying before the 9/11

Commission or volunteering to steer public policy debates about new safety rules for skyscrapers or how America could revamp its intelligence agencies to protect itself from future terrorist attacks. Most retired silently into private emotional caves, nurturing their wounded lives and trying to make sense of the fact that someone they loved had been randomly killed in the name of a political and theological agenda.

In some ways, I found that the most devastating legacy of 9/11 was the damage those attacks did to ordinary people who were left to wonder why their loved ones died—innocents murdered, with the suicide-killers claiming their bloody act gave them a ticket to a heavenly paradise with lush gardens and a long line of beautiful virgins to tend to their desires. No answers or explanations really made sense. Not one. And, after chronicling the personal stories of victims from the 9/11 attacks for several years, I kept returning to the same question that haunted me that first day at "Ground Zero": What should I make of all this?

On many weekends, I began to take long walks through the town I call home, Teaneck, New Jersey. Invariably, I found myself stopping at the local library, sometimes finding a half hour of peace by browsing the shelves of history books or novels. As I left the library to head home, I usually walked along the edge of a parking lot and past the municipal offices that keep track of taxes, traffic tickets and building permits. And there, in the shade of a katsura tree, I often stopped by a statue of a young woman bending to smell a rosebush.

The statue is called *An Unfinished Life*.

It commemorates a woman who had been killed in a terrorist attack a few years earlier.

I had seen this statue before. Indeed, I had stopped to study it occasionally over the years and to read the plaque on its stone base. But after the 9/11 attacks, I found myself pausing more often to reflect on the woman smelling the roses and what her unfinished life meant.

Her name was Sara, and five years before the 9/11 attacks, she had been killed by a Palestinian suicide bomber in Jerusalem who embraced the same brand of radicalized Islamist martyrdom theology as the al-Qaeda operatives who killed themselves and thousands of others by flying hijacked commercial jetliners into the World Trade Center. As a newspaper columnist, I wrote about her death soon after it occurred, focusing primarily on the irony that she had written sympathetic essays in college about Islam and the plight of displaced Palestinians, yet had died less than a year after her college graduation at the hands of a Palestinian who believed he would be granted his special martyr's place in heaven by killing himself and innocent people.

But how had America responded to Sara's death? How had the world? More importantly, could Sara's story, which took place before the 9/11 attacks, teach us lessons about the so-called "War on Terrorism" that erupted with the 9/11 attacks and seems to slog forward with no end in sight into the twenty-first century?

Like most journalists at the time, I moved on to other stories and other subjects not long after Sara was killed. For the most part, Sara's story disappeared from the media, eclipsed by other terrorist attacks of the 1990s and the passage of time that can make the news media I love and admire so much seem so callous and shallow, lacking in context and memory.

As America continued to cope years later with the fallout from its worst terrorist attack on September 11, 2001, I decided to look back. What I discovered was a piece of history that had been largely overlooked in the years after the 9/11 attacks and as America embarked on its "War on Terrorism." In some ways, this piece of history offered a lesson—a prescription, perhaps—of what was to come after 9/11. It also offered a warning of what to avoid.

During the late 1990s, more than a dozen Americans died in terrorist attacks in the Middle East along with hundreds of Israelis and Palestinians, often at the hands of suicide bombers who blew themselves up along with their victims as an act of Islamic spiritual fulfillment and political defiance. But the bombers who died usually did not act alone. What about those who planned or financed the attacks and built the bombs that killed so many people? Were any of them held accountable?

And what of the families of those American victims? What happened to them?

I decided to start with one attack—the bombing of a commuter bus on Jerusalem's Jaffa Road on February 25, 1996.

Sara died in that bombing.

But, as I was to discover, her legacy and life were hardly unfinished.

———

As we left Jerusalem and drove to the prison in the Negev, I thought of Sara and her unfinished life—and untimely death. What should I make of it—now?

After an hour's drive, we left the cooler hill-country temperatures behind and rolled into the outskirts of Beersheba, the ancient stop for caravans from Egypt. We could feel the heat now. The air seemed dry and dusty. The sun had already climbed high into the azure sky. Before us, the rocky Negev and its lumpy, treeless landscape stretched into a hazy, undefined horizon.

We passed several concrete box homes along the roadway with satellite TV dishes on their roofs, and rolled over a gentle hill. Beyond a palm grove, a Bedouin herder guided four camels toward a watering hole. After another hill, we saw Eshel Prison rising from the sand and rocks. We parked and walked to the front gate.

Minutes later, after passing through a metal detector, I was ushered into a small meeting room with a wooden table and several folding chairs. Lt. Col. Ian H. Domnitz of the Israeli Prison Service smiled and shook my hand.

"Hassan Salameh will be here in a minute," he said. "Then you'll have a chance to introduce yourself. We don't know if he'll talk to you. He has no idea you are coming."

Unlike their American counterparts, Israeli prisons have a unique system for allowing journalists to speak to inmates. In America, journalists are generally required to submit a letter to prison officials, explaining why they want to interview an inmate. If prison officials approve, the letter is then passed to the inmate—or perhaps to the inmate's lawyer—who then makes a final decision. In Israel, if prison officials approve a visit by a journalist, the inmate is simply told that he has a "visitor."

The inmate is brought to a room, and the journalist has a minute or two to explain the purpose of the visit. At that point the inmate has a choice: To talk or to tell the journalist to get lost.

With forty-six life sentences to serve for a series of bombings he orchestrated during the mid-1990s, Hassan Salameh was arguably one of Israel's most notorious terrorists. He not only recruited young men to be suicide bombers; he built the bombs and selected the targets. But I wanted to talk to Salameh about just one incident, the bombing of a Jaffa Road commuter bus in Jerusalem a decade earlier.

I heard a steel door slam, then the shuffle of feet and the chunky clang of leg irons growing louder in the hallway. The door to the meeting room opened, and Hassan Salameh paused for a second or two and looked around the room. Then, he stepped forward. The guards removed his handcuffs and leg irons.

Thinking about this moment during the car ride from Jerusalem, I figured I would be able to ask at least one question before Salameh decided to speak or return to his cell. And so, I thought of the young woman from New Jersey—the woman depicted as smelling roses in the statue near the library of her hometown. An Unfinished Life.

I opened my notebook and turned on my recorder.

I looked into Salameh's eyes.

"Do you know the name Sara Duker?" I asked.

"Yes," he said, quickly and unflinchingly.

"Why did you kill her?" I asked.

# PART I

# FIRE

# CHAPTER 1

Sara wanted to catch an early bus that morning. Although she had been out late the night before, meeting with a women's prayer group in central Jerusalem, she awoke before dawn in the apartment she shared with several young women on the bottom floor of a boxy, four-story concrete building across the street from an Israeli Health Ministry annex and down the block from a synagogue.

It was February 25, 1996, a Sunday, around six o'clock in the morning. The sun was not scheduled to rise for another twelve minutes. A persistent shroud of thick clouds and chilly mist hugged the city and forecasters said the weather probably wouldn't change much that day. It was, after all, still winter in Jerusalem. The dry sands of the Judean desert were less than thirty minutes away by car, on the ancient, arid roads that led to Jericho, the Jordan River, and the Dead Sea. But in February, Jerusalem's sharp hills and rock-strewn valleys were captive to the kind daily dose of dampness and clouds that seemed more suited to a New England fishing town.

On most days, Sara preferred long, flowery skirts, floppy hats and purple sneakers for her five-foot-two, one-hundred-pound frame. It was, friends often remarked, an iconic look for her, projecting an ethereal, carefree aura that masked the quiet, laser-sharp seriousness she brought to her science research and writing. On this day, though, the weather and trip she was about to take dictated a more functional wardrobe.

Sara pulled on a windbreaker, jeans and a pair of dark brown Vasque hiking boots. She slid her US passport into the windbreaker's left pocket along with an ID card from her new research job at Jerusalem's Hebrew University. Her right pocket held her wallet containing her New Jersey driver's license and Social Security card, an Israeli twenty-shekel note and a twenty-dollar American Express travelers cheque. She strapped a belt pack around her waist with another $210 in travelers cheques and a credit card, and packed a blue shoulder bag with computer printouts, pens, a handful of bus passes, and a water bill, presumably for her landlord when she returned. She slipped her graduation ring from Columbia University's Barnard College on her left ring finger, and looped a gold chain around her neck that held a hand-shaped pendant called a *hamsa*, the ancient symbol revered by Jews, Christians, and Muslims alike to keep away evil.

Then she stepped outside to catch a bus.

By her side was her boyfriend, Matt, who had walked from his apartment a mile away to join her that morning.

Sara Duker of Teaneck, New Jersey, and Matthew Eisenfeld of West Hartford, Connecticut, had been dating for almost two years. She was twenty-two years old and planning to embark on postgraduate studies in environmental science, perhaps in Israel or back in the United States. He turned twenty-five three weeks earlier, and was halfway through his second year of studies to become a rabbi.

In recent months, though, both had begun to seriously discuss marriage. Sara had not settled on a timeline yet, but, in a letter to Matt, she wrote that she was "realizing more and more what I want for my life, even if only in faint spurts," and while "both of us are moving to the fast track, we'll both become closer to grasping the distant things we seek."

Matt was more sure of what he wanted. He already confided to a rabbi that he hoped to marry Sara within the year and regularly repeated similar sentiments to friends. "He loved her deeply. I think Sara was a combination of brilliance, utterly devoid of pretension, and fun," said Shai Held, one of Matt's roommates in Jerusalem. Perhaps with a wedding on his mind and a future life with Sara, Matt had recently jotted down a list of goals on a piece of paper that he hung on the wall of the bedroom of the apartment he shared with Held and another rabbinical student. "Above all, we need to be happy," Matt wrote. "There is not enough time allotted to us to waste time in misery."

Their days in Jerusalem had been jammed mostly by work—Sara's with meticulous research at the basement microbiology lab on the Givat Ram campus of Hebrew University; Matt's with long hours of scriptural study as part of his year-old immersion at the Schechter Institute of Jewish Studies just down the hill from Sara's university lab. They tried to reserve a piece of each day for each other, if only for a short conversation or a stroll along the mile or so of winding tree-lined residential streets between Matt's apartment in Jerusalem's Rehavia neighborhood and Sara's near the city's San Simon section.

As much as academics had become the center of their routine, each also set aside pieces of their days to nurture their spiritual sides, too. After dinner the night before, Sara walked twenty minutes to the apartment of another American woman, Aliza Berger, who had moved to Israel and was building a career as a translator. Sara and Aliza shared a common interest in trying to find new ways to pray together as Jewish women. But at the same time, they were not religious revolutionaries; they wanted to remain close to Judaism's ancient rules that governed women's roles.

This sort of struggle for Jewish women was not unusual. By the mid-1990s, the spirit of feminism that had altered long-standing customs of politics, business, marriage, academics and other major elements of society had also begun to challenge some of the most fundamental traditions of most religions, from Christianity to Islam and Judaism. Beginning in college, Sara began to focus much of her efforts on toppling some of the walls that barred women from taking greater leadership roles in synagogue services.

Soon after arriving in Israel in the fall of 1995, Sara joined with Aliza and other Jewish women to recite morning prayers together on the Sabbath. But Aliza and several women in the group wondered if Sara was a bit too progressive. When Sara prayed, she draped a *tallit*—a prayer shawl—over her head, a ritual traditionally reserved only for Jewish men. Among some Jews, Sara's decision to pray with a tallit was considered far too radical or at least venturing into uncharted theological ground that had not been mapped by rabbis and scholars. To others, Sara's tallit was merely another example of how Judaism was adapting to modern times. Progressive synagogues had been welcoming women as rabbis for more than a decade and promoting egalitarian styles of worship with men and women. Only a few years earlier, Judaism's Conservative branch, which occupied the theological and liturgical middle ground between the Reform movement and the Orthodox branch, began ordaining women as rabbis. A core foundation of the Conservative movement was that Jews, while adhering to precepts of the Torah, should also adapt to modern life in ways that made sense. So, for instance, while Orthodox Jews customarily refrained from driving cars or using electrical appliances on the Sabbath, some Conservative Jews felt that such conveniences were necessary to modern life. With that sort of mindset, some felt it was only a matter of time before women in Conservative synagogues would pray regularly with tallits.

Certainly Sara already felt that way. At the same time, she also harbored an abiding respect for Judaism's most fundamental traditions. Though she attended an Orthodox-focused high school in New Jersey, her family belonged to a Conservative synagogue. By the 1980s, Sara's synagogue embraced a more egalitarian style of worship in which women took on greater roles in rituals and in the leadership of the congregation. Not surprisingly perhaps, Sara frequently led services at Barnard College that included men and women.

In college, she began praying with a tallit. But like other Jewish women who embarked on this new ritual, Sara adopted a slightly different approach—namely, in what her tallit looked like. Men's tallits, for instance, were traditionally white with black or blue stripes. To signal their sexual difference or perhaps independence and fashion flair, some women had embraced other colors. In Jerusalem, Sara's tallit was multi-colored—purple, with shades of lavender and blue, and with green stripes. "It was clear that she was comfortable with this," said Ayala Levin, who was one of the organizers of the women's group and who was weighing whether to wear a tallit, too. "Many people come to Jerusalem and wonder if this is going to have a spiritual effect on them. She was comfortable and happy in her own skin. You could see that. It showed through."

Earlier that day, the women gathered in a third-floor room at Jerusalem's Pardes Institute of Jewish Studies for morning Sabbath prayers. Sara walked to a podium and gently placed her tallit over her hair. Then, in a soft but confident voice, she steadily recited the opening Hebrew psalms of the traditional Sabbath ritual. Sara was the only woman in the room wearing a tallit that morning. As Ayala Levin watched from across the room, she marveled at how Sara's voice grew stronger. "She glowed and had a dynamism about her," Levin said.

Several women were not as impressed, though, and felt Sara had gone too far. Others, including a few who even supported Sara's wearing of a tallit, feared that the gesture might seem too progressive—too radically feminist, perhaps—and would turn off some women who had recently shown up.

On Saturday evening, after sunset and the end of the Sabbath, the women gathered at Aliza Berger's apartment to talk about the issue. Before the meeting began, Sara chatted easily with several women, describing the bus trip she planned the next morning with Matt. Then, she took a seat on a sofa.

Rahel Jaskow settled into a chair to Sara's right. Jaskow had not made a decision yet to wear a tallit but she was open to it. She prayed often with Sara on Friday nights at a neighborhood synagogue. And, after one evening service in which Sara wore her tallit, the two women walked out together.

Sara seemed aware that her tallit had been noticed. As she left the synagogue, she turned to Jaskow.

"Wow," said Sara. "I've caused quite a stir."

Sitting now, in Berger's apartment, Jaskow wondered what Sara might say.

Sara asked the women if she could speak first. She wanted to leave early.

Sara began by describing her commitment to Judaism and how she wanted to keep her faith as a guiding force of her life as a scientist and as a woman. Then she meticulously noted how Jewish traditions and scriptures had described the tallit as a method for Jews to fully express themselves in prayer. Sara wanted that complete expression. Why should she be denied because of her sex?

As she spoke, Rahel found herself transfixed by Sara's words, especially Sara's gentle phrasing and careful, scientific logic. Rahel noticed Sara's hair, brown, curly, flowing freely. She had admired Sara's hair before. But tonight it was different. As Ayala Levin had seen hours earlier during the morning prayers, Rahel Jaskow noticed now that Sara seemed to glow. "I caught this glimpse of her hair and there seemed to be a light around it," Rahel said. "I thought nothing of it at the time. I wondered if the glow was maybe a trick of the light in the room. But at the same time, it seemed to me that Sara had a great beauty about her that night."

Sara finished and stood up, explaining again that she was leaving early the next morning with Matt. As she walked to the door, the women called out together, "Have a great time."

After the door closed and Sara walked down the stairs to the street, the women thought about what she had said—and, perhaps just as important, the passion and soulfulness of her message. "Pure sincerity," said Aliza Berger.

That night, the eight women at Berger's apartment cast votes. They would permit women to wear tallits in their morning prayer services. But Sara never knew about the vote. She was home, packing and getting ready for bed.

Before Sara closed her eyes, she picked up the phone and dialed the number for her mother's cousin, Rivkah Fishman, and her husband, Joel, who lived in a nearby apartment. It was almost 11:30 p.m.

Rivkah was already in bed, reading a book, and reached for the phone on a bedside table.

"Hi, Rivkah. It's me."

Rivkah instantly recognized Sara's lilting voice. The Fishmans had a son and daughter of their own, but they had grown to think of Sara as a daughter. A decade before, after her father had died, Sara visited the Fishmans in Jerusalem with her mother and younger sisters. A few years after that, Sara dropped by again, this time with stories of how she was conducting biological research in the Red Sea.

On the phone, Sara's voice was light, airy. She seemed excited, but apologized for calling so late. She told Rivkah and Joel that she wanted them to know she was leaving early on Sunday for the beginning of a three-day vacation trek with Matt to neighboring Jordan—a long-awaited respite and reward for several months of intense study and work in Jerusalem.

"Be sure to see Petra," Rivkah said, mentioning the ancient Nabataean city that had been carved more than 2,300 years ago into a rocky canyon east of the Dead Sea.

Sara said Petra was on the itinerary that she and Matt had planned.

Rivkah mentioned one last request: Be sure to take photographs.

Sara said she would, then casually explained that she and Matt needed to catch several buses to get to Petra. The first leg of their journey, she said, was a short ride on a Jerusalem commuter bus to the city's central bus terminal on Jaffa Road.

⁂

The next morning, as Sara left her apartment with Matt to walk to a nearby commuter bus stop, a man stepped from a small apartment on the other side of Jerusalem and slipped into the passenger seat of a blue Opel sedan.

He was nineteen, a vocational trade student who grew up some thirty miles away in al-Fawwar, a Palestinian refugee community of roughly 6,500 residents near the West Bank city of Hebron. The man had left al-Fawwar a few days earlier, without telling his parents or his six brothers and four sisters where he was going. He traveled first to a mosque in Ramallah, and then was driven to a rented apartment in the Palestinian enclave of Abu Dis on the eastern edge of Jerusalem's Mount of Olives.

The man slept little as he waited for dawn on Sunday. Those who saw him later recalled that he seemed energetic and happy. He had prayed much of the night, reciting meditations in Arabic and reading from the Koran. He then showered, shaved, and dressed in new clothes purchased for him a few days earlier in the bustling Palestinian-owned shops on Salah al-Din Street in East Jerusalem that sell jeans, T-shirts, jackets, and all manner of baseball caps. His goal, acquaintances said, was to look like an Israeli student.

Over his shoulder, he carried a small black vinyl duffle bag that had been packed with approximately twenty pounds of explosives, extracted from American-made antitank land mines dug up near the Egyptian border in the Sinai Desert. During the night, as the young man prayed in the apartment, another man wired the explosives to detonate with the push of a button that had been attached to the shoulder strap on the duffle bag.

The bomb-maker handed the bag to the young man, and reviewed final instructions. Get on a commuter bus crowded with passengers. Don't draw attention to yourself. Wait a few minutes. Invoke Allah's name. Push the button. Expect to enter paradise.

"He was calm," the bomb-maker, Hassan Salameh, would say later of the young man with the shoulder bag. "He was ready. He was more calm than me."

The Opel's driver, a Palestinian security officer who was secretly affiliated with the militant Islamic Resistance Movement—also known as Hamas—navigated the narrow roads around the Mount of Olives, then rolled past the ancient Jewish cemetery, the gnarled, centuries-old olive trees in the Garden of Gethsemane and the stone arches of the Church of All Nations that enshrines the rock where Jesus of Nazareth is said to have prayed the night before he was crucified by Roman authorities. The road flattened out slightly and the Opel turned and crossed the ravine known as the Kidron Valley, then weaved through a series of hilly turns and passed under the northern walls to the Old City of Jerusalem and the gold Dome of the Rock mosque, which enshrines yet another historic rock that had been the centerpiece of the Holy of Holies in temples built by the ancient Israelites.

After another mile, the car stopped on Jaffa Road. The young man got out, carrying his black bag.

He walked to a bus stop and waited for the next commuter bus.

— ~ —

Fifty miles away, in the dusty, seaside Palestinian mecca known as Gaza City, one of the Middle East's most trusted diplomats awoke that Sunday and changed his travel plans.

Terje Roed-Larsen had come a long way from his youth amid the snow and frigid winds of Bergen, Norway. Now forty-eight years old, the gregarious Norwegian had become a familiar figure in the Middle East. As a sociologist in the 1980s, who had studied living conditions for Palestinians in the West Bank and along the Gaza Strip, and now as a diplomat and key architect of the 1993 Oslo Peace Accords, Larsen had earned the respect of both Israelis and Palestinians.

For many on both sides, the Oslo "process"—as it came to be known when it was signed in 1993 at the White House in Washington, DC, with President Bill Clinton, Israeli Prime Minister Yitzhak Rabin, and Palestinian leader Yasser Arafat—was considered the long-awaited breakthrough that would lead to a final peace agreement between two peoples who had fought for decades over the same rocky landscape. In return for an end to bombings and shootings by Palestinians, Israel offered to give back pieces of the West Bank, East Jerusalem, and the Gaza Strip that it had seized during the Six Day War in 1967. By February 1996, however, the land-for-peace process had hardly become an overwhelming success so Larsen was back in the Middle East, trying to keep the peace accords he had worked so hard to formulate from falling apart.

He left his diplomatic post with the Norwegian foreign ministry to take on a new job with the United Nations as its special representative to the fledgling Palestinian government and coordinator for UN aid to the West Bank, the Gaza Strip, and in East Jerusalem—the so-called "Palestinian territories."

As the UN's primary link to the Palestinians, Larsen held the equivalent rank of assistant UN secretary general and had several choices on where he could live. Each was fraught with political trip wires. There were Jerusalem and Tel Aviv, of course—centrally located, with easy access to the world's diplomatic community, not to mention the UN's offices and, in general, more modern homes. But Jerusalem and Tel Aviv had obvious disadvantages; they were located in Israel. If Larsen lived in Israel, he risked losing credibility with the Palestinians. He felt that his job demanded that he should live in the Palestinian territories.

Living in the Palestinian territories meant that Larsen had fewer choices for a home. An obvious possibility was Ramallah, the bustling Palestinian capital that had enveloped several hillsides about ten miles north of Jerusalem in the middle of the West Bank lands that many devout Jews now called by their ancient names of "Judea" and "Samaria" and that Palestinians referred to simply as "Palestine." But Larsen chose Gaza City, the dusty seaside stop on the road to Egypt that was now crowded with more than a half a million Palestinians. Another 1.1 million Palestinians lived elsewhere in the twenty-five-mile-long Gaza Strip, many clustered in what the UN still referred to as refugee camps, even though the tent villages established to care for Palestinians who left Israel after its founding in the late 1940s had now been replaced by concrete box homes along streets barely wide enough for a compact car to pass through. Gaza City was the business and political center of the Gaza Strip and if the United Nations representative wanted to be close to some of the most rampant problems affecting Palestinians, Gaza City was the place to be.

Larsen's residence was hardly cramped, dusty, or connected to the omnipresent poverty and hardship of Gaza's camps, though. He lived near the beach, in the city's former diplomatic neighborhood. From Larsen's home, the view, like so many in the Middle East, could be deceiving. If he gazed toward the Mediterranean, Larsen could sense the water's peaceful ebb and flow. Toward land, however, Gaza City was still a place where gunmen roamed, bombs exploded randomly, and assassins of all types lurked. It was, indeed, a dangerous place to call home. But perhaps the most significant reason Larsen chose Gaza City as his primary residence was the presence of one man he had grown to know well in recent years—Yasser Arafat.

Larsen's house was on the same block as Arafat's. These two key players in the Middle East conflict were neighbors. If they needed to talk, they didn't need to call on a convoy of armored SUVs, with a phalanx of burly, heavily armed bodyguards. They could simply open the front door and walk down the street.

Arafat was a night owl. He rarely held meetings when the sun was up. So on the evening of Saturday, February 24, 1996, as Sara Duker walked from her apartment in Jerusalem to meet with a Jewish women's prayer group, Larsen left his seaside villa in Gaza City and strolled up the block to meet with Arafat—a meeting that would impact Larsen's Sunday schedule.

Larsen did not have a fixed agenda when he spoke with Arafat that night—certainly nothing important that Larsen could recall when he described the evening get-together years later. It was, after all, not uncommon for Larsen to drop in on Arafat, if only to measure the mood of the mercurial voice of the Palestinian people and perhaps talk about the various twists and turns in the Oslo peace process.

Certainly the last few years had not been easy. Only months before the formal signing of the Oslo accords in a dramatic 1993 ceremony at the White House, Palestinian militants unveiled a new tactical weapon—suicide bombings, carried out by religious militants who espoused a radical Islamic theology that promised an instant path to paradise for any "martyr" who killed so-called "infidels." To the bombers, these infidels were Israelis and their crime was invading Muslim lands, which included Israel itself, the West Bank, the Gaza Strip, and East Jerusalem.

In that first bombing, a Palestinian operative drove a pickup truck loaded with explosives up to an Israeli bus that had stopped at a roadside cafe near Jericho. The Palestinian then detonated the explosives, killing himself and setting fire to the Israeli bus. No passengers were killed and only two were slightly injured. But that singular event was the beginning of one of the bloodiest periods in the long-running Israeli-Palestinian conflict. For Larsen and other diplomats—including many Israelis—a vexing concern was the fact that the suicide bombings were largely the work of two of the most radicalized groups in Gaza and the West Bank—Palestinian Islamic Jihad and Hamas.

Suicide martyrdom was not entirely new to Islam. But when it occurred throughout history—and by no means was it common—it was largely the work of intensely militant factions of Shiite Muslims. Most Palestinians were Sunni Muslims. And while neither the leaders of Palestinian Islamic Jihad or Hamas had come forward yet with detailed explanations of why their groups had embraced suicide martyrdom, counterterror experts in Israel and the United States pointed to the 1992 deportation of more than four hundred Palestinian militants to Lebanon as a watershed event. When sent to Lebanon, the displaced Palestinian militants were cared for by members of the Hezbollah party, largely Shiite, with the hefty financial backing of the Islamic Republic of Iran.

Hezbollah militants had long promoted suicide bombing as a tactic, with the most dramatic example being the bombing of the US Marine barracks in 1983 in which 220 Marines, eighteen Navy sailors and three US army soldiers had been killed. A year after deporting the Palestinian militants to Lebanon, Israel relented and allowed them to return to the West Bank and to the Gaza Strip. Within months, the first suicide bombing took place.

To Israel's primary counterterror agency, the General Security Service—better known as Shin Bet—that initial suicide bombing was hardly accidental. "The Palestinians had adopted the tactics of the Shiites," one of Shin Bet's top analysts, Barak Ben-Zur, would say later. But few members of Shin Bet could foresee the carnage that was to come.

Certainly, Terje Roed-Larsen did not see the ominous trend. On that Saturday in late February 1996, when he met with Arafat, suicide bombings were not as much of an immediate concern. Yes, there had been other suicide attacks, including one less than a year earlier in the Gaza Strip when a twenty-year-old American student from Brandeis University, Alisa Flatow of West Orange, New Jersey, had been killed by a suicide bomber who drove an explosives-laden pickup truck into an Israeli bus. Alisa Flatow had been a student at the same North Jersey Jewish high school as Sara Duker and had come to Israel while in college to deepen her knowledge of Judaism. While Alisa's father, Stephen Flatow, had begun to give emotional speeches across America about his daughter's murder, the issue of suicide bombings had not gained the kind of diplomatic or political traction yet that it would in years to come.

In fact, Palestinian militants had not attempted a suicide bombing in months. And six weeks earlier, Shin Bet agents killed the chief Palestinian bomb-maker for suicide operations, Yahya Ayyash, who had been nicknamed "The Engineer" because of his expertise in assembling explosives. Ayyash's bomb-making fingerprints seemed to be everywhere. Shin Bet investigators said he played a direct role in at least five bombings. But his influence had become even more widespread. Ayyash recruited other bomb-makers and passed on his skills at building deadly explosives. Shin Bet believed he had been indirectly involved in as many as a dozen other attacks. One of his compatriots played a supporting role in the plot that killed Alisa Flatow. And Israeli agents also had discovered that Ayyash had designed a "suicide vest" for bombers to hide explosives under their coats.

"Ayyash was to Israelis what Osama bin Laden later became to Americans," an Israeli counterterrorism agent explained.

In early January 1996, Shin Bet investigators tracked Ayyash to the Gaza Strip and planted a cell phone loaded with explosives in the home where he was staying. When Ayyash put the phone to his ear to make a call, an Israeli counterterrorism official monitoring the phone from an electronic listening post in Israel pushed a button. The phone exploded, killing Ayyash instantly.

Ayyash's funeral on the following day in Gaza City became a cascade of anger against Israel. More than one hundred thousand Palestinians crowded into Gaza City's dusty streets. In the following days, a variety of Palestinian radical groups vowed to avenge Ayyash's killing with some sort of terrorist operation against Israel.

But no attacks took place—not immediately. By early February, from its vast web of Palestinian contacts and double agents within the Gaza Strip and on the West Bank, Shin Bet picked up a variety of signals that Hamas was organizing some sort of bombing attack. But where and when? Shin Bet had no precise details, only a vague warning.

By February 11, Israeli military and counterterror leaders decided that the warnings had become too ominous. Roads to Israel from the Gaza Strip and the West Bank were sealed, blocking some fifty thousand Palestinian workers from commuting to jobs in Israel and thousands of others from visiting relatives. Israeli leaders said that the goal was to stop any terrorist teams from sneaking across the border.

But the roadblocks were too late. On Friday, February 2, Hassan Salameh ate lunch with his family, then told his wife, whom he had married only four months before, that he needed to report to work at a plastics factory.

Salameh left but never came home. Hamas operatives drove him to a desert road near a fence that separates Israel from the Gaza Strip. As night fell and after Israeli military patrols passed by, Salameh slipped under the fence and crossed into Israel, carrying a satchel of explosives.

He hid in an orange grove for the next week. Then on February 12— the day after Israel sealed its borders—Salameh met with Hamas activists in Hebron to recruit a team of operatives who would help him mount an attack.

The Shin Bet, while extremely worried about warning signs of a revenge mission for Ayyash's death, had no idea yet of Salameh's plans—or even that Salameh had crossed the border. Earlier that week, Ami Ayalon, a former Israeli Navy admiral whose heroism as a commando had earned him Israel's equivalent of the Medal of Honor, took command of Shin Bet. As he reflected on the moment years later, Ayalon remembered how the focus of the agency was not so much on the Palestinian threat but on what he feared at the time was a rising tide of "Israeli fundamentalism."

Four months earlier, Israeli Prime Minister Yitzhak Rabin had been assassinated by an Israeli who had become disgruntled with the Olso process and the turnover of pieces of the West Bank and the Gaza Strip to the Palestinians. To some devoutly religious Israelis—whom Ayalon and others considered to be fundamentalists—the West Bank, along with Israel itself and the Gaza Strip, was the original land of Israel that God had given to Abraham and his descendants. To give this land away was considered a religious sacrilege.

Such was the mindset of Rabin's assassin. Increasingly, it seemed to be a view embraced by a small number of Israeli extremists who sometimes attacked Palestinians. Two years earlier, on February 25, 1994, in the ancient city of Hebron, an American-born Israeli doctor, Baruch Goldstein, carried a semiautomatic rifle into the mosque that adjoins a small synagogue above the Cave of Patriarchs, which Jews, Christians, and Muslims all venerate as the burial place of such spiritual figures as Abraham, Isaac, Jacob, Sarah, Rebecca, and Leah. Witnesses say Goldsein said nothing as he aimed his rifle and meticulously shot twenty-nine Muslim worshippers to death and wounded another 125. He stopped only after onlookers overpowered him with a fire extinguisher and then beat him to death.

Terje Roed-Larsen was well versed in the wide variety of increasingly complicated and volatile problems that had emerged in recent months in Israel. But when he entered Arafat's residence that Saturday evening, he merely wanted to talk about a few mundane concerns involving living conditions for Palestinians in Gaza. The issue had been an abiding concern for Larsen. And that night he did not find an answer with Arafat.

As Larsen got up to leave, however, the conversation changed in a way that startled Larsen. Arafat asked Larsen what he planned to do the next day—Sunday, February 25, 1996.

Larsen told Arafat that he was thinking of spending the day in Jerusalem. Arafat paused. The Palestinian leader seemed concerned but somewhat at a loss for words. Larsen knew Arafat often spoke in cryptic ways—not always explaining clearly what was on his mind but nevertheless sending signals. This time was no exception.

"Why don't you stay away from Jerusalem on Sunday," Arafat told Larsen.

Larsen left and went home.

What exactly did Arafat mean? The Palestinian leader's words were unspecific—far too vague. But it was the tone of Arafat's voice that bothered Larsen.

Larsen pondered Arafat's warning through the night. On Sunday morning, he canceled his trip to Jerusalem and decided to say put in Gaza City.

Around 6:30 in the morning on that Sunday, Sara Duker and Matt Eisenfeld stood at a corner bus stop that was just down the hill from Sara's apartment and near a vegetable market.

Minutes later, a red and white commuter bus pulled up. Matt and Sara got on. They paid their fares and shuffled toward the back where a group of soldiers, home on weekend leaves, stood with duffels and backpacks. The bus turned onto Emek Refaim Street, a busy, winding thoroughfare that runs from the city's southern neighborhoods and eventually approaches the walls of Jerusalem's "Old City." Matt grabbed a seat by a window on the driver's side of the bus. Sara sat down next to him, on the aisle.

From a seat across the aisle and near the bus's rear door, Leah Stein Mousa, a hospital administrator who grew up in New York City but had lived more than two decades in Jerusalem's San Simon neighborhood, watched the young couple settle into their seats. "I could tell they were Americans because they spoke English," Mousa later remembered, still bearing traces of her New York accent. "I could also see they were in love."

If there is a bus that defines Jerusalem, it is the one Sara and Matt rode that day. The Number 18 bus, often simply called "the 18," is the numeric symbol for the Hebrew word, *Chai*—to life. Much like New York City's "A" subway line—the so-called "A Train" immortalized by the bouncy tune written by Billy Strayhorn that became a staple of the Duke Ellington orchestra—the Number 18 bus, operated by Israel's Egged bus line, is a transportation icon, traversing Jerusalem's diverse neighborhoods, like a thread that connects different pieces of colorful fabric. The Number 18 bus route starts on the western edges of Jerusalem and winds through the hills near Mount Herzl, then loops through the working class streets of San Simon and skirts the edge of the industrial zone of Talpiot before turning onto Emek Rafaim Street and cutting through the German Colony, home of many diplomats, academics, and journalists. After the bus climbs a series of hills toward the limestone walls of Jerusalem's Old City and the Jaffa Gate, it turns onto Jaffa Road, and passes city hall, the police station and several miles of small shops and cafes before rolling into Jerusalem's Central Bus Station.

The passengers are generally a demographic equivalent of a tossed salad—proud Arabs whose families may have fled to West Bank refugee camps after Israel's founding in 1948, students from Hasidic schools whose families have persevered in Jerusalem for centuries, Israeli soldiers home on weekend leaves and Christian backpackers from Europe or the United States trying to trace the steps of Jesus of Nazareth and his first-century disciples. On any given day, the bus might also be filled with clerks, grocers, government bureaucrats, students, and tourists—a cross-section of Jerusalem's workers.

Sara Duker had long marveled at the mix of lives and personalities on Jerusalem's buses. A few weeks before, in an e-mail to friends at Barnard College in Manhattan, she wrote: "Those of you who have been here before know that bus-riding is a quintessential Israeli experience—the opportunity to come into contract with the true national character."

February 25, 1996 was no different on the Number 18 bus.

Yonatan Barnea, a twenty-year-old Israeli soldier who lived in the German Colony, was heading back to his base. His father, Nahum, one of Israel's most influential newspaper columnists, rose early and drove his son to the bus stop, then headed to his office to see what kind of news would emerge that day.

At another stop, Jeffery Sosland, an American graduate student who was in Israel to study how the region's limited water resources had impacted politics, also got on in the German Colony. Like Matt and Sara, he was also heading to Jordan. But he planned to catch a charter bus at a stop closer to the Old City. Matt and Sara were heading to the Central Bus Terminal.

Jana Kushnirov, a thirty-six-year-old mother who emigrated from the Ukraine three years earlier, got on at another stop with her thirty-seven-year-old husband, Anatoli. The couple was looking for a new apartment that morning and left their two children, an eight-year-old boy and five-month-old girl, with a babysitter. At other stops there was Peretz Gantz, sixty-one, who escaped the Nazis as a teenager; Daniel Biton, forty-three, a gardener; Masuda Amar, a fifty-nine-year-old grandmother of five; Wael Jumah Kawasmeh, a twenty-three-year-old Palestinian from East Jerusalem who planned to marry in a month; and Ira Weinstein, fifty-three, a butcher who had grown up in New York City and had moved to Israel.

Sara and Matt, while only in their twenties, were experienced travelers, accustomed to moving easily among the kind of diverse group of passengers who boarded the Number 18 bus that morning. During the previous summer, Sara had flown to California and Siberia on a research trip. A few years earlier Matt had spent several weeks in China.

On this day, they planned to take the Number 18 bus to Jerusalem's Central Bus Terminal. From there, they figured they could board another bus that would take them down the spine of the Negev Desert to the Israeli port city of Eilat on the Red Sea. They would cross into Jordan and catch yet another bus to the archeological sites at Petra.

In many ways, their trip to Jordan was a key sign of how well the Oslo peace process was working. For the first time in decades, Israeli Jews could cross into Jordan and feel safe. And yet, Sara and Matt both knew that Israel, and the surrounding areas, could erupt in violence at any moment.

On this same day two years earlier, while waiting for morning prayers to begin at a yeshiva in the Israeli community of Efrat in the West Bank, Matt and a friend, Edward Bernstein, watched in silence as a line of ambulances raced toward Hebron to care for those who had been wounded in the shooting by Baruch Goldstein. "Matt was very upset. We all were," Bernstein recalled.

Two days after that attack, Sara, who had just begun to date Matt and was spending a semester sabbatical from college immersing herself in Jewish studies in Jerusalem, wrote in her diary how the Hebron shootings had made her "nervous." She attended a peace rally, then mused in her diary that Jews and Muslims "should be able to coexist." Less than a week later, she recorded another milestone in her diary, after taking a walk near Jaffa Road. "I had my first bomb scare," Sara wrote.

Now in Jerusalem again, Matt and Sara had not been close to any bombings. Indeed, there had been no significant suicide attacks in Israel since the previous summer. But there were still reasons to be worried.

Two months earlier Matt had sipped coffee in the study room of the Schechter Institute in Jerusalem and studied the newspaper coverage of the Shin Bet killing of Yahya Ayyash. It was obviously a triumphant moment for Israel's security forces.

Matt fell silent as he read about the exploding cell phone that killed Ayyash—a story that seemed more like a plot from a James Bond movie than an actual police operation. Then Matt looked up at his friend and fellow rabbinical student across the table, Shai Held. "Lots of people are cheering about this," Matt said. "But someone is going to die for this."

At five-foot-five, Matt Eisenfeld still had the wiry, muscular frame that had made him a stand-out high school wrestler and track and cross-country runner back in West Hartford, Connecticut. But now, in Jerusalem, in his second year of studies to become a rabbi, he had started to grow a beard—not heavy and thick yet, but distinctive and studious nonetheless. He joked with friends that he let his whiskers grow because he had grown tired of shaving. But Matt's scruffy beard was, on some level, a sign of the seriousness he brought to his religious calling and the fact that he was stepping into a new phase of his adult life.

"I'm smack dab in the middle of my twenties," he wrote in a letter to his younger sister, Amy, when he turned twenty-five three weeks earlier. Matt seemed surprised, perhaps a bit bedeviled that he had reached a quarter-century of life, and yet he also seemed to embrace the fact that he had embarked on a new, richer and more serious life as a rabbi. "A friend asked me if I felt different," Matt wrote to Amy, then a student at Washington University in St. Louis. The friend meant it as a joke, perhaps just one of those conversational lines that emerges at important birthdays and other milestones of life, Matt said. But he took it as a moment to reflect on how his life was, indeed, changing. "I answered I did feel different," he wrote, adding in jest, "I am expecting my beard to change color any minute now."

Like Sara that morning, Matt dressed to fight off the February chill, with a green coat with brown collar atop a gray fleece vest jacket and black jeans. Over his shoulder, he carried a backpack with two Talmud volumes and a spiral notebook containing his ideas—some written in Hebrew, some in English—for an instructional Haggadah he had been assembling to use at a seder during the upcoming Passover holidays and a visit by his parents. He also brought along a leather book about two inches thick, which included, among other prayers, a meditation on peace.

The Number 18 pulled up to Jaffa Road. Beyond the windows on the right side of the bus, passengers could see the walls of the Old City and the Jaffa Gate. The bus turned left on Jaffa Road and headed north for several blocks and stopped at a series of bus shelters outside Jerusalem's City Hall.

The sidewalk was crowded that morning with commuters awaiting buses. A group of passengers got off, including Jeffery Sosland, the American graduate student who was researching water resources. He walked south for a few blocks in search of a charter company that would take him to Jordan.

No one seemed to pay any attention to a man who got on the Number 18 at the City Hall bus stop. The man was dressed like an Israeli student and carried a duffel bag.

The man found a seat in the middle of the bus—next to the rear door that passengers used to exit.

The bus doors closed and the Number 18 eased into the Jaffa Road traffic. The bus passed the police station. It crossed Zion Square, then passed by the streets leading to the vegetable stands of the Mahane Yehuda market and the rows of small clothing stores.

After another mile, the bus approached a major intersection—Sarei Yisrael Street. Leah Stein Mousa rose from her seat and walked to the rear exit door and stepped into the well to get off the bus quickly. The man with the duffel bag sat silently to Mousa's left, separated from her by a clear plastic partition.

The bus pulled up to a stop on the corner of Jaffa Road and Sarei Yisrael Street. Another bus rolled up close behind. A white van stopped just to the left of both buses. On the right, twenty-four-year-old Avi Huja touched the brakes in his white Mitsubishi van. Huja could have pulled up next to the Number 18. But he stopped a few feet behind the bus in the right-hand lane.

Inside the bus, as she waited for the door to open, Leah Mousa noticed someone stand up to her left. It was the young man with the duffel bag.

He was holding the bag in front of his chest as if he was carrying a satchel of groceries. After pausing a moment, he stepped into the aisle of the bus and yelled, "Allahu Akbar"—Arabic for "God is great."

Then he pushed a button.

# CHAPTER 2

THE WORST SOUND AFTER A TERRORIST BOMBING IS NO SOUND—SILENCE.
It is the telltale sign of death, say Jerusalem's most experienced emergency
medics. Silence means that those closest to the blast have been killed or
hurt so badly that they can't even scream in pain or shout for help. And
if a bomb explodes on a crowded thoroughfare such as Jerusalem's Jaffa
Road during a morning rush hour, silence means the casualty count will
be high.

On February 25, 1996, David Sofer, an eighteen-year-old ambulance
driver and emergency medic, heard the unmistakable metallic thud of the
blast as he walked east on Sarei Yisrael Street toward the junction of Jaffa
Road.

Then came the silence.

"Oh, no," Sofer thought to himself. "Not another one."

It was 6:45 a.m. Sofer, a devout Orthodox Jew, had just left the yeshiva
where he frequently studied and participated in morning prayers. His shift
at the ambulance station not far from Jerusalem's Central Bus Terminal
near Jaffa Road was not scheduled to begin for another fifteen minutes. He
figured he would enjoy a quiet walk as the dawn broke over his city.

But as he left the prayer service and stepped onto the sidewalk, Sofer
felt the ground shake. Smoke rose into the morning sky about four hundred meters away and Sofer, who had recently begun his mandatory military service in the Israeli army, wondered for a moment whether a missile
had struck a building. With his dark eyes and olive skin, Sofer would
eventually earn a spot in the elite Duvdevan commando unit that infiltrated Palestinian neighborhoods on the West Bank or in the Gaza Strip.
Instinctively and without waiting for orders or even checking his radio, he
broke into a run toward the smoke. As he drew closer, he found himself
composing a mental checklist of what he should do when he reached the
scene. First, he would look for anyone seriously injured. Then, he would
determine who needed attention first.

He ran across a bridge and saw the Number 18 bus—then felt the silence.

"It was quiet," he said. "And it was a very scary moment. You expect to see movement. You expect to see people running. But as I was coming closer, I felt like I walked into a cemetery. Nobody was moving."

The bomb in the black bag had done its job. "The bus went up in the air," a witness said. The blast and its orange fireball tore off the bus roof, peeling back the steel and tossing it behind the rear windows and into another bus as if it were tinfoil.

But the black bag contained more than just explosives. Packed around the bomb were several pounds of nails, screws and steel ball bearings. When the bomb exploded, the nails, screws and ball bearings sprayed from the bag, shredding the bus and beyond with a steely shower of shrapnel. The glass in all the windows was gone—shattered and scattered across Jaffa Road. Passengers had no time to duck or even realize what had happened, police said. The bus's seats were riddled with pellets. So were the bodies. In the back of the bus, a man in a white shirt sat lifeless in his seat, leaning forward slightly, his right hand reaching through a window. Several seats away, a bloody, severed hand hung from a bent and jagged steel window frame.

For those nearby—or those like David Sofer who ran to the scene hoping to save passengers—it was moment of quick decisions amid gruesome chaos. But it was also a moment to realize how little could be done for the victims, as Michael Dahan noted when he saw the wreckage. "There were only pieces of bodies all over," said Dahan, a thirty-two-year-old former Israeli soldier who was one of the first to arrive on the scene. "We gave people water. What more can you do? Some were dying right there."

The blast-cloud of shattered glass, twisted metal, and ripped flesh sprayed through car and apartment windows. It covered parts of nearby roofs and clung to the branches of trees that lined Jaffa Road. A head rolled onto the sidewalk near a pedestrian, Yigal Kara. A headless corpse lay on the street a few feet from the bus. A body had flown past Yitzhak Rubin, a ticket inspector, and landed fifty meters away. Inside his Mitsubishi van, which he stopped just to the right and behind the Number

18 as he waited for the traffic light on Sarei Yisraeli Street to change, Avi Huja felt the rush of hot air from the blast. He opened the door of his van and ran down the block, away from the burning bus. After collecting himself a few minutes later, Huja turned and ran back. As he approached the bus, he found a female soldier lying on the street, screaming in pain, with one of her legs blown off. Huja and another man wrapped a tourniquet on the woman's leg to try to stop the bleeding, and then carried her to the sidewalk. Nearby, Arik Cohen, an Israeli Air Force corporal, stood in disbelief. Cohen had been asleep in an apartment. He ran to the scene in his pajamas and found a police car smeared with blood and body parts scattered on the street.

Flames licked the sides of the bus. Avi Rivivo, who happened to be walking by as the bomb detonated, tried to approach the bus but felt something odd under his feet. He looked down and noticed he was stepping on fingers and legs. "It was like entering the gates of hell," he said later.

A twenty-two-year-old Israeli soldier, Shmulik Avital, who had been riding on the bus behind the Number 18, leaped from his seat and scrambled out the door. As he tried to climb aboard the Number 18, though, he was stopped by a burst of black smoke. Momentarily blinded, he stepped back—then again tried to board the crippled bus. He dragged an injured woman from her seat, then returned to carry a soldier whose hair was on fire.

Avital would be credited with carrying six people to safety. But after an hour, he collapsed on the sidewalk, crying and apologizing out loud for not being able to save more people. "What could I have done?" he said. "I'm only human. I'm only human."

David Sofer ran to the front door of the bus. Smoke still poured from the rear seats where the bomb had exploded.

He climbed into the bus. The driver was still in his seat—dead. A woman, who seemed to have just paid her fare, had fallen over the driver—also dead.

Sofer stepped over the woman and squeezed into the aisle between the seats and stopped and looked at the scene for a second or two. He could see the entire length of the bus now, all the seats, all the passengers.

Many were still in their seats, "all sitting up," he recalled.

And they all seemed to be dead. All of them. No one screamed in pain. No one even seemed to be moaning.

Sofer inched toward the back of the bus. More paramedics arrived on the scene now, many trying to climb into the bus and others just standing in shock as they surveyed the scene before them.

Sofer tried to watch where he placed his feet. As he shimmied toward the back of the bus, he passed a woman in a seat. Her lips moved. Was she still alive? Sofer did not know. He reached down anyway and lifted the woman up, then turned, called to the paramedics outside the bus and handed the woman to them through a broken window.

Sofer whirled and retraced his steps to the main door of the bus. As the paramedic who found the woman, it was his job to make sure she was placed in an ambulance and taken to the hospital. But as he followed the other paramedics who were carrying the woman to an ambulance, he passed the body of another woman laying face down on the sidewalk, about thirty yards from the bus.

Sofer figured the woman was dead and that another paramedic had removed her from the bus and placed her on this patch of sidewalk. Or perhaps she had been walking along the sidewalk and had been hit by debris from the blast and had been killed.

As Sofer walked by, he heard a gasp—a desperate attempt to breathe. He stopped and looked down. The woman on the sidewalk was trying to breathe. He heard another gasp, then a frantic gulping and sucking for air. Sofer bent over. He turned the woman over and called for stretcher.

It was Leah Stein Mousa.

She had been blown from the back door of the bus to this spot. Another paramedic ran up with a stretcher. Sofer and the other paramedic carefully lifted Mousa and placed her on the stretcher and carried her to an ambulance. The other paramedic slid into the driver's seat of the ambulance and turned a key to start the engine. Sofer jumped into the back.

Mousa was still breathing. Sofer hoped he could at least get her to a hospital.

In the rear of the bus, silent, a young couple was still in the seats they took when they stepped onto the bus less than thirty minutes earlier.

Matt and Sara.

They were not moving.

━━━

Ami Ayalon wanted to get to the office early. He had taken over the reins of Israel's Shin Bet counterterror security agency only three days before. Sunday would be the start of his first full week on the job. A Shin Bet driver picked up Ayalon at his house near the northern Israeli port city of Haifa. As the car rolled south along a highway toward Tel Aviv, Ayalon monitored the radio and thought about his day ahead.

One of Shin Bet's duties was to protect Israeli's highest ranking officials. It had been only four months since an Israeli extremist had shot and killed Prime Minister Yitzhak Rabin. And since the assassination, the agency had taken its share of criticism over whether it paid too much attention to Palestinian terrorists and had not monitored the activities of some Jewish extremists.

As he rode in the car toward Tel Aviv, Ayalon expected he might be organizing plans to improve Shin Bet's surveillance of the Israelis who were so opposed the peace process that Rabin had started with the Palestinians and Yasser Arafat that they might resort to violence against their own government. Just after 6:45 a.m., however, Ayalon heard a brief, but numbing report.

Bomb explosion on a bus. Jaffa Road. Jerusalem. Many casualties.

Ayalon told his driver to find the quickest road to Jerusalem. His morning office meetings could wait. Ayalon wanted to get to the scene of the explosion.

In Ramallah, ten miles to the north of Jaffa Road, another man also monitored the radio. Hassan Salameh was not taking any phone calls. He knew he was about to become one of the most sought-after fugitives in Israel, the West Bank, and the Gaza Strip. It was, he would say later, a role he happily embraced. And just after 6:45 a.m., Salameh heard the news he was hoping for. The bomb he had built the night before and had given to the young man from the refugee camp had worked. The Number 18 bus was on fire.

Now Salameh waited for another piece of news.

During the night before, at the rented apartment in Abu Dis, Salameh had assembled a second bomb. He also met with a second suicide bomber—another young Palestinian man from the West Bank. Just after the first bomber left in the blue Opel sedan for the bus stop on Jaffa Road, a second bomber was picked up by a Hamas operative in a white pickup truck and driven to the Israeli city of Ashkelon, not far from the border to the Gaza Strip. The second bomber wore a far different disguise than the young man who carried the bomb to the Jaffa Road bus. On instructions from Salameh, the second bomber dressed in the uniform of an Israeli soldier. His target was a bus stop near Ashkelon where Israeli soldiers often gathered in large numbers to await buses to military bases in southern Israel.

Salameh knew the thirty-mile trip to Ashkelon would take longer. There were also more chances to get caught, perhaps in a random checkpoint set up by the Israeli police who might find something suspicious about the young man in the uniform of an Israeli soldier.

Salameh had still not heard from the second bomber or from his driver.

On the western edge of Jerusalem, another man also waited. As soon as he heard the news that a terrorist bomb had exploded on Jaffa Road, Dr. Avraham "Avi" Rivkind rushed to his post as chief trauma surgeon at Hadassah University Hospital Ein Kerem. Hadassah is so large that it has two branches in Jerusalem—the Ein Kerem hospital on the western side of the city and another complex atop Mount Scopus on Jerusalem's eastern border overlooking the West Bank. On this day, it would have been quicker and shorter for ambulances to make the trip to Hadassah's Mount Scopus branch. But Hadassah's Ein Kerem complex had a more extensive trauma unit. It also had Avi Rivkind.

Rivkind, a lanky man with an angular face and piercing eyes, knew the day ahead would be long. He also knew the casualties could be numerous and gruesome. Rivkind began his career several decades before as an Israeli army surgeon. He did not expect to become one of the world's foremost experts in treating victims of bombings or shootings. That expertise was thrust upon him, first in patching up Israeli soldiers who had been wounded in his nation's wars, then in caring for the steady stream of civilians—Israeli and Palestinian—who had been injured in terrorist bombings or shootouts. He knew from personal experience what a bullet from a semiautomatic AK47 or M16 could do to human flesh when it ripped through a body. He also knew how even the smallest pieces of shrapnel could cut through muscle and bone.

As a reminder of the kind of wounds he had learned to deal with, Rivkind kept an array of small screws, ball bearings and nails in a plastic medicine bottle on the desk of his hospital office—pieces of shrapnel that he had removed from the legs, arms, abdomens and heads of soldiers and civilians who had been brought to his trauma unit. Rivkind also knew that treating victims of terrorist attacks, especially bombings, was not like other doctor-patient relationships. There was little time for one-on-one consultation, little bedside manner. Decisions about which patients to treat first and how to treat them were made quickly, instinctively. Large teams of physicians and nurses were needed, and Rivkind took pride in knowing how to organize his teams to care for mass numbers of casualties. But he could never master one part of that preparation. "You can not prepare yourself emotionally," he said. "Every time there is a terrorist bombing, there is a chance that one of the victims will be someone you know."

Soon after arriving at the hospital, Rivkind ordered his teams of doctors and nurses to assemble by the driveway that led to the Hadassah Ein Kerem's emergency room. He listened for the sirens and waited.

Several miles away, as he rode in the back of the ambulance, David Sofer knew he had to make a crucial decision. On the stretcher, Leah Stein Mousa, her face blackened by fire and her clothes streaked by greasy soot, was breathing heavily now—gasping even more desperately for air. Her pulse began to drop.

Sofer knew that the best place for Mousa was Hadassah Ein Kerem—and Avi Rivkind's team of trauma experts. But the hospital was still a ten-minute ride. Sofer sensed that Mousa might die on the roads to Hadassah.

He looked up and yelled to the ambulance driver.

"Let's go to Shaare Zedek," Sofer said, referring to another of Jerusalem's hospitals.

Although it was closer to the bomb site than Hadassah Ein Kerem, Shaare Zedek Medical Center did not have the advanced trauma ward that Hadassah had at that time. Sofer knew that. But he also knew that Leah Mousa's life was slipping away. Thinking quickly, he reasoned that if doctors at Shaare Zedek could stabilize Mousa, maybe she could be moved to Hadassah at a later time.

Sofer had radioed ahead, and a team of doctors and nurses ran to the ambulance as it rolled up the driveway to Shaare Zedek's emergency room doors. Sofer got out, reached for Mousa's stretcher as the nurses and doctors lifted it from the ambulance, then backed away and watched them rush her through the hospital doors.

Only thirty minutes before, he had left morning prayers at his yeshiva. Now, as the emergency room doors closed, Sofer wondered if the woman he had accidentally found on the sidewalk would live or die. He wanted to stay and take care of Mousa. But he knew others at the hospital would do that. He had been trained to not get too emotionally involved with patients. Otherwise he would not be able to focus his attention and energy on other bomb victims. So he slipped into the passenger seat of the ambulance and told the driver to go back to Jaffa Road. Still, he made a mental note to himself to return and check on the woman he had found on the sidewalk.

❧

Koby Zrihen worked his police radio as he sped through Jerusalem's streets, summoning a team of fellow police detectives to the Jaffa Road bomb scene as quickly as possible. Being a police detective in Jerusalem is unlike an investigator's job in most other big cities. In New York City, London, and Paris, police detectives handle all manner of crimes, from murders to street muggings to break-ins and thefts. Their job is to collect evidence and trace the whereabouts of the criminals. In Jerusalem, Zrihen was well schooled in the art of collecting evidence and tracking down crooks. He knew how to assess fingerprints, how to analyze even the smallest pieces of evidence, how to interview witnesses and suspects. But what made him different was that the primary focus of most of his investigative work was chasing suspected terrorists.

He parked his car near the intersection of Jaffa Road and Sarei Yisrael Street. Several ambulances had already arrived and medics were carrying away wounded. Zrihen walked slowly toward the blackened skeleton of the bus, his eyes combing the scene.

The bodies of the dead—or pieces of the bodies—seemed everywhere, scattered across the street or piled atop one another in the bus. The wail of sirens from fire trucks and more ambulances grew louder, and Zrihen found himself looking down to avoid stepping on severed fingers, hands, and feet. Along the sidewalks, people gathered in small knots, some of them crying now.

His job was not to rescue the wounded or pick up the dead. Zrihen had to quickly figure out if there was any evidence amid this carnage that might offer a clue to where the bomb came from and who set it off. Years before, he had commanded a platoon of tanks in the Israeli army. In his police work, he still relied on some of the skills he learned in the military—about how to quickly assess a battlefield and find the signs that were important amid those that were not. And yet, he could not ignore the fact that this was no ordinary battlefield. Yes, a bomb had exploded. And yes, an orange fireball had swept through a bus, killing many in the same gruesome way he had seen men die in combat. But these were his fellow citizens—and most were civilians.

"You are finding yourself doing something no human being wants to deal with," Zrihen recalled. "You mind is empty and kind of full."

He noticed the smell of death, faint at first, then stronger as he walked closer to the bus skeleton. He knew this smell from previous bombings. It was somewhat sweet but it was also laced with the unmistakable tinge of fire.

Zrihen tried to ignore the crying of the onlookers, the gruesome array of bodies and severed limbs, the smell. His mind raced. How would he find any clues to the bomber amid this chaos?

He watched as his investigators organized themselves into search teams. Several walked southward on Jaffa Road, in the same direction the bus had come. Others climbed through the bus. Still others searched the asphalt immediately adjacent to the bus.

The street was covered with paper—from soldiers' duffel bags, from students' backpacks, from women's purses and men's briefcases. Each piece had to be searched. Then, the detectives had to examine the bodies themselves and the body parts. Did any of these pieces of paper offer a clue to the identity of the bomber? Zrihen hoped they would.

When a bomb explodes, it leaves all sorts of clues, especially on the bodies of the dead who are close enough to the bomb to absorb the brunt of the explosion. Zrihen was especially interested in bodies—or parts of bodies—that were charred the most. They were probably closest to the blast. Maybe there was a clue there.

It had been almost thirty minutes since Zrihen drove up to the bomb scene. The wounded had been removed within the first twenty minutes. Now the bus and nearby streets were swarming with dozens of people— medics still checking on the dead, Shin Bet agents, journalists, firefight-ers, cops, soldiers, and members of the Zihuy Korbanot Ason (ZAKA), which have one of the world's most unusual jobs: wiping up blood and picking up body parts so they can be properly prepared for burial. While the instincts of the first-responders and others were well intentioned, Zrihen also knew that the onslaught of people on a crime scene often contaminates evidence or, in some cases, destroys it. Unlike in the United States, where police and the FBI typically seal off a crime scene and sometimes wait hours to even remove the dead or clean up the body parts so that investigators can meticulously search for evidence, Israeli crime scenes tend to be far more chaotic and are wiped clean within hours.

The level of chaos had continued to rise. A doctor at Hadassah Ein Kerem Hospital called a medic on the scene. One of the victims of the bus explosion had lost an ear in the blast. The doctor felt he might be able to reattach the ear to the wounded man at the hospital. But he needed to have the ear. Could the medics search the bomb scene for an ear? And, if they found one, could they drive it to the hospital? Within minutes, medics found an ear. They packed it in ice inside a cooler then two other medics drove the cooler to Hadassah Hospital.

It was the kind of story that underscores the courage and dedication of Israeli's ambulance service, not to mention the unique care and surgical expertise of trauma doctors and staff at Hadassah Hospital. For a meticu-lous cop like Koby Zrihen, however, it was the kind of intrusion that might disrupt a crime scene and perhaps damage much-needed evidence.

Zrihen studied the bus floor. He knew from past experience that a suicide bomber often detonates a bomb in two ways—by picking up a bomb-laden bag and holding it to his chest or by simply leaving it on the bus floor and pressing a button. If the bomb exploded on the bus floor, Zrihen knew there would be a hole.

He scanned the entire bus, under the seats—or what was left of them—and especially in the back where most of the passengers had died.

No holes in the floor.

Zrihen made a quick mental calculation. He looked down Jaffa Road. About one hundred feet away, investigators had found the charred head of a young man with a thin face. The head appeared to have been violently ripped from its body. Was this young man close to the explosion? Also, while the face had been badly burned, investigators thought it had features that were typical of Palestinians. Zrihen's investigators took a DNA sample from the head, which might help identify the man.

Then came another clue. Near the bus, Zrihen's investigators found an ID card for a nineteen-year-old Palestinian from the al-Fawwar refugee camp near Hebron, almost thirty miles away. The name on the card did not offer any immediate clue—Majdi Abu Wardeh. But Zrihen wondered nonetheless why a nineteen-year-old Palestinian man would be so far from his home and taking a bus on Jaffa Road at 6:45 a.m. on a Sunday. And was this the ID card for the young man whose head had been found minutes earlier?

Ami Ayalon, the new Shin Bet chief, was now on the scene. He, too, thought that the badly burned head and the ID card of the nineteen-year-old Palestinian man from the West Bank refugee camp might be important clues. Shin Bet's Jerusalem chief, Yisrael Hasson agreed. Shin Bet agents knew the West Bank well and were familiar with the al-Fawwar camp where the young man was from.

In recent months, however, Shin Bet had deliberately scaled back its West Bank monitoring, deferring and trusting instead the newly formed Palestinian security police under Yasser Arafat. The new relationship had been uneasy and rocky. The Shin Bet mistrusted Arafat—and many of his close advisors. Far too many Palestinian security officers had been former guerrilla fighters. Shin Bet feared that far too many still kept close ties to Hamas and Islamic Jihad. But the Oslo Peace process essentially set up a system of self-governance in the Palestinian terrorities. That self-governance meant the Palestinians would handle police matters—most of them, anyway. On this day, as Ami Ayalon and Yisrael Hasson walked through the rubble at the Jaffa Road bomb scene, both knew that Shin Bet had to take an active role in checking on the identity of the nineteen-year-old man from the al-Fawwar camp.

Maybe it was a coincidence that this young man happened to be on the Number 18 bus. Then again, maybe this was the clue that Shin Bet needed to track down the origins of this bomb plot. Perhaps the young man's parents could shed light on why he had come to Jerusalem so early on this Sunday and why he had taken a bus. Ayalon and Hasson dispatched several agents to al-Fawwar. Besides talking to the parents, the agents were told to obtain DNA samples from the parents.

The ambulance with David Sofer in the passenger seat rolled up to the intersection of Jaffa Road and Sarei Yisrael Street. With a siren blaring and lights flashing atop the ambulance, Sofer was able to return to the bomb scene in less than ten minutes after leaving Leah Mousa at Shaare Zedek Medical Center. As the ambulance stopped, Sofer got out and walked toward the blackened wreckage.

More paramedics had arrived. So had more police and Shin Bet agents. Two police officers with bomb-sniffing dogs stood in the middle of the intersection of Sarei Yisrael Street and Jaffa Road, waiting to see if they were needed to search for other explosives. One of the dogs—a brown, mixed breed—was lying on the asphalt. Nearby, three men chatted by the back door of a white ambulance van. Four other men leaned against the side of the van—all apparently waiting for instructions.

Sofer looked at the bus. Crews of crime scene analysts and paramedics were still trying to remove the dead, some of whom were still upright in their seats, their heads slumped forward or to one side. Sofer knew the body count would be high.

Just after 7:30 a.m., police radios jumped to life with a new, ominous report: Another terrorist bomb had exploded—this one, at a bus stop thirty miles away, in Ashkelon, where several dozen soldiers were waiting. The bomber, a Palestinian man who died in the explosion, was dressed as a soldier.

Here, amid the carnage on Jaffa Road, Sofer tried to ignore the news that another bombing had taken place. Other medics would surely respond to that explosion and tend to the wounded and dead. For now, he had more work to do.

Sofer stepped into the bus again. Its floor was littered with the scraps of daily life—purses, backpacks, papers, books, eyeglasses, hats, shoes. Men from the ZAKA organization were now quietly walking from seat to seat, searching for body parts and wiping up bits of flesh and small pools of blood. Sofer inched toward the back seats, where some dead passengers were still in their seats.

Medics picked up the bodies of several dead soldiers. Sofer noticed a name tag on a young soldier's uniform: "Yonatan Barnea," the son of the prominent Israeli newspaper columnist. Sofer wondered if Nahum Barnea knew about his son yet. He turned and looked to another seat, and a young woman. Medics had not removed her body.

Sofer hesitated, struck by how young and beautiful she seemed. He leaned forward and picked her up, then turned to carry her off the bus. As he stepped off the bus, Sofer wondered about the woman and where she came from—what drew her to this bus on this morning.

"She is someone's daughter," Sofer thought as he walked with the woman's body to a waiting ambulance. "She must have a family somewhere."

# CHAPTER 3

TEN HOURS AFTER THE FIREBALL RIPPED APART THE NUMBER 18 BUS ON Jaffa Road, a telephone rang almost 6,000 miles away in the second-floor bedroom of a colonial-style house on a tree-lined street in the New York City suburb of Teaneck, New Jersey. It was almost ten o'clock, Sunday morning, February 25, 1996. Arline Duker had slept longer than usual and was making her bed as she reached for the receiver and heard a woman's voice—Kathleen Riley, the United States Consul in Jerusalem.

"Is this Arline Duker?" Riley asked.

"Yes."

"Are you the mother of Sara Duker?"

"Yes."

"And she's in Israel?"

"Yes . . ."

Arline had been out late the night before at a party at a synagogue on the other side of town to celebrate the bar mitzvah of a friend's son. Around 11:30 p.m., she found herself at a table with several friends, exchanging news about their children—especially Sara. Nine months before, Sara had arrived for Sabbath services at the synagogue with her boyfriend, Matthew Eisenfeld, and the sight of such a vibrant couple so obviously in love inevitably sparked all manner of speculation of whether a wedding was in the near future.

As her friends listened, Arline explained that Sara was in Jerusalem where Matthew was also pursuing his rabbinical studies. Then she glanced at her watch. It was seven hours later in Jerusalem—around 6:30 on Sunday morning there. Arline realized she had not spoken to Sara on the telephone in two weeks. For a moment, she wondered if she should rush home and call her daughter. Then, Arline thought better of it. Sara would probably want to sleep late. With the bar mitzvah party winding down, Arline wanted to get to bed, too. There would be plenty of time on Sunday afternoon to call Sara.

Arline, of course, had no idea that as she spoke to her friends at the bar mitzvah party that Sara was walking from her apartment with Matthew to catch the Number 18 bus and embark on a short vacation to Jordan. As midnight approached and she continued chatting with the friends, Arline felt a sense of motherly pride at how well her family seemed to be doing.

It had not been an easy path for her. A dozen years before, Arline lost her husband, Ben-Zion, to brain cancer. The two had met in the early 1970s when Arline was enrolled in graduate courses at Columbia University's Teachers College. When he died in October 1984, Ben-Zion was just forty-two. Arline was thirty-nine, with three daughters to raise.

Ariella, the youngest, was only three at the time of her father's death, and Arline's middle daughter, Tamara, had just turned eight. Sara, the oldest at eleven years, had been especially close to her father. As Arline liked to say later, Ben-Zion taught Sara to read, and, in conversations on their father-daughter walks to the synagogue on Saturday mornings, he passed on a love of Judaism to his daughter that seemed to become a permanent part of her personality.

After Ben-Zion died, Arline noticed that Sara threw herself into her schoolwork with a deeper sense of seriousness. Sara still maintained a girlish sense of serendipity, mostly evident in her penchant for flowery skirts and purple sneakers, but, as even some of her friends noticed, she seemed driven to build a strong and independent life for herself. Now twenty-two years old and a graduate of Arline's alma mater, Barnard College at Columbia University, Sara seemed to have reached a new and stable plateau.

Arline often marveled at how Sara seemed equipped with a seriousness that she balanced with a deep sensitivity to those around her. In some ways, Sara seemed far older than she was and was already making strides to support herself, establish a career, and perhaps marry and have a family. Arline felt a sense of accomplishment—and, at times, quiet relief—at the steady path that Sara seemed to have forged. While in Jerusalem only a few months, Sara had not only found a full-time job at the Hebrew University biology lab, but also had organized an environmental group and was planning a campaign to improve the city's slipshod methods of recycling plastic and other trash. Arline also was proud of how her daughter had embraced her place in Judaism, trying, like many young Jewish women in the mid-1990s, to balance her faith's traditions with modern women's roles in work and at home. "I was always amazed at how much she managed to get done," Arline said years later.

In some ways, Arline could have been talking about herself. After her husband died, Arline left her teaching career and returned to graduate school for a degree in social work. She enjoyed the challenge and pace of teaching, first in the New York City public schools then later in several Jewish private schools. But her husband's death had given Arline a new appreciation of the needs of grief-stricken people—and how important a sensitive, attentive counselor could be. She embarked on a new path as a therapist, first with a Bergen County government agency, then with her own counseling practice not far from her home.

Now, on this Sunday morning, Arline found herself in a somewhat odd predicament after so many years of raising three daughters. The house was quiet and she was alone. Tamara, now twenty, had also left for studies in Israel, at a university in the southern Israeli city of Beersheba. Arline's youngest, fourteen-year-old Ariella, had spent the night at a sleepover party at a friend's house.

In the preceding days, a much-welcomed thaw broke through the frigid winter chill that had enveloped the New York City region for months. Forecasters even predicted that temperatures in the region might reach sixty degrees that day. But any notion that Arline might have a relaxing day ahead, with perhaps a quiet walk in a park or a leisurely breakfast, evaporated when she answered her bedroom phone.

From her office at the US Consulate on Nablus Road and just a few hundred yards from the stone arch of the Damascus Gate to Jerusalem's Old City, Kathleen Riley supervised a wide array of tasks, from keeping track of visas to helping US citizens who lost passports. Her most difficult job was making the sort of telephone call she placed on Sunday morning to Arline Duker's house in Teaneck, New Jersey.

Riley had entered the US State Department's diplomatic corps a decade earlier and had already been posted in tense spots, including Haiti and Egypt. She took over the consular chief's job in Jerusalem in 1993, amid the hopeful feeling that the Oslo Peace Accords might finally provide the blueprint for resolving the grinding conflict between Palestinians and Israelis. Riley quickly realized that finding some measure of peace was not easy. While she felt safe on most days, she had also learned to listen for the sounds of trouble. "If you hear something and then a lot of sirens," she said, "you assume something bad happened."

On that morning, just before 7 a.m., in her home on Mount Scopus, Riley heard a dull thud on the other side of Jerusalem—the bomb on the Number 18 bus on Jaffa Road. Riley had heard that sound before and knew what it meant. She made a mental note to have her staff call Israeli police by mid-morning to check whether any Americans were among the casualties.

It was now almost 5 p.m. Riley faced one the most painful tasks of any American diplomat. "You have to go into your office and shut the door and sit for a few minutes and get ready to pass some of the worst news that anybody is going to get in their life." On that day, Riley harbored an additional concern. "You also want to be sure you do it before it gets on the news."

In Teaneck, Arline had not been listening to the radio or watching TV. She had no idea that a bomb had torn apart a bus in Jerusalem. But as Riley asked about Sara, Arline felt her mind race. Was Sara in trouble? Was there some difficulty with her passport perhaps? Did she get arrested with that new environmental group she joined, perhaps chaining herself to a tractor in some sort of protest?

"Have you heard the news reports today?" Riley asked.

Arline's mind accelerated. Oh, my God. What are you talking about?

"I just woke up," Arline said. "I haven't heard any news."

"There's been a terrorist attack in Jerusalem," Riley said.

Arline fell silent. Oh, my God, she thought. Riley also paused, and the words, "terrorist attack," seemed to hang within the phone line like a heavy curtain over a window. After a second or two, Arline asked: "Is Sara alright?"

"She was on the bus that was blown up in the attack," Riley said.

"Is she alright?" Arline asked again.

Riley hesitated, then answered, trying to keep her voice calm and measured.

"I'm sorry to tell you that your daughter died in the attack."

The words could not be clearer. Your daughter died in the attack. For all its delicate and careful negotiations with high-level diplomats from other nations, the US State Department sometimes has to communicate in ways that are not nuanced. Kathleen Riley knew that there was no easy way to pass on this kind of message. As she spoke, Riley tried to gauge how Arline Duker was handling the sudden news that Sara had been killed. In the past, when she had to make similar calls to other American families, Riley had been yelled at by a suddenly grief-stricken relative or told she was surely mistaken and lying. As she listened on the phone on that Sunday morning, Riley felt Arline Duker was doing her best to remain calm.

The truth is that Arline felt numb as she held the phone, handcuffed momentarily by the desire to scream, the need for more information and simple disbelief. Sara? Dead? In a terrorist attack?

"I just couldn't take it in," Arline remembered.

As a counselor—as a wife who had lost a husband—Arline knew all too well that delivering news about a death, especially the death of a child, was not easy. No amount of sugar coating or emotional niceties can soften the impact of what needs to be said. And so, the words are often clumsy and constrained. When the news is delivered over the telephone, it takes on an even colder feeling.

Perhaps just as clumsy and difficult is how to answer such news. For Arline, a single, stunned word leaped into her mind.

"What?" she said. "What? What?"

Then, after a pause, Arline asked: "Are you sure?"

"Yes," Riley said. "She has been identified."

In such moments, psychologists say the human mind sometimes wraps itself in a protective shield, as if the news is about someone else—someone not connected to you. Sometimes, a person receiving such shockingly terrible news does not immediately collapse emotionally, but briefly has the presence of mind to remain calm and ask succinct questions.

Arline thought of Matthew and whether Sara was with him.

"Was she with somebody?" Arline asked.

"Yes," Riley said.

"Matthew Eisenfeld?" Arline asked. "Is he okay?"

"No," Riley answered. "He was also killed in the attack."

Arline found herself fighting harder to stay calm.

"Do his parents know?" she asked in a steady voice.

"Yes, we spoke to the parents," Riley said.

Arline stopped. The weight of the news—a terrorist bomb, her daughter and Matthew both dead—began to sink in.

She needed to ask one more question.

"Are you absolutely sure?" Arline asked. "Are you sure there is no mistake."

Riley said she was sure. After the Israeli police called to say that they had found Sara's and Matthew's US passports, Riley had dispatched one of her staffers to the morgue. A few hours later, Israeli authorities positively identified the bodies of Sara and Matthew.

Riley sensed that Arline was trying to figure out what to do next. Riley asked Arline if she was alone or whether she had anyone at home with her.

"No I'm here by myself," Arline said.

"I think you ought to have somebody with you," Riley said.

Riley said she would call back later in the day, but she asked Arline to write down her name and telephone number.

"Wait a minute, wait a minute," Arline interrupted. "I have another daughter in Israel."

Tamara. Did she know? How to tell her? Arline felt her voice rising. She mentioned to Riley that Tamara was studying at Ben-Gurion University in Beersheba.

"Somebody has to tell her," Arline said of Tamara. "I can't call her. I can't even figure this out myself. I don't know what I'm going to do. Somebody has to tell my daughter. I don't want her to find out on the news."

As quickly as she felt herself falling apart, Arline regained control and assembled a plan to reach out to Tamara. She thought of a cousin in

Jerusalem—Rivkah Fishman and her husband, Joel—and another cousin at Ben-Gurion University. Perhaps they could help to notify Tamara.

Arline quickly found Rivkah's phone number and passed it to Riley. "I'll take care of this," Riley said, promising to call back later.

Looking back on that conversation years later, Arline could appreciate how difficult it must have been for Riley to make that phone call and deliver such news. Likewise, there is no unpainful way to take in such news.

Arline hung up the phone. Then she screamed.

And then something else happened—something that she can't explain even after years of contemplating it. Arline stopped screaming and began to organize herself and the day ahead. Call Ariella. Call her rabbi, her friends, the neighbors, her parents. Plan a funeral. Plan something to say when friends called.

She reached for the phone. Before she did anything else, she needed to make one call to a number in West Hartford, Connecticut, to Vicki and Len Eisenfeld.

Kathleen Riley said she had already called the Eisenfelds five hours earlier, because Matt's body had been positively identified sooner than Sara's. As he heard the phone ring by his bedside around 4:30 in the morning, Len was not alarmed or surprised. As a physician specializing in caring for critically ill babies, he had grown accustomed to phone calls at all hours of the night, delivering even the worst kind of news. "It's no big deal for the phone to ring," he recalled years later when he thought back to the moment.

Riley's voice was steady and measured. She asked if Len was the father of Matthew Eisenfeld.

"Yes," he said.

"Did you hear what happened?" Riley said.

"No."

"There's been a bus bombing in Jerusalem," Riley continued, then adding that Matthew had been killed.

Len exhaled.

"Whew," he said, falling silent. After pausing for a second or two, he asked Riley, "Would you please talk to my wife?"

As a doctor, Len had plenty of experience in telling parents that a child had died. But years before, he privately promised himself that he would never place himself in the position of having to tell his wife such news about Matthew or their daughter Amy. "I had already rehearsed in my mind that I never wanted to tell Vicki that one of our children had died," Len said.

Vicki was already awake and stirring next to her husband in the bed. She turned on the light. She was accustomed to Len speaking on the phone in the middle of the night with nurses or other physicians about serious medical problems with young children at the hospital. But this time, his tone was different. What's more, Len was not on call that night. "His voice sounded a little weird," she thought, especially when she heard Len ask the caller to "talk to my wife."

Len handed Vicki the receiver.

"What? Tell me what?" she asked. "What's going on?"

Kathleen Riley identified herself again and explained that she was calling about the bombing of a bus in Jerusalem. Had Vicki heard about it yet?

Vicki remembers her mind racing. Had I heard? Heard what?

"As fast as I wonder why she is calling me, my heart is reaching for Matthew, for my son and the sleep falls away completely," she remembers thinking. "I think he must be hurt. I wonder what hospital he is in and how fast I can get there."

As Vicki listened to Riley repeat the story about the bus bombing in Jerusalem and tried to weigh the impact of the message that her son had been killed, she remembered feeling strangely detached and rational, as if all this was happening to someone else and she was just an observer. "Somewhere I was thinking that this was crazy," Vicki said.

She was, of course, receiving the worst kind of news for any parent—that her child had died. And yet, Vicki found herself managing to remain steadily focused. "I didn't know where my voice is coming from," Vicki recalled. "I heard myself. But I seemed to be somewhere outside of myself. My voice sounded calm and familiar, but the words I was saying couldn't possibly have made sense."

Suddenly, Vicki interrupted Riley.

"What am I supposed to do?"

Riley asked Vicki where she and Len wanted to bury Matt. It was an abrupt question but not entirely unreasonable. One of the most difficult concerns when a US citizen dies in a foreign country is determining what the family back home wants to do with the body.

"I don't know," Vicki answered. "I never thought of that before. In Israel? At home? Okay, at home. How do I bring him home? Shall I just hop on a plane and come pick him up?"

The questions were popping up fast now in Vicki's mind.

"Was Matt with anyone?" Vicki asked.

The question seemed to startle Kathleen Riley. "Who do you think he was with?" she asked.

Vicki mentioned Sara Duker.

Riley wrote down the name, then said several victims had still not been identified. But she promised to check on the name and get back to her.

Vicki paused. Another question flashed through her mind: Suppose this call is some sort of dream, perhaps a perverted prank?

"Excuse me," Vicki asked Riley. "Can I call you back?"

Riley gave Vicki her phone number.

Vicki hung up. "Who do you call?" she remembers asking out loud.

Vicki phoned her brother, a lawyer in another Connecticut town, about an hour's drive from West Hartford. She told him she received a call from the US consulate in Jerusalem and that Matthew had been killed.

"I think it's real," she said. "What am I supposed to do?"

Meanwhile, Len was looking for the phone number to Sara's apartment in Jerusalem. Len knew that Sara lived with several other young women. Maybe they might know more.

He dialed the international telephone code for Israel, then the number to Sara's apartment. The phone rang and rang. No answer.

Vicki and Len then called Kathleen Riley.

In the brief period since they had talked, Riley was able to check with Israeli authorities on whether Sara had been on the bus—and, yes, Sara had died too.

Riley asked Len and Vicki not to call Arline—not immediately, anyway. Riley would make the call.

It was not even six o'clock in the morning yet in Connecticut. The sun would not rise for another hour. Len and Vicki pondered what they should do next. There are no guidelines for what just happened, no manual entitled, "How to Behave When Your Child Is Murdered."

"I deal with medical emergencies all the time, in life and death situations," Len said later. "I can usually think pretty clearly right on the spot."

As a doctor, he had watched scores of parents take in the news that a child had died. Sometimes Len had delivered the news himself. And as he reflected on those moments, Len recalled sometimes rehearsing how he would react if he ever had to receive the news that Matthew or Amy had died.

You can't prepare for the kind of telephone call that Len and Vicki had just received, even if you have been schooled in the meticulous rational thinking that experienced physicians employ.

"It's like the wind being knocked out of you," Len said.

He walked downstairs and fell into a chair. "My favorite chair," he remembered.

Len leaned back and felt the familiar comfort of the cushions nestling his back and arms. And then, he felt the heavy, somber weight of the moment again. Matthew had been killed. His Matthew. His son. Blown up by terrorists on a bus.

Suddenly Len felt another weight—his own mortality. As he watched Matthew graduate from Yale several years earlier and then enter into rabbinical school and meet a charming young woman named Sara, Len had felt he would be planning for a wedding, his son's ordination to the rabbinate, perhaps even for the arrival of grandchildren. And now that arc of life had been suddenly broken—literally blown apart. As he sat in his chair, Len thought, *I'm forty-nine years old at this point. At least I don't have much longer to live and I don't have to deal with this for too many years.*

Just after ten o'clock, the phone rang again. Len and Vicki recognized the familiar voice of Arline Duker.

The three had become close as they watched their children's relationship blossom. Len and Vicki picked up separate phone extensions so they could both speak to Arline.

As parents, they had privately become excited in recent months—without telling Matt and Sara, of course—how they looked forward to planning a wedding. Indeed, each had privately envisioned the day when their children would come to them to announce that they were planning to marry.

"We had a life where there were certain expectations and plans and things and suddenly our kids are dead," Arline said. Now they had to plan a funeral. "How are we going to live now?" she asked.

———

Just before midnight on Saturday, at almost the same moment that Arline Duker was speaking about Sara to her friends at the bar mitzvah party in Teaneck, another telephone rang, this time in a home in the Maryland suburbs of Washington, DC. Dennis Ross, the Clinton administration's special Middle East envoy and one of the principal players from the US in the Oslo peace process, picked up the receiver and was greeted by a familiar voice, the US ambassador to Israel, Martin Indyk.

Ross and Indyk came from far different parts of the world. Ross, the son of a Jewish mother and Catholic stepfather, had been raised in the San Francisco suburbs of Marin County and studied at the University of California at Los Angeles; Indyk, London-born and raised in Australia in a Jewish family, had been a student in Jerusalem when the 1973 Yom Kippur War erupted and even volunteered to help with the Israeli war effort. Both men knew each other well, though. Just as important, both trusted the other's judgment and observations. In the 1980s, Ross and Indyk cofounded a Washington think tank that specialized in Middle East policy studies. And in the Clinton administration, both had risen to become influential voices within the White House and the State Department on the often unpredictable winds that swept across Israel and the other nations in the Middle East.

As he picked up the phone and heard his friend's voice, Ross was fully aware that Indyk would not call him so late in the evening—and so early on Sunday morning from Israel—unless he had something important to discuss. Years later, Ross remembered checking the time. It was around 11:50 p.m. Saturday—6:50 a.m. on Sunday in Israel. The bomb on Jaffa Road had detonated a mere five minutes earlier.

Indyk did not mince words, Ross recalled. The ambassador told Ross a commuter bus in downtown Jerusalem had been blown up by a suicide bomber. Casualties were likely to be high.

Neither man knew yet that two American citizens had been killed and that several others had been wounded. That news would reach them a few hours later. Both nevertheless sensed that this bombing could be an ominous sign of things to come. When the second bomb exploded less than an hour later in Ashkelon, Ross's and Indyk's worst fears were confirmed. After months of remaining quiet, Hamas was back on the attack, with more suicide bombers. That these bombs exploded only a few months before Israel's scheduled elections was no coincidence, they felt.

Israel's electorate had become increasingly restless during the three years since the Oslo Peace Accords had been signed. The accords aimed to accomplish many goals, including the ultimate establishment of a Palestinian nation. But they were also supposed to usher in a new era of nonviolence in which Jews and Arabs would be free to visit each other's neighborhoods and towns without being attacked. It was this kind of hope that prompted Sara Duker and Matt Eisenfeld to plan a trip to Jordan—an Arab nation—to see the archeological ruins of Petra. Only a few years before, no Israelis, probably no Jews from any nation, would have dreamed of making such a trip.

But such hopes had been unraveling little by little, much to the dismay of Ross and Indyk. While the Oslo accords were supposed to be the pathway to building a Palestinian state, the assassination of Prime Minister Yitzhak Rabin demonstrated that not all Israelis were happy with that goal.

Besides those who believed that Israel had historical and theological ties to the West Bank and the Gaza Strip and should not give up the land, a large number of Israelis also worried that a Palestinian nation in those territories would be an all-too-tempting launching pad for attacks by militants affiliated with Hamas and Islamic Jihad. For some time, Indyk had been monitoring intelligence reports that described how Iranian operatives were trying to convince Palestinians—especially Hamas loyalists—to launch more attacks. He wondered now whether these two bombings were somehow linked to Iran.

At the heart of the Oslo process, and specifically Israeli's pledge to rescind its claims to the West Bank and the Gaza Strip, was a promise that each side would stop attacking the other. But those attacks and retaliations had not stopped. In April 1995, Alisa Flatow of New Jersey had been killed along with seven Israeli soldiers in a bus attack by a Palestinian suicide bomber. In August 1995, a suicide bomber killed five more people, including an American teacher from Connecticut, in another attack on a bus. Between those bombings, Palestinian operatives even tried to kill Israelis with bombs aboard donkey carts in the Gaza Strip. No Israelis died in the donkey cart bombings. But investigators from Shin Bet would later learn that Hassan Salameh had helped to build at least one of the bombs in those donkey carts. They also discovered that a compatriot of Salameh's—a previously little-known figure named Adnan al-Ghoul—had been part of the team of Palestinian operatives who carried out the bombing that killed Alisa Flatow. And al-Ghoul was linked to an even more notorious Palestinian operative—Yahya Ayyash, the so-called "Engineer."

In the years to come, such links between Salameh, Ayyash, and their compatriots would seem far more ominous. For now, however, most Israel investigators viewed the array of Palestinian operatives and bomb-makers as operating independently of each other.

Israel's counterterrorist agencies, meanwhile, had not been idle. Agents from Shin Bet and Israel's foreign intelligence agency, Mossad, had struck back with dramatic results. In September, outside a hotel on the island of Malta, a Mossad team, with its assassin aboard a motorcycle, gunned down the leader of the Palestinian cell responsible for the bombing that killed Alisa Flatow. Then came the assassination of Ayyash in January with an exploding cell phone.

During this time, an articulate and passionate American voice emerged who spoke in uniquely personal terms about the continuing attacks by Palestinians. In the months after Alisa's death, Stephen Flatow, a New Jersey lawyer, had begun to give a series of speeches to Jewish groups across America about what terrorism had done to his family—and what it meant for the future of Israel and the success of the Oslo peace process.

Dennis Ross knew Flatow was not the only American to raise concerns about whether it was a good idea to pursue the Oslo negotiations amid so much violence in Israel. Indeed, Flatow was touching on a basic question that many US officials had been asking: If Palestinian leaders can't control terrorist elements within their population, why should Israel entertain the idea of giving back large swaths of the West Bank and the Gaza Strip?

It was Ross's job to try to keep some notion of hope for peace alive. He feared that violence and discord could increase otherwise. In Israel, the successor to Yitzhak Rabin as Prime Minister, Shimon Peres, had gone to great lengths to assure his nation, and Ross, that he was personally committed to the Oslo process. But Peres's most formidable opponent, Benjamin Netanyahu, a US-educated conservative, had emerged as a major critic of the Oslo process, raising a basic question that resonated with many Israelis: Why should Israel trust the Palestinians if Palestinians continued to launch suicide attacks?

As Peres settled into his prime minister's job after the death of Rabin, he had a twenty-point lead over Netanyahu in Israeli opinion polls. Unlike the United States, where elections at all levels of government are generally conducted on a firm schedule, Israel's government is more flexible. National elections are scheduled every four years, but Israeli leaders can call for early elections. In December 1995, with such a large lead in the opinion surveys, Peres decided to roll the political dice. He announced that Israeli elections would take place the following May—far earlier than they were supposed to be held. Peres even flew to Washington to personally tell President Clinton of his plans.

Dennis Ross admired Peres in many ways. Ross saw Peres as a skillful diplomat, an insightful observer and a brilliant strategist who had been one of the primary forces in helping to develop Israel's top-secret nuclear weapons stockpile. But as a politician who depended on the backing of ordinary Israelis, Ross felt that Peres lacked fundamental skills needed to ensure his success with voters. He was also an uninspiring speaker. And while Peres had nurtured a keen instinct for long-term diplomatic strategy, Ross felt that he seemed remarkably deficient in being able to foresee the kinds of pitfalls that could hurt his own political career inside Israel. When Ross learned of Peres's decision to schedule elections in May, he turned to an Israeli official he knew and asked a question that still haunted him: "That's fine if Shimon wants to have an election, but what if two bombs go off?"

On the phone with Martin Indyk and hearing of the bombing on Jaffa Road, Ross recalled how he had asked that question. Ross knew how delicate the Oslo agreement was, in particular how even the most unexpected remark or attack by either side could derail the progress he had worked so hard for. He had been up late on Saturday, studying reports about negotiations he was trying to broker between the Israelis and Syrians. But as Indyk described the Jaffa Road attack to him, Ross wondered if this incident might become the first step to unraveling Shimon Peres's career as Israeli prime minister. And if Peres was thrown out of office, Ross feared what might become of the Oslo accords. An hour after Indyk's call, Ross's fears about Peres worsened. A second bomb blew up beside the soldiers' bus stop near Ashkelon.

In Israel, Martin Indyk shared similar fears about Oslo's future. For months, Indyk had been reviewing intelligence reports indicating that Iran would try to derail the Oslo process. To the Iranians, the creation of a stable Palestinian nation—and an even more stable and strong Israel— was not good news. The reports that Indyk saw portrayed Iran as favoring as much discord as possible in the region. And when it came to the Palestinians and Israelis, discord meant only one thing: bloodshed.

Ten months earlier, Indyk met with Stephen Flatow, who had come to Israel to escort his daughter's body home to New Jersey. It was a powerful moment for Indyk. As the US ambassador to Israel, he had been obviously aware of the increase in Palestinian suicide bombings. But now those bombings were killing Americans, too. Now, ten months after Alisa Flatow's killing, Indyk was about to learn that two more Americans had died. "As the American ambassador, I felt responsible for US citizens in the country," Indyk said. "It was very personal for me. These were people under my care."

In Washington, Ross called Secretary of State Warren Christopher soon after finishing his conversaton with Indyk. The White House and State Department were already aware of the Jaffa Road bombing. But another crisis had emerged, a crisis that would later play a role in how US officials responded to the Jaffa Road attack.

～

Just after 3 p.m. on Saturday, February 24, two fighter jets lifted off from an air force base in Fidel Castro's Republic of Cuba. Armed with missiles, the two Russian-designed supersonic Migs roared over the Straits of Florida. Their target: Three privately owned planes from the United States, piloted by volunteers from the anti-Castro group that called itself "Brothers to the Rescue."

Based in Florida and staffed by Cubans who fled to the US to escape Castro's dictatorial regime, the Brothers' stated goal was to patrol the Straits of Florida in search of other Cubans trying to sail the ninety-mile stretch of shark-infested waters in the hope of landing in Florida.

The Brothers were formed five years earlier after a much-publicized story of a Cuban exile who sailed away from his homeland in a leaky boat and later died of dehydration. The group increased its patrols in 1993, after thousands of Cubans attempted to make the trip to Florida in rickety boats. Many were rescued by US Coast Guard patrol boats, then taken to the American naval base at Guantanamo Bay, Cuba, where they lived in tents and other temporary structures not far from the same plot of arid, beachfront land where US authorities would later hold hundreds of Muslims who had been captured in Afghanistan and other nations after the 9/11 attacks. But despite extensive patrols by the Coast Guard, some boats sank and their passengers drowned. The Brothers hoped to stop those sorts of tragedies. From their patrol planes, the Brothers pilots would search for escaping boats, then radio the US Coast Guard to rescue them.

What seemed like a purely humanitarian mission, however, quickly became controversial, to Cuban officials, anyway. Since May 1994, Cuban air force officials said they logged numerous incidents in which the Brothers planes had flown into Cuban airspace without permission. In one incident, Cuban authorities said a Brothers plane flew low over Havana, releasing anti-Castro leaflets. Back in the US, federal aviation officials warned the Brothers that their planes might be attacked by the Cuban air force if they ventured too close to Cuba. The Brothers insisted they were unafraid. "You must understand," said Jose Basulto, the group's leader. "I have a mission in life to perform."

Basulto's rescue flights over dangerous international waters were widely praised. But venturing into Cuban air space was asking for trouble, and placing the US government in a difficult position. What if the Cubans attacked Basulto's planes?

In early January 1996, tensions between Cuban authorities and the Brothers increased after the Cuban air force accused the Brothers of flying into Cuban airspace and releasing more anti-Castro leaflets on two different days, an assertion still in dispute years later. The Brothers don't deny dropping the leaflets; they claim they released half a million of them over the Straits of Florida and well beyond the twelve-mile Cuban territorial limit, but that a strong wind blew the papers over the Cuban mainland. Cuban officials later offered what they claimed to be unassailable proof—from a spy they planted within the Brothers organization—that the leaflets were dropped ten miles from the Cuban coast, two miles within Cuban air space.

On February 24, when Cuban radar operators detected another group of Brothers planes heading toward Cuba, the Cuban air force was ready. As one Mig circled overhead, another fired two missiles, striking two of the Brothers planes, sending them plummeting into the water and instantly killing four Brothers volunteers who were at the controls. The third Brothers Cessna, piloted by Basulto, escaped and returned to Florida with an eyewitness report of the Cuban attack that immediately set off widespread protests among the Miami-based community of anti-Castro Cuban exiles.

Cuban authorities announced that they were defending their homeland from an illegal incursion. But while it seems likely at least one of the Brothers Cessnas briefly crossed into Cuban air space, US radar showed that all three of the Brothers planes were well outside Cuba's territorial line when the missiles were fired—a fact later confirmed by an international investigation that used independent radar data from ships sailing in the area.

As they sorted through the radar reports on that Saturday and weighed the diplomatic and political complexities of what the attack could mean, President Bill Clinton's staff of national security advisors quickly reached a conclusion: The United States could not remain quiet. America had to respond. With Clinton running for reelection in November 1996, the White House was determined not to look weak or indecisive. At the same time, the White House response should be meaningful and effective.

Richard Nuccio, the administration's top security advisor on Cuban issues, was weighing all of these concerns as he arrived at the White House on Saturday afternoon. In some ways, he was not surprised by the news that the Cuban air force had attacked the Brothers to the Rescue planes. He had long feared such a confrontation.

Nuccio was born in Teaneck, New Jersey, at a hospital only blocks from Sara Duker's home, though he had long since moved away from northern New Jersey. From years of studying the Cuban government, he knew that Castro did not flinch from using brute force, even if it meant shooting missiles at unarmed civilian planes. Likewise, Nuccio also understood the deep anger of many Cuban Americans toward Castro.

Next to Miami, northern New Jersey was home to America's second largest Cuban community. And Nuccio's reputation as one of Washington's foremost Cuba experts grew when he worked for Rep. Robert Torricelli, a North Jersey democrat whose district included a large Cuban community. Torricelli, who later won a Senate seat, had long been a champion of Cuban exiles—and was even well known inside Cuba for his anti-Castro speeches to American audiences. When Torricelli visited Cuban refugees during the summer of 1993 at the US Navy base at Guantanamo Bay, Cuba, a group of Cubans lifted the congressman on their shoulders and carried him around their camp. As one of Torricelli's aides and a staffer with a House foreign affairs subcommittee that specialized in Cuban issues, Nuccio met numerous exiles who had been imprisoned by Castro or had their property taken by his henchmen. And after listening to their stories, he had come to admire their passionate desire to rid their homeland of Castro's communism and to plant new seeds of democracy. But at the same time, Nuccio feared that an incident between Cuba and a Brothers plane could push America into a wider confrontation with Castro.

When Nuccio entered the Situation Room in the West Wing, information about the attacks was still coming in. The White House was awaiting absolute confirmation on the names of the dead and the positions of the Brothers planes when they were attacked. But, after listening to a briefing by two US military officers, Nuccio sensed in his gut that Castro had touched off a major international incident by ordering the Migs to attack unarmed American aircraft. "This was my first full-scale crisis," Nuccio wrote in his journal.

He left the Situation Room and went upstairs to speak with Sandy Berger, Clinton's deputy national security advisor. "We're going to need some options for the president," Nuccio remembers Berger telling him.

Berger declined to be interviewed for this book. But Nuccio kept detailed notes of their conversations. What follows is based on Nuccio's account.

Nuccio said Berger told him that staffers had already scheduled a meeting Sunday morning to discuss possible responses and that they would would meet with Clinton in the afternoon. "I think we have to move quickly on this, don't you?" Berger said.

"Of course, Sandy, but what kind of options are you talking about?"

Nuccio remembers Berger looking at him in disbelief.

"Sanctions against the regime," Berger said. "Military responses. Americans may have been killed."

Nuccio had long been frustrated by some of the risks that the Brothers group and other Cuban Americans had been taking as a way to protest Castro's brutal policies. "Sandy, these people have been playing with fire," Nuccio said. "They got exactly what they were hoping to produce. If we respond militarily, they will have succeeded in producing the crisis they've been looking for."

Berger's frustration brimmed too, Nuccio said. "Rick, are you telling me the United States should stand by and let Castro kill American citizens?" he said.

Nuccio promised to sketch out a list of policy options overnight. But he did not feel confident that a clear and effective strategy would evolve. Nuccio felt that the Brothers had been trying to provoke Castro. Now that Castro had acted, should the US march headlong into a war?

A day later, on Sunday, when Nuccio returned to the White House, he realized he was not the only White House advisor who harbored intense reservations about how strongly the US should respond to Castro. The skeptics included Joint Chiefs Chairman General John Shalikashvili. As the others settled into chairs around a table, Nuccio took a seat along the wall—a "back bencher," as he described his role.

Overnight, the White House had received news of the bombings in Israel—and the deaths of Sara Duker and Matthew Eisenfeld. By midday on Sunday, several hours after the Duker and Eisenfeld families had been called by Kathleen Riley, President Clinton issued a statement that called the bombings "brutal acts of terror" by "enemies of peace" and pledging that the US "stands alongside Israel and with all the peacemakers, as together we continue our work for a comprehensive and lasting settlement for all the peoples of the Middle East."

Inside the West Wing on Sunday, Nuccio noticed that the attacks in Israel were barely mentioned by anyone on the president's national security staff. Cuba seemed to be the top priority. "Because it was an election year," Nuccio recalled, "everything was in context of the upcoming election." And while Election Day was still eight months away, the Florida presidential primary was only two weeks away. Already Senator Bob Dole, a vocal Clinton critic and a Republican presidential candidate who was trying to court Miami's anti-Castro Cuban exile community was calling for a tough response to Castro from the White House. But the central problem was obvious to everyone at the meeting: How tough could Clinton actually be?

Shalikashvili explained that the US military had many options, but that an attack by American forces in Cuba posed major problems. An invasion would require large numbers of US troops, with a sustained ground war. Air Force attacks might prove to be useless, because Castro kept his fighter jets in fortified bunkers. A Naval blockade would likely hurt Cuban civilians instead of punishing its military elite.

The group next considered economic sanctions. But the US had already imposed a widespread economic embargo on Cuba. Not many other economic options were available, though Republicans in Congress had been pressuring to extend those sanctions with passage of the proposed Helms-Burton Act.

The group raised one more possibility: What about making Castro pay by taking financial assets that had been frozen in US banks during the early 1960s?

In general, the idea of taking another nation's property or, in this case, financial investments, as punishment was considered poor policy. Yes, it might be a way of quickly imposing a punishment—the equivalent of a monetary fine—against a rogue foreign state. But, as most experienced diplomats had long maintained, such quick-fix punishments could set dangerous precedents that might lead to retributions against American assets in other countries. If the US took billions in financial investments from a misbehaving nation, what would stop that nation, or others, from taking US property overseas? What's more, since the 1970s, US laws specifically gave "foreign sovereign immunity" to most nations, meaning that the US could seize assets or property of foreign nations only in specific cases and generally after the matter had been argued in court. Changing that policy would require new laws.

Despite these concerns, Nuccio found that the idea of making Cuba pay with some sort of financial fine for its attack on the Brothers to the Rescue planes quickly became a popular option within the White House. At 4 p.m. on Monday President Clinton stepped to the podium in the White House briefing room to announce how America would respond to the downing of the Brothers planes. There would be no military strike, no blockade. Clinton said America's ambassador to the United Nations, Madeleine Albright, had called an emergency session of the UN security council to condemn Cuba and to "present the case for sanctions" until Cuba "agrees to abide by its obligation to respect civilian aircraft and until it compensates the families of the victims."

Then, Clinton announced a four-point plan for action by the federal government. He called for travel restrictions, an upgrade in anti-Castro radio broadcasts, and pledged that he would no longer oppose but now supported an extension of the embargo as part of the Helms-Burton Act. But most notable and, ultimately, most controversial, was Clinton's first recommendation—to compensate the families of the Brothers pilots with Cuban government funds that had been withheld years before by the US government.

"I am asking that Congress pass legislation that will provide immediate compensation to the families, something to which they are entitled under international law, out of Cuba's blocked assets here in the United States," Clinton said.

The president offered no details about how much money was available or exactly what international laws he was referring to. But as a post-script Clinton added:

"If Congress passes this legislation, we can provide the compensation immediately."

They did not know it at the time, but Clinton's words would ultimately become a major driving force for the parents of Sara Duker and Matthew Eisenfeld, and for the parents of Alisa Flatow, as they sought accountability and justice for the murders of their children.

They too wanted the killers of their children to pay. On this day, however, they had no idea how much Fidel Castro and the Brothers to the Rescue would play a role in helping them achieve that goal.

First, someone had to find the killers.

In Jerusalem, Israeli police and Shin Bet agents were already on the trail of the bombers. But it was a confused, complex and frustratingly familiar trail.

Within hours of the explosions, Hamas claimed responsibility for the attacks. But there was no single, reliable message from Hamas. A leaflet, purportedly prepared by Hamas, proclaimed that "the attacks were a painful blow" in retaliation for Israel's assassination of Yahya "The Engineer" Ayyash. The leaflet also promised that future attacks would be canceled if Israel promised to stop hunting for Hamas fugitives and released the group's members who had been jailed for previous attacks. Other messages, allegedly from Hamas, contained no such promise, but nonetheless offered more information on the motivation for the attacks.

Anonymous callers, who said they were Hamas members, contacted Israel Radio's Arabic service and the Reuters news agency and repeated that the bombings were meant to avenge the death of Ayyash. But the callers also pointed out that the attacks were meant to coincide with the second anniversary of the killings of the twenty-nine Muslim worshippers in Hebron by Baruch Goldstein.

Beyond those brief and strident statements, Israeli investigators faced a more formidable dilemma. Besides the suicide bomber, who else was involved in the bombing plot?

Shin Bet and Israel's National Police knew from experience that suicide bombers rarely acted alone or on impulse. A suicide bombing often involved weeks of planning, suitcases full of cash and explosives, and a tightly knit, well-trained team of operatives that included scouts, drivers, guards, and a bomb-maker who doubled as the ringleader and recruited suicide bombers. As suicide bombings increased in Israel and researchers began to study the phenomenon, they discovered that the bomber was often the youngest, least experienced, and most politically naïve member of the team. And while the suicide bomber usually died in an attack, the others escaped.

So where were the other operatives who carried out Sunday's bombings on Jaffa Road and at the bus stop in Ashkelon? And were they planning other attacks?

Investigators had the name of the bomber—Majdi Abu Wardeh—from an ID card they found at the Jaffa Road bombing. And they knew that Wardeh had grown up in the al-Fawwar refugee camp near Hebron. But when Shin Bet agents arrived at the camp and found Wardeh's parents in a small concrete home halfway up a narrow street on the side of a hill, they found few leads.

Wardeh's father, Muhammed, a teacher, and his mother, Intesar, said they had been looking for their son for two days. "He left on Friday, and he told us he was going to Israel to work," Muhammed said, explaining that he did not feel his son would participate in a suicide bombing.

By late Sunday, however, Muhammed and Intesar Wardeh had no choice but to accept the terrible truth that their son had blown himself up aboard a bus in Jerusalem that morning. The parents gave the Shin

Bet agents DNA, which had been linked to the charred head found near the bus wreckage on Jaffa Road. Also, from talking to their son's friends, Muhammed and Intesar learned that their son had not gone to Jerusalem directly but had gone to Ramallah with his cousin, Mohammad.

Shin Bet agents were already contacting sources in Ramallah, focusing in particular on a Hamas cell at the city's Birzeit University. After questioning several students affiliated with the university, Shin Bet contacted two Palestinian security officers, one of whom turned out to be the driver of the blue Opel that brought Majdi Abu Wardeh to the Jaffa Road bus stop. After a lengthy interrogation, the driver offered a name of a Hamas operative they had not heard of before—Hassan Salameh.

Now, where was Salameh?

In Jerusalem, Israeli Prime Minister Shimon Peres called a news conference to discuss the bombings. He said Israel still supported the Oslo peace process and would continue to negotiate with the Palestinians—and also hunt for terrorists. "We will keep all the commitments we made, and neither the Hamas nor anyone else will move us from this," he added. "At the same time, no one will stop us from acting against Hamas with all means and in all ways."

Yet the day's attacks had clearly changed the tone of Israel's support for the Oslo process. And even as Peres repeated his allegiance to the process for which he shared a Nobel peace prize with his predecessor, Yitzhak Rabin, and with Yasser Arafat, he still seemed subdued and resigned to even more pain.

"I know deep in my heart that on the way to win peace, we shall have to pay a heavy toll for it," Peres said.

Late in the afternoon, Peres toured the Jaffa Road bombing scene, guarded by dozens of police. Until now, Peres had maintained a formidable lead against his challenger in the upcoming elections, Benjamin Netanyahu. Some polls still placed Peres more than 20 points ahead of Netanyahu. Others said the gap had fallen to 10 points. Whatever the case, Peres still had a clear lead, analysts said. And while Netanyahu quickly made a point of announcing in the hours after the Jaffa Road and Ashkelon bombings that he would not criticize Peres on this day and in the coming days for the attacks, Peres seemed suddenly vulnerable. It was as if the bombings—especially the attack in the heart of Jerusalem's bustling Jaffa Road business district—had ripped off an emotional scab and reminded Israelis that the Oslo peace process had not really brought peace.

As Peres walked toward the blackened frame of the Number 18 bus, a crowd of onlookers booed.

"With blood and fire, we will throw out Peres," several shouted.

"Peres go home," others yelled.

"Murderer."

"Traitor."

Still others chanted "Peres is next"—what many believed to be a sordid reference to the fact that Peres's predecessor, Yitzhak Rabin, had been shot to death by an Israeli who wanted to put a halt to the Oslo process.

Later in the day, Peres announced he was again sealing the borders between Israel and the Palestinian territories on the West Bank and in the Gaza Strip.

In Gaza City, Terje Roed-Larsen heard about the bombing in Jerusalem that morning, soon after waking up, and instantly remembered the warning he received the day before from Yasser Arafat. As he recalled years later, the news stunned him, but not necessarily because yet another bloody attack had taken place and innocent people had been killed. As an experienced Middle East diplomat, Larsen had seen far too much killing in the region, much of it to avenge earlier killings. He knew the cycle of death and, in particular, how frustrating it had become to men like him who had dedicated so many years trying to convince both sides to end the shootings and bombings and to embark on the difficult journey of building secure nation-states. What shocked Larsen was Arafat's warning and what it meant.

Larsen knew that one of the great hazards of Middle East negotiations was having to deal with the mysterious and often elusive and unpredictable Arafat who, with his pistol on his hip and his military uniform, still fancied himself as a guerrilla fighter and yet also wanted to be seen as a respectable diplomat who was as comfortable talking with a US president at the White House or chatting with world leaders at the United Nations in New York City as he was in rallying a crowd of several thousand Palestinians in Ramallah to resist the Israeli occupation of the West Bank.

Israel's leaders knew this firsthand. Shimon Peres's staff of advisors came to see Arafat not so much as a trustworthy ally or even a respected adversary but as an often-devious player who publicly proclaimed himself as a man of peace but chose to ignore some of the more violent Palestinian groups. "Arafat knew the impact of terror," said Peres's close friend and confidant Avi Gill. "And Arafat always held on to the violent option." What worried Avi Gill and others in Shimon Peres's inner circle was whether Iran's operatives had infiltrated Hamas and other radical Palestinian groups—and, if so, what Arafat planned to do about it.

In Gaza, following the bombing of the Number18 bus, Terje Roed-Larsen was not weighing the possible machinations of Iran. He was trying to sort out the meaning of Arafat's seemingly direct, yet typically cryptic warning. In all of his encounters with the Palestinian leader, Larsen had rarely experienced anything quite like the brief conversation on Saturday in which Arafat urged him to avoid Jerusalem on Sunday. To Larsen, Arafat's tone held even greater meaning than his words. In Larsen's mind, Arafat was delivering a warning. And now that a bomb had exploded, indeed, a bomb that would clearly cause Israel's conservatives to again question the wisdom of pursing the Oslo peace process, Larsen had come face to face with one of the deepest concerns shared by many diplomats who came to the Middle East with good intentions only to find themselves mired in rhetorical quicksand and an emotional maze that blurred history, theology, politics, and language.

Did Arafat, the recipient of a Nobel peace prize, know that this terrorist bombing was going to take place? If so, how could Larsen ever trust him again? And on a more practical note, should Larsen confront Arafat?

"I felt Arafat had knowledge beforehand that this attack was going to happen," Larsen said years later.

For now, however, Larsen decided to keep quiet.

⚊⚊

Apart from the massive hunt for the bombers by police and Shin Bet agents, the jockeying of various political factions for leverage and the looming debates about assigning blame for this latest attack, a delicate and gruesome question had still not been answered by nightfall. How many people had died in the bombing?

When terrorist attacks take place in Israel, the counting of the dead—and, more importantly, the identification of them—inevitably falls to the group of men and women who work in a series of tan, flat-roofed, cinderblock buildings that are located behind a walled compound on the outskirts of the ancient city of Jaffa, near Tel Aviv. Officially, the compound is called the National Institute of Forensic Medicine or sometimes the Abu Kabir Forensic Institute as a reference to its location in the community of Abu Kabir. But to Israelis, it carries a far more mundane name—the national morgue.

The bodies of Matthew Eisenfeld and Sara Duker were brought to the morgue in an Israeli ambulance, then placed in what their autopsy reports described as a "refrigeration chamber" to await an examination by a pathologist.

At 11 a.m., the institute's director, Dr. Yehuda Hiss, removed Sara's body and brought it to an autopsy room. In an adjoining room, another pathologist, Dr. Esther Daniels Phillips, began to examine Matt's body.

Neither doctor chose to perform a complete autopsy, which would involve examining Matt's and Sara's internal organs, though both doctors took photographs and x-rays. Hiss had learned from years as a battlefield physician with the Israeli Defense Forces, that the cause of death after a bombing is often so obvious that there is no need to examine a victim's heart, liver, and brain. "Often the shock of a blast has a severe impact on the human body," Hiss explained. "Someone can be killed by a blast that takes place fifteen meters away or farther."

As Hiss looked down on Sara's body, he made note in his records that she was still wearing her belt pouch containing her credit card and bank card, along with the travelers cheques she brought for the trip to Petra. One of her hiking boots was missing. And her left earring had become detached and entangled in her hair. But her watch, still attached to her left wrist, was ticking.

Matt was still wearing his green coat with the brown collar and his black Reebok shoes. But, unlike Sara, who appeared to have been killed instantly, Dr. Phillips found that paramedics had placed an IV needle into Matt's right forearm. Did this mean that Matt was still alive when paramedics arrived at the scene? At the moment, the question seemed pointless. After all, Matt had died. But in the years to come, that tiny needle hole in Matt's arm would be viewed by some as evidence that he had suffered before he died.

At the morgue that day, the conclusion of how Matt and Sara died was clear. Both doctors resorted to identical phrasing in their reports. "Death," they wrote, "was caused by explosion of explosive material."

They would use that same phrase often that day as other bodies were brought to the morgue.

By nightfall, the bodies had been counted and identified. Twenty-five people had been killed on the Number 18 bus, along with the bomber, Majdi Abu Wardeh. (Another badly burned bus rider, Ira Weinstein, a dual Israeli-US citizen, would die six weeks later, bringing the total to twenty-six.) In the Ashkelon bombing, one bus rider had been killed, along with the bomber.

It was the highest single-day death toll in Israel from a terrorist attack in more than two decades.

—◦—

On Sunday evening, the doorbell sounded and Arline Duker opened her front door. Two men stood on the porch. Arline knew one man well—a rabbi from Sara's high school. She had seen the other man on television and had come to admire him for his eloquence and passion.

"I'm Stephen Flatow," the man said.

Arline felt relieved to see him. She did not need to be reminded that only ten months earlier Flatow's daughter, Alisa, had been killed by a suicide bomber who crashed an explosives-filled van into the side of a bus on the Gaza Strip.

Arline also knew that Flatow, a powerfully built man with round shoulders, thick forearms, and penetrating eyes, had made a point of not remaining quiet about his daughter's death, either in comments to the media or in appearances. Could Arline take on such a role? Arline sensed that, like Alisa Flatow, Matt and Sara would become symbols of the tragic randomness of terrorism and the growing problems with Oslo peace process as a path to real peace in the Middle East.

During the day, in brief moments when she was able to set aside the shock and emotional sadness over losing Sara, Arline thought how the attack on the Number 18 bus would change her life. TV news trucks had already parked on the street. News reporters knocked on the door. Photographers clustered on the sidewalk. Arline felt an intense desire to protect herself and her two other daughters. Yet, she was also resigned that her family would be in the public eye for at least the near future.

"This is going to be a very public experience," Arline remembered thinking to herself. "My life as I know it is going to be over."

She invited Flatow into the living room.

"You speak a lot," she asked, surprised somewhat by her directness. "How do you do that?"

"You find ways," Flatow began.

In a calm voice, he told Arline that he found some measure of comfort and healing by talking about his daughter's death. He did not want Alisa's life, or murder, to be forgotten. And so, he said he accepted as many invitations as possible to speak. And if contacted by the news media, he offered comments on the peace process.

"It doesn't mean you have to do that, too," Flatow said. "Don't do something because somebody is telling you that you have to."

Flatow's self-confidence was comforting—even somewhat empowering to Arline. Here, in Flatow, was a father who had not descended into such a deep despair over his daughter's death that his life and family had been paralyzed. Flatow had seized the tragedy of his daughter's killing as an opportunity to draw attention to deeper issues of terrorism and how to hold terrorists accountable.

"I just wanted to let Arline know that I was there to support her," Flatow said later. "She was not alone."

"I had seen him walking and talking and being active," Arline remembered. "He seemed like such a powerful person and had such composure. But I sensed he was dying inside. Yet he didn't disintegrate. And I said, 'Okay, it's possible to live with this devastation. You don't have to die.'" After forty-five minutes, Flatow left. As she reflected later on his visit and words of advice, Arline remember how a thought flashed through her mind: "Okay. It's possible somehow."

What Stephen Flatow did not mention that night was that he had already convinced himself of the need to hold his daughter's killers accountable for what they had done. In time, Flatow would become a key guidepost as Arline Duker and Vicki and Len Eisenfeld also ventured down that same path and asked the most basic of all questions when anyone is murdered:

Who did this?

# CHAPTER 4

THE MATCHING PINE COFFINS LAY SIDE BY SIDE, SEEMINGLY SUSPENDED in time and space above the freshly dug grave. It had been three days since Kathleen Riley called Arline Duker and Len and Vicki Eisenfeld, three days of trying to balance the emotional riptides over the killing of Sara and Matt while weighing such pragmatic logistical decisions as how to bring the bodies back to the United States, what sorts of funeral services to organize and what, if anything, they should say when the TV news crews knocked on their front doors. One decision, however, seemed obvious and inevitable to both families, perhaps even easy in the midst of such a wrenching time.

Matt and Sara would never be joined together as husband and wife, but the obvious closeness of their relationship and the fact that they died together, seated side by side on the Number 18 bus, meant, in the minds of their families, that they should remain together, side by side. And so the Dukers and Eisenfelds agreed that the bodies of their children would lie next to each other forever in the same grave, in a Jewish cemetery nestled in the rolling hills on the outskirts of Hartford, Connecticut, a few miles from the home where Matt grew up.

The joint burial of Sara and Matt underscored the tragedy of their deaths, and the sight of the two coffins together, about to be lowered into the same grave, was like a powerful emotional magnet that brought together all the sorrow and anger that the bombing had touched off. Here, in a quiet Connecticut cemetery, were the side-by-side symbols of how senseless murder was now woven into the fabric of life in the Middle East. The journey to the cemetery and the emotions that accompanied it, however, began two days earlier at an airport warehouse in Israel.

A death can produce emotional tides that wash through the layers of families, friends, colleagues, and even those who may have had only a chance encounter with the person who died. Sometimes those personal tides are strong; sometimes they are nuanced and remarkably subtle.

The deaths of Sara and Matt—and especially the brutal way they were killed—touched off a wide array of responses in the media, on their college and seminary campuses in America and Israel, in homes of friends across the world. But their deaths also set off political ripples too that brushed up against a range of public figures in Israel and in the United States, and touched on some of the most complex issues of the Middle East peace process. So perhaps it was not surprising that the first memorial service for Sara and Matt—a hastily organized good-bye ceremony at Israel's Ben Gurion Airport on Monday—had two parts. One ceremony focused on the personal; the other on the political.

After doctors at Israel's national morgue completed their autopsies, wrote their reports and catalogued the clothing and personal belongings, the bodies of Sara and Matt were placed in separate coffins and driven to the airport, a few miles north of Tel Aviv. Just after 2 p.m., on Monday, a van from the morgue pulled onto the tarmac and drove to a warehouse, stacked high with boxes and other cartons to be shipped across the globe. Several dozen friends and colleagues of Matt and Sara stood in silence as airport handlers opened the doors of the van, then removed two coffins and placed them on the warehouse floor.

The gathering was not supposed to be a funeral service for Sara and Matt—that would take place in America. But many friends and colleagues in Israel felt the need to come to the airport, if only to offer a silent good-bye and perhaps recall what Sara and Matt meant to them.

A rabbi who had grown close to Matt, Menachem Schrader, stepped forward and turned to the group. Schrader grew up in the New York City borough of Queens, just across the East River from Manhattan. But he moved to Israel as a young man to teach Hebrew scriptures and bore the soft-spoken demeanor of someone who had spent much time quietly reflecting on the meaning of life's ups and downs, as chronicled in thousands of years of Jewish writings.

Two years earlier, as Matt watched a stream of ambulances rush down the Hebron Road to try to save Palestinian victims of the shooting at the Cave of the Patriarchs, Schrader had been his primary teacher. Schrader had an unusually personal connection to the shootings. The gunman, Baruch Goldstein, had been Schrader's personal physician. "He was deeply depressed," Schrader said of Goldstein recalling the incident. "It was such a needless act."

After that shooting, Schrader, the scriptural scholar, and Matt, the eager student, grew closer. During their year together, Matt looked to Schrader for guidance on a delicate topic he had been wrestling with: Whether to become an Orthodox rabbi or to remain with the more egalitarian branch of Conservative Judaism where Sara seemed to feel most comfortable.

In time, Matt left Schrader's school and enrolled at the Jewish Theological Seminary in Manhattan, a Conservative institution that had embraced egalitarian roles for women and that sits like a proud castle on the northern edge of the Columbia campus and across the street from its Christian counterpart, Union Theological Seminary.

Matt kept in touch with Schrader. Six months before returning to Israel and his studies at the Schechter Institute, the Jerusalem branch of Jewish Theological Seminary, Matt wrote a four-page, handwritten letter to Schrader in which he touched on an entirely new topic—his desire to marry Sara someday. "We speak about marriage often," Matt wrote. "If all goes well, I could see being engaged within the next year, to be married the following summer. I pray to bring it about, and to do so quickly if this relationship is correct."

Schrader kept Matt's letter. When he learned that Matt had been killed along with Sara, Schrader thought of the wide-open trust that his former student displayed as he confided how much he dreamed of making a life with Sara and encouraging her work as a scientist. Before driving to the airport and anticipating that he might have an opportunity to speak at a memorial service to Sara and Matt, Schrader took out three pages of blank computer paper and began to sketch out his memories of the promising rabbinical student he had mentored and the young research scientist that Matt wanted to marry. In hand-printed block letters, and sprinkling an occasional Hebrew word or two amid his English sentences, Schrader recounted a meeting he attended less than a month before at Matt's apartment in Jerusalem, in which Matt gave a formal presentation to fellow rabbinical students and friends on a Talmud tractate that he had been studying. For any rabbinical scholar, a detailed and meticulous study of an entire Talmud tractate took considerable effort. Among his colleagues at the Schechter Institute, Matt was the first to complete one. And the fact that Matt took on this particular endeavor as an independent project to be done on his own time underscored how monumental was his achievement. Schrader also was impressed by the subject of the Talmud tractate that Matt had selected: marriage and the ideals that Judaism inspired in husbands and wives.

When rabbinical scholars complete their study of a section of the Talmud, it's customary to make a presentation of what they have learned to a gathering—or *siyum*—of fellow students.

On that evening for the siyum, Matt's apartment brimmed with friends and fellow students. Along the wall, a table held bottles of wine. Another table was crammed with plates of food, including a vegetarian dish Sara had created. Matt took a seat near the table with wine and looked out on the apartment living room and his friends and fellow students.

Sara watched Matt intently from a nearby chair.

Rabbi Schrader watched them both, admiring how much his former student had grown and how promising his future looked, not only as a rabbi but as a man with Sara as his partner.

Now, standing silently in the airport warehouse, with the coffins of Matt and Sara, were some of those same friends and fellow students who attended Matt's siyum only weeks earlier. Schrader could feel their collective sorrow filling the warehouse as they waited for him to speak.

He began by remembering the siyum—and the happiness and pride that so many felt that evening for Matt. "Matt had the crowd completely engrossed in his presentation," Schrader said. "For a brief moment, I saw the power which could have been, the teacher who could have taught, the mentor who was already serving as a model for his friends."

Schrader then turned his thoughts to Sara—and what she meant to Matt.

"For Matt, Sara was a dream," Schrader said. "A dream for which Matt waited to realize with great anticipation. A dream Matt waited with great patience."

Schrader did not need to remind everyone how broken that dream had now become.

Several hours later, another farewell ceremony took place. For this, the coffins were draped in US flags and moved to the tarmac near the door of a baggage compartment of an Israeli El Al jetliner that was scheduled to fly that night to John F. Kennedy International Airport in New York City.

Ambassador Martin Indyk stepped from his car and walked to a small podium. Two bombings that seemed to have been orchestrated to take place the same day had unearthed a wave of unease among Middle East diplomats about the stability of the Oslo process. But to Indyk such concerns seemed secondary now with the sight of the two coffins on the tarmac. Not only had two Americans died in one of those bombings, but two others who had dual US and Israeli citizenships—Leah Stein Mousa and Ira Weinstein—were being treated in Jerusalem hospitals for life-threatening burns and other wounds.

"Friends," said Indyk. "We are gathered here to send Matthew and Sara on their last journey back to their parents for their burial in the United States. They were two of America's finest, the best, the brightest. One from Yale, the other from Barnard. One a rabbi, the other a research scientist. They came here together to celebrate their love of Israel. They leave here in caskets. They were good friends who, bright and early yesterday morning, were starting out on a trip to Jordan in order to taste the fruits of peace, when a fanatical suicide bomber ended their lives along with the lives of twenty-three Israelis—snuffed out their futures that a mere twenty-four hours ago looked so bright and full of promise."

Indyk offered his official condolences "on behalf of the United States government, President Clinton and Secretary of State Warren Christopher." He reiterated his hope to "close the circle of peace and to go on with the fight against terror." He then returned to a personal theme. "It is not in the natural order of things for parents to bury their children," Indyk said. "I pray, I know, the day will come when this will not happen again."

Schrader's soft-spoken eloquence and Indyk's measured phrasing set a tone for what would come in the following days. The coffins, still draped in American flags, were loaded into the belly of a jetliner for the eleven-hour flight to New York.

Almost forty hours later, on Wednesday afternoon, with a stiff New England breeze rattling the bare branches of the maples and oaks that lined the perimeter of the Temple Beth El cemetery in Avon, Connecticut, and with the sun blocked by a somber blanket of gray clouds, Sara's and Matt's remains arrived at their final resting place.

A traditional Jewish funeral is governed by exacting symbolism and customs that date back thousands of years. But the final rite—the burial itself—is uniquely personal and intimate. Friends and family do not rely on the help of cemetery workers to shovel dirt atop the coffins after they are lowered into the earth. The *k'vurah*—the Hebrew name for the filling in of the grave with dirt—is performed by family and friends. The rite is so intricately choreographed that those who pick up a shovel are instructed to turn the shovel backwards so as not to show their enthusiasm for what they are doing. Also, the shovels are not handed from one person to the next but are merely shoved into the ground when one person is finished so that another person can grab the shovel.

Such gestures and the act of tossing dirt atop a coffin in the grave is not considered a burden. This final rite is seen as a labor of love for friends and relatives, a "mitzvah" and gift that cannot be reciprocated, which helps to bring a sense of spiritual closure that allows the soul to be released.

Arline Duker and her daughters, Tamara and Ariella, stood silently with the Eisenfelds and their daughter, Amy, and hundreds of mourners who clustered on the neatly trimmed grass to await the moment when the coffins would be lowered and covered with dirt. As mourners recited the last prayers of Judaism's ancient burial rite, the symbolism of what Sara and Matthew might have become was made clearer. Death cut short their lives together, separating them from friends and family. But in eternity, they would always be united, side by side.

In eulogizing the couple during Sara's funeral the day before at Teaneck's Congregation Beth Shalom, Rabbi Kenneth Berger called the decision to bury the couple together "a fitting end to a great love story." Now in the cemetery, as he gazed at the matching coffins, Matt's family rabbi, Stanley Kessler, echoed Rabbi Berger's sentiments. "It's so appropriate that they be buried near each other," Rabbi Kessler told one of the dozens of news reporters who covered the burial. "Their souls are surely intertwined for all eternity."

Even before this final trip to the cemetery, Sara and Matt had become noteworthy figures in the news media, in America, and across the world. Obviously, there were other victims in the bombing of the Number 18 bus on Jaffa Road, some with deeply tragic stories. The dead included soldiers, a Holocaust survivor, recent immigrants to Israel from Romania, a Palestinian commuting to work, and a husband and wife who had come to Israel from the Ukraine and were taking the bus to look at a new apartment. When they died, the couple left behind an eight-year-old son who promised, when interviewed by Israeli television just after his parents were buried in Jerusalem, to try to remember them as best he could.

"How do I see things? I think things will be okay," the boy said, sounding far older than he was. "I already missed them yesterday. But I'll have to get over it."

The deaths and lives of Sara and Matthew and their budding relationship seemed to capture a deeper essence of the tragedy, though. Sara and Matt were bright, handsome, and, of course, in love. In a sense, they were seen as a modern day Romeo and Juliet. But unlike the Shakespearean characters, Sara and Matt were not victims of misguided suicides that stemmed from a pointless family feud. They were killed in a suicide-murder that seemed equally pointless and had been carried out by a young Palestinian man misguided by a theology that called for the deaths of innocent people in the name of a larger political and theological cause.

As touching as it seemed to bury Sara and Matt together, the fact that they died so uselessly and violently seemed to add an unspoken emotional weight that each mourner carried through the funerals and to the cemetery.

During Sara's funeral, Rabbi Berger drew attention to the inexplicable tragic nature of their deaths by referencing the Book of Job and how the central character, Job, a good man who attempts to lead an exemplary life, looked heavenward and asked why God seemed to have abandoned him.

"Today we stand here with Job," said Rabbi Berger. "We know there are no answers, no words with which to mitigate the pain or console the inconsolable. It's so hard to believe that Sara's life ended so suddenly and tragically. All we can do is sit here today with each other and remember the light that Sara and Matt brought to our lives and to the world."

What also captured the world's attention—and underscored the tragedy and its irony even more—was that Sara and Matt had been outspoken, in the US and in Israel, about their desire for Israelis and Palestinians to live in peace. When Prime Minister Yitzhak Rabin had been assassinated five months earlier, Matt's seminary colleagues selected him to speak at a memorial service, in part because he wanted to talk about the need to find a peaceful solution to Israeli-Palestinian conflict. In an essay she wrote a year earlier to win a grant to help fund her trip to Israel, Sara pointed out the importance for Israelis to treat their Arab neighbors with respect.

"Extremism characterizes political debate with deep rifts between religious and secular Jews," wrote Sara. "And no matter what our national and religious beliefs regarding the West Bank and Gaza, there are few Jews who do not experience at least some discomfort with Israeli policies toward the Palestinian Arabs."

Watching the families and others gather, Colette Avital, the Israeli counsel general based in New York City, felt the sadness of the moment envelop her. As an experienced diplomat, Avital knew it was her job to keep her emotions under wraps in moments like this and to offer a brief message of condolence and sorrow. But seeing the two coffins together and knowing the story of how Sara and Matthew were considering marriage, Avital realized that this was not a moment to remain distant.

"The idea of two young people, very much in love and very much looking forward to their future and—poof—they no longer exist is something that hits you on a personal level," Avital remembered thinking.

Earlier, during a service at the Eisenfeld family's synagogue, Avital spoke of how the deaths seemed to touch her and indeed everyone so intimately. "There are times when words escape the most eloquent of speakers, when the unexpected events of our lives overtake our ability to understand. Today is such a day," she said. "For how could I have imagined the day that I would stand here, representing the government of Israel, at this service for two young, wonderful human beings who have now joined the long list of our victims. Yesterday, I stood stunned with the thousands of mourners who came to pay a last resounding tribute to

Sara Duker. Yesterday, in Israel, we lowered the bodies of our loved ones into the warm soil of Israel."

Avital mentioned a twenty-year-old female soldier, Hofit Ayash, who died in the suicide bombing attack at Ashkelon forty-five minutes after the Number 18 bus exploded. Ayash planned to marry in June. She recently completed her military service and was only at the bus stop in Ashkelon because she was traveling to her army base one last time to return her gear and say good-bye to friends.

Avital then mentioned Peretz Gantz, sixty-one, a Holocaust survivor, who died on the Number 18 bus; then Boris Sharpolinsky, sixty-four, a new immigrant from Ukraine; Celine Zaguri, nineteen, and in Israel only six weeks; Yonatan Barnea, the son of the journalist Nahum Barnea, who ran from his office near Jaffa Road to the scene to cover the story, only to realize that his son was dead; the eight-year-old boy who lost both parents.

Finally, she turned to Matt and Sara.

Avital recounted how Matt spoke to his seminary classmates about the importance of continuing the peace process after the assassination of Yitzhak Rabin. She mentioned Sara's environmental work in Russia during the previous summer.

"The tragedy that stole Matthew and Sara from you, from their sisters, from their friends, from their people cannot be reversed. We cannot even say, 'Let them not have died in vain.' For their deaths were as senseless as the act that took away their lives. The terrorist who strapped around him twenty pounds of explosives did not make individual distinctions. What we can do is to ensure that Matthew and Sara did not live in vain."

As with countless other funerals after countless other tragic deaths across the arc of human history, the relatives and friends of Sara Duker and Matthew Eisenfeld understood that a burial of someone you love and admire is not just a time for mourning. It is a time for telling stories, too—or simply remembering those now gone.

In his office in Hong Kong, where he worked for a branch of the J.P. Morgan investment banking conglomerate, Xiao-Guang Sun picked up the phone and heard a familiar voice—a friend from Yale, named Josh. Matt and Sara were dead, Josh said. Killed in a bus bombing in Jerualem.

Raised in China, Xiao came to the United States in his final year of high school along with his father, a university professor. After a year in a New England prep school, Xiao found himself at Yale, barely understanding English and with no friends.

On his first day, Xiao met Matt Eisenfeld and the two immediately became close. That connection continued even after Xiao transferred to the Massachusetts Institute of Technology after just one year at Yale. Xiao spent holidays at the Eisenfeld home in West Hartford. When he returned to Asia after graduating from MIT, Xiao and Matt kept up a regular correspondence. When Xiao's girlfriend recently accepted his marriage proposal, one of the first friends he told was Matt.

When the telephone rang at his desk at J.P. Morgan, Xiao already knew about the bus bombing in Jerusalem. He typically began his days by devouring the *South China Morning Post*, an English-language daily that served Hong Kong. And as he read an account of the bombing, Xiao thought of Matt.

"I can't say it was superstition," Xiao said. "But I did think: 'Well, Matt is there. What's going on there?'"

Now he knew. Xiao got off the phone, left his office and walked to a nearby park and sat on a bench in silence, his mind tracing how his life had intersected with Matt's. "I couldn't come to the reality of what happened," he said. "It was the first death in my life of someone I knew well."

Xiao remembered having a drink with Matt in a Manhattan bar near Columbus Circle only the summer before when he had flown from Hong Kong on a business trip. He thought of a postcard a year earlier from Matt. Then Xiao thought of his last communication, a letter Matt wrote two months earlier. In jagged handwriting that covered two pages, Matt congratulated Xiao on his upcoming wedding and sketched out his life in Israel—rising at 5:30 for morning prayers and spending weekends with Sara—while also hinting of the country's internal troubles. "Needless to say, this has been a difficult year in some ways," Matt wrote. "Prime Minister Yitzhak Rabin was killed a month ago, sending us all into depression. It's hard to act when such terrible things happen, but one must.

One must continue to contribute to one's community, perhaps with more energy than before."

That hopeful look into the future was typical of Matt, Xiao thought. So were Matt's final lines: "Tell me the date of your wedding! And send me an invitation! Sara might even come too!"

Across continents and oceans, other friends of Sara and Matt settled into the same ritual of remembrance.

In Austin, Texas, another of Matt's Yale roommates, Ted Scott, thought of the letter he had also received recently in which Matt mentioned that he and Sara planned to travel to Jordan. "Now that there is peace, this type of travel is safe," Matt wrote.

At Barnard College, where she was finishing her senior year of studies, Oshrat Carmiel, recalled Sara's whimsical wardrobe—especially her love of Keds purple sneakers—that camouflaged her intense intellect. "She wanted to be different," Carmiel said. "She was very proud of being very smart. She was not going to hide that. There was a part of her that was emboldened. It wasn't in your face. It was how she presented herself. She just wanted to do something different."

"Everything about her was petite, but when she was ready to announce a thought she spoke with force," Carmiel said. "It was easy to dismiss her. It was easy to think that she was the soft, quiet person. It takes a while that you have this creeping realization that this is a person with a serious intellect."

Another friend of Sara's at Barnard, Celia Deutsch, had just stepped off the subway at the Columbia University stop when a colleague stopped her.

"I'm so sorry," the colleague told Deutsch.

"What?" Deutsch said.

It was the Monday morning after the bombing, and Deutsch had not yet heard the news about Sara and Matt.

Deutsch and Sara had bonded in a unique way the previous year. Deutsch, a Roman Catholic nun and religion professor at Barnard, was an expert in ancient Jewish scriptures. Sara had been selected for a special Barnard program—Centennial Scholars—that required her to write a research paper. Sara had chosen to examine the writings of a first-century rabbi, Elisha ben Abuyah. She asked Deutsch to guide her.

With the news that her former student was dead, Deutsch's mind raced back to the hours she had spent talking with Sara the previous year about Judaism and the rich tradition of scripture.

"She had a liberty of mind," Deutsch said years later. "In my mind, I kept seeing her."

Many others felt the same way. The news that Sara and Matt had been killed unleashed a steady torrent of memories that seemed to grow in the days leading up to their joint burial. The sharing of memories seemed almost to bring them to life again. But of course, the very act of speaking of a memory was a stark reminder that only the memories were left now, mixed now with the conflicting emotions of anger and disbelief over what had taken place.

At Sara's funeral in Teaneck, Tal Weinberger, who befriended Sara in high school and Matt at Yale and then watched their relationship blossom, stepped to the podium in the front of the synagogue, and paused for a moment as she looked out over the crowd that included New Jersey Governor Christine Todd Whitman. "The only reason I can stand up here and talk reasonably calmly is because I'm still in denial," Weinberger said. "I always imagine all the milestones of my life with Sara in the background. I still haven't realized that I won't be at her wedding and that we won't be able to babysit for each other's kids."

In a letter read to the congregation, Sara's younger sisters, Tamara and Ariella, invoked their sister's love of purple sneakers and how she had taken a job recently in Jerusalem as a housecleaner to earn extra money but had been fired for incompetence. "For those who would use her death as an excuse to blame and hate, we can only say that our sister never hated anyone and would never have wanted to contribute to the hate in this world," the sisters wrote.

At Matt's funeral, Cantor Joseph Ness wept as he sang a dirge. Matt's uncle, Larry Port, told reporters outside that "if Matt were still here, he would want the peace process to continue. He believed in it strongly." Matt's friend and roommate, Shai Held, recalled how Matt and Sara regularly prayed together. And yet, as Held also noted, Matt's spirituality was not without its lighthearted moments. Matt loved studying the Torah, said Held. But he also loved an occasional sip of whiskey.

Matt's sister, Amy, too choked up to speak, wrote a letter that was read to the congregation in which she described how her brother helped her with a newspaper route. The two siblings piled newspapers in a wheelbarrow, then walked the streets of their hometown. But Amy conceded she quickly tired. "Because I was always exhausted, it became our routine that I would get into the wheelbarrow and Matt would push me uphill, the rest of the way home," she wrote. "Matt will never push me home again."

Rabbi Benjamin Segal, the president of Jerusalem's Schechter Institute where Matt was studying, called his promising student "a gentle soul with a very fine mind." Then, Segal turned his thoughts to both Matt and Sara. "Such wonderful young people who could have been great leaders, great people, are lost," he said. "It's an old story."

And so it went.

⌒

The memories multiplied as the funerals unfolded, told often in brief stories that touched on Sara's whimsy or Matt's ability to listen when someone needed to vent, stories of their spirituality, their academic pursuits, their careful nurturing of friendships and even their acceptance of strangers.

One story, repeated often in public and in private discussions among their friends, involved a homeless woman at the Columbia campus who was befriended by Matt and Sara as they walked to their classes during the year before they left for Jerusalem. The woman's name was Annie.

The Columbia campus, which sits atop a series of craggy hills called Morningside Heights on Manhattan's Upper West Side and is flanked by the massive Episcopal Cathedral of St. John the Divine on one side and the tomb of President Ulysses S. Grant on the other, has been home to an extraordinarily diverse population. Dwight Eisenhower walked the campus as its president. Barack Obama was there as a student. Other noteworthy residents included beat poet Allen Ginsberg, choreographer Twyla Tharp, author-monk Thomas Merton, singer Suzanne Vega, the Yankees' Lou Gehrig, comedian Joan Rivers, and an endless list of writers, philosophers, mathematicians, revolutionaries, performers, physicists, artists, sociologists, and dreamers. In World War II, the Manhattan Project, which led to the invention of the atomic bomb, was born on the Columbia campus. In the late 1960s, Columbia was also home to one of the most radicalized of student groups in a time when almost every college campus brimmed with radicals.

But like almost every other New York City neighborhood, the campus was also a magnet for its share of homeless, or street people.

It was wintertime on the Columbia campus. Sara was winding up her courses at Barnard College and diving into work with Sister Celia Deutsch on her final thesis before graduation; Matt was midway through the first year of his studies at Jewish Theological Seminary.

Annie seemed to have no real home, except the streets. She spent her days sitting on a patch of sidewalk near the corner of 121st Street and Broadway, just up the block from the seminary and a few steps from a cafe where students often gathered for a cup of coffee.

Sara and Matt often walked by Annie's spot—Sara to attend the egalitarian prayer group at the seminary and Matt on his way to classes there. Friends are not sure whether Sara or Matt spoke to Annie first or, indeed, whether the two of them stopped and talked to her at the same time. At Barnard, Sara had volunteered to work with a campus group that visited with homeless people and brought them food. Sometimes, friends said, Sara even brought food from the Barnard and Columbia dining halls.

Annie seemed to touch Sara and Matt deeply. Some friends say it was Annie's vulnerability. She was thin, worn, fragile, in her mid-fifties but looking much older because she had spent so many days and nights living on New York's streets. Others said it was Annie's friendly nature that reached out to Matt and Sara.

Far too many homeless people in New York City are often handcuffed by addictions to drugs and alcohol or are plagued by various mental illnesses, so that they can seem angry, unapproachable, even dangerous to strangers. Annie was different. She was also a bit of an entrepreneur. Unlike many homeless who simply hold out a cup and beg for spare change from passersby, Annie had set up a business. She knitted small bookmarks for students.

Sara and Matt spoke frequently about Annie to their friends, especially about the hardships the homeless woman faced. She had several illnesses, including breast cancer, recalled seminary student Matthew Berkowitz, who became Matt's roommate a year later in Jerusalem. Many students simply passed by Annie, often feeling sorry for her or giving her a modest donation, but never speaking to her.

Matt and Sara brought the news of Annie's health problems to the other students.

"I remember feeling so shocked," said Berkowitz when told about Annie's sicknesses. "Matt and Sara found this out because they were the kinds of people who wanted to find this out."

On one especially cold morning, Matt brought Annie to an apartment he shared with several rabbinical students. "Matt offered her a cup of tea," said Edward Bernstein. "Even in a community of idealistic people, with people looking to go into the rabbinate or into Jewish education or just trying to believe that they wanted to make the world a better place, Matt stood out."

Matt and Sara told friends they were frustrated; they wanted to do more for Annie.

One day, they came up with an idea, which would be recalled again and again at their memorial services after their deaths because it summed up so well their mix of ideals and practicality.

Sara and Matt felt that Annie needed to make more money on her own. And if she could knit bookmarks, could she knit other items? Sara and Matt felt that the nearby Jewish Theological Seminary was a natural customer base for what could be a small business venture knitting yarmulkes or Jewish skullcaps for male students. Many seminary students wore yarmulkes—or, as they often called them, *kippots* or *kippahs*. Among college students at least, knitted yarmulkes were popular, especially if they were colorful.

"I remember going to Barnard and seeing homeless people," Arline Duker said of her own experience as a student there. "But I don't remember any of us getting to know them the way our kids did."

Sara and Matt approached Annie with the idea and she agreed. Sara bought yarn, then she and Matt took orders from the seminary students for the custom-made yarmulkes from Annie. The hand-knitted yarmulkes were an instant success, although not the sort that would suddenly propel Annie into a comfortable life. Annie earned less than $100 on the project, students said. But as many friends remembered, the inherent value and meaning of the story for others was far greater.

"They shared this passion for acts of loving kindness and social justice," said another rabbinical student, Michael Bernstein, who was one of Matt's roommates at the seminary when he and Sara befriended Annie. "That was a big part of who they were."

———

Less than a year after leaving the Jewish Theological Seminary for studies in Israel, Michael Bernstein saw Sara and Matt again—this time, with an entirely different topic on their minds. In Jerusalem, on a Sunday afternoon several weeks before they were killed, Matt and Sara dropped by the apartment that Bernstein shared with his wife, Tracie.

Like Matt, Michael Bernstein had come to Jerusalem for a year of intense scripture study at the Schechter Institute. The two rabbinical students were not merely close friends, they were frequent study partners in the complicated analysis of Torah and Talmud passages that rabbinical students customarily engage in. But on this day, Matt and Sara had not come to the Bernstein's apartment to discuss scripture or to reminisce about Annie.

The couples talked about life in Jerusalem, especially how they were adjusting to the language differences, bus schedules, new apartments and roommates, and the food. But the Bernsteins sensed this was not a casual visit. Matt had indicated as much when he telephoned several days earlier. "They basically called up and said 'We want to ask you a question,'" Bernstein remembered.

Michael and Tracie Bernstein had been married six months earlier, a joyful ceremony in America that Sara and Matt attended. Now Matt and Sara had a simple question: What was great about getting married?

Michael and Tracie were not surprised by the question. They knew how open Matt and Sara were—open enough, certainly, to ask a newly married couple about their decision to marry and why they valued going through the formality of a wedding as opposed to just living together.

The Bernsteins sensed that Matt and Sara were on the cusp of getting engaged and wanted advice and encouragement. "Their relationship was so deep because they were very honest and very real," Bernstein said years later. "They were the kind of friends that you knew you could talk to about anything."

As he looked across the table on that Sunday afternoon in Jerusalem, Michael Bernstein felt honored by the question Matt and Sara had brought to him and Tracie. The question itself was grounded in a sense of trust that the two couples shared. Michael and Tracie knew that Sara and Matt already demonstrated the kind of unspoken and intimate closeness of a couple who had pursued their own interests and yet still managed to find time to nurture a deep love for each other. At the same time, Matt and Sara also seemed unafraid to open themselves up to their friends. "The question did not reveal a skepticism about marriage, but instead showed how they approached their relationship with depth and thoughtfulness," Bernstein wrote years later in a Facebook posting in which he described the meeting. "They were both suffused with great compassion for others and a talent for putting their dreams into action. And somehow, more than anything else, they loved each other."

The conversation about marriage drifted from the sublime and humorous—what each partner might discover about the other's habits—to the deeply spiritual and how Michael and Tracie felt marriage made Judaism more meaningful. As the lunch ended, Michael and Tracie were quite sure that they would be hearing fairly soon of a new engagement—Matt's and Sara's.

---

On the Sunday that Matt and Sara began their trek to Jordan by catching the Number 18 bus, Matt's roommate, Matt Berkowitz, was also traveling. A few days earlier, Berkowitz and his fiancé, Miriam, left for a short trip of their own. Instead of Jordan, Matt and Miriam decided to head to the Israeli community of Kiryat Gat on the edge of the Negev desert.

Matt and Miriam spent Saturday night in Kiryat Gat. When they awoke on Sunday, Matt and Miriam heard some of the residents talking about a bus bombing in Jerusalem and checked the television news. "Chaos," Berkowitz said of the footage he watched.

Neither Matt nor Miriam had any idea that Matt and Sara were already dead. "It was a time before cell phones," Berkowitz said years later.

The next day, Matt Berkowitz and Miriam caught a ride into the Israeli resort of Eilat on the Red Sea. It was Monday now; the bombing on Jaffa Road and the other blast in Ashkelon dominated the Israeli newspapers. Berkowitz walked to a newsstand and scanned the headlines—and, then, his eye caught sight of photographs of two familiar faces.

Matt and Sara.

---

The *New York Times* featured the deaths of Sara and Matt in a front-page obituary that accompanied a long news story about the bus bombing and its potential impact on the peace process. "They were in love with their faith and with each other, and they died together as the victims of hate," wrote the *Times*'s John Sullivan in the story's first paragraph that appeared under the headline, "2 US Students Found Faith, Love and Death."

The story continued inside the newspaper and featured Sara's and Matt's college graduation photos. It pointed out Sara's and Matt's Ivy League college pedigrees. It mentioned their wide array of friends and their outspoken commitment to the Middle East peace process. But many who were interviewed said how empty they felt after hearing of the deaths.

"For a terrorist to kill her just kills me," said Barnard Dean Dorothy Denburg. "She was such a quiet person and a gentle person. She was very committed to peace in the Mideast."

Likewise, Matt's dean at Jewish Theological Seminary, Rabbi William Lebeau, asked, "What could be the meaning of the violence like this, the utter waste of his life and the lives of all who were killed? What could be the value of destroying such a life?"

That question by Rabbi Lebeau would come to loom large in years to come. The *Times*'s front page unknowingly offered a foreshadowing of the how the deaths of four Cuban Americans over the Florida Straits the day before would one day be connected to the deaths of the two young Americans on the Number 18 bus on Jaffa Road. Placed on that front page next to the *Times*'s main news account of the Israel bombings—"2 Suicide Bombings in Israel Kill 25 and Hurt 77, Highest Such Toll"—and next to a photograph of the blackened skeleton of the Number 18 bus, was a news story explaining that President Bill Clinton, facing Republican criticism that he was not tough enough, was weighing a variety of options to punish Cuba and Fidel Castro for ordering its air force to shoot down the two unarmed planes flown by Brothers to the Rescue. "This is an act of war," said a Cuban-American activist. "Mr. Clinton has a lot to think about tonight."

In its evening news program on Monday, National Public Radio devoted a segment to Sara and Matt. In Israel, where obviously many Israelis had perished, too, the deaths and promising lives of Sara and Matt resonated. "The Heart Is Broken," proclaimed a headline in the popular Israeli newspaper *Yedioth Ahronoth*.

Israeli television news, in between segments assessing how the bombings would affect the upcoming elections, continued to broadcast images from the bombing site, where a memorial had candles arranged to spell out the Hebrew word for "enough."

"It was one of those mornings when you had to say, 'Thank God I wasn't there,'" said TV news anchor Mike Greenspan. "By the end of the day, an entire nation was weeping."

In his newscast, Greenspan mentioned several victims. He also reported that Israelis shot and killed a Palestinian-American motorist who crashed into a Jerusalem bus stop on Monday. It was not even known at that point whether the crash was a deliberate act of terrorism or simply an accident. But the killing of the motorist revealed how tense Israel had become in the wake of such horrific bombings.

—◦—

Later that day, Prime Minister Shimon Peres stepped into the well of the Knesset to brief Israel's legislators on the bombings and their aftermath. Peres began by asking for his nation to try to stay calm. Then he turned to the incident hours earlier in which the Palestinian-driven car crashed into a bus stop. "It may be a terrorist attack," said Peres, "but until everything is checked, there is no room for guesswork."

The problem for Peres was that disturbing stories were already spreading fast about the Palestinian driver, Ahmed Abdel Hamid Hamida, who moved to the Middle East eight months before from the Los Angeles suburb of Rowland Heights, where he ran a grocery store. He reportedly returned to the West Bank to dedicate himself to Islam, and, according to the Israeli newspaper *Haaretz*, he told friends that morning when he left in his Fiat: "You will see me tonight on television." Adding to the possibility that Hamida had deliberately crashed his car into the bus stop was the fact that witnesses told Israeli police that as he ran the red light he veered directly toward the bus stop.

Peres was not known as a man brimming with mirth and lightheartedness. His somber expression bore witness to the fact he was involved in some of his nation's most important security decisions during threats of invasion from Egypt, Iraq, and Syria and through years of near-constant attacks by squads of Arab guerrillas who would sneak across the border and attack some of Israel's most vulnerable towns. On this day, however, Peres appeared even more pensive and grim. Throughout his career, he had tried to fight against the notion that he was not tough enough against Israel's Arab neighbors even though he had worked for years to help Israel's military acquire an arsenal of nuclear bombs. Now, as he was entering an election campaign while a significant minority of Israeli voters questioned whether the Oslo peace process had really made Israel safer, Peres seemed desperate to show that he could protect his nation from attacks.

He pledged that he would not suspend Israel's involvement in the Oslo peace process, but would strike out at the terrorists where and when Israel's security service found them. Israel was facing "diabolical suicide bombers" who were "targeting all Israelis," he warned. But where would the next attack take place? And when? What Peres did not tell the Knesset was that his own intelligence specialists told him that their informers were now warning them of other suicide bombings being planned by Hamas and its violent cousin, Islamic Jihad, in the near future.

Peres turned his attention to the Palestinian government and Yasser Arafat and warned that Arafat's election victory the month before would become meaningless if he allowed "a minority of armed men" to "torpedo his policies." The Palestinian Authority, said Peres, faced a critical decision: Disarm the terrorists affiliated with Hamas and Islamic Jihad or face the prospect of losing power to those groups.

The Israeli government had already reached out to Arafat and his security officers for help in tracking down the terrorists behind the bombings. Earlier that day, Arafat had even written a letter of condolence to the Dukers and Eisenfelds. But no one had been arrested yet.

From the Knesset podium, Peres paused, then turned his thoughts to the peace process. He promised not to halt Israel's participation in the ongoing Oslo negotiations that included a pledge to withdraw Israeli military units from the city of Hebron in the coming weeks. But before finishing, Peres repeated his promise to attack and arrest terrorists too.

Peres walked back to his seat in a front row on the Knesset's left side and as he sat down, Benjamin Netanyahu rose from a seat in a nearby row.

Netanyahu was already well known to Americans. As Israel's United Nation's ambassador in the late 1980s, he was a frequent guest on American television talk shows. He was well versed in Israeli policy. What also made Netanyahu popular was that he had a near-perfect command of the English language with almost no hint of an Israeli accent. To some, he sounded more American than Israeli.

This was no accident. Netanyahu's father, Benzion, a noted history professor and father of three sons, was brought to the United States by several colleges and universities in the 1950s and again in the late 1960s. Benzion's middle son, Benjamin—or "Bibi" as close friends called him—graduated from a high school near Philadelphia. After serving in the Israeli army, Benjamin came back to America to study at MIT.

At the podium, Netanyahu nodded toward Peres and looked out at the other ministers in the Knesset. Netanyahu said that this was no time for recrimination by Israeli politicians—even those who were campaigning against each other to win an election and control of the government. "Israel must stand united to defeat those who would destroy her," Netanyahu said.

Netanyahu turned to Peres. "Shimon, fight these terrorists with all Israel's might. Fight them and you will have our full support. No matter what government, we will never allow the terrorists to succeed."

In a Jerusalem TV studio, Israeli news anchor Michael Greens-pan summarized the speeches by Peres and Netanyahu, then turned to the story of Matt and Sara. Like his journalistic colleagues in America, Greenspan viewed the deaths of the young Americans as emblematic of the overall tragedy, and he invited Edward Bernstein, one of Matt's fellow students at the Schechter Institute and a former roommate in New York, to the studio to share some thoughts.

Greenspan asked about Matt and Sara and how their deaths affected the other American students.

"They were probably going to get married," Bernstein said, his voice falling off. He fell silent for a second or two, then added:

"They died together and they're going to be buried together. That might be the one beautiful thing about this."

—◡—

After burying their loved ones at a cemetery, Jews customarily begin a weeklong period of mourning called "shiva." Arline Duker retured to Teaneck and met with relatives, friends, neighbors, political figures, and journalists who stopped by to pay respects. Likewise, in West Hartford, Vicki and Len Eisenfeld welcomed a stream of visitors.

Shiva is not just a time for condolences. Often, it is a time to take stock of the life that was lost—and, in the case of Matt and Sara, how their lives were ended.

One day during shiva, Vicki Eisenfeld found herself pondering a concern that had been building quietly inside her. She was, of course, deeply saddened that Matt and Sara had been killed. She was also upset that their deaths were no accident.

But what could be done about this?

The Eisenfelds had received a letter of condolence from Stephen Fla-tow. "We stand with you," Flatow wrote in his brief letter, which was read at Matt's funeral.

Flatow also was wrestling with the same dilemma as Vicki Eisenfeld: What could be done about this killing? Like Vicki, he saw no clear answer.

In the days after Matt's death, Vicki often found herself struggling to contain her anger. And midway through the shiva period, she finally spoke up. Sitting in her living room, she turned to several guests and asked, "What can we do about this?"

The bluntness of the question seemed to startle several guests.

"What do you mean?" someone asked.

Vicki said that representatives of Hamas had claimed responsibility for the bombing of the Number 18 bus. Israeli investigators had not announced any suspects' names. But, as Vicki pointed out, Hamas was a well-known group, with a headquarters and a variety of spokesmen in the Gaza Strip and elsewhere.

"What can we do about this?" she asked again, pausing and adding yet another question: "Why can't we take them to court?"

An attorney who had been listening spoke up.

"You can't take Hamas to court," he said.

"Why not?" said Vicki.

———◆———

In Jerusalem, Hamas struck again.

Again, it was a Sunday morning—the first Sunday after Sara and Matt were killed, March 3, 1996. Again, it was Jaffa Road. Again, it was the Number 18 bus.

And again, it was a bomb made by Hassan Salameh, given to a young Palestinian man who boarded the Number 18 bus near Jerusalem's city hall and believed he was giving his life to the will of Allah. Nineteen people died, all Israelis. More than three dozen were injured.

Rabbi William Lebeau had just stepped through the doors of the King Solomon Hotel and onto the sidewalk to breathe in the morning air before beginning a two-mile walk to the Schechter Institute and a memorial service for Sara and Matt. Lebeau had gone to the funerals in America. But as dean of the Jewish Theological Seminary, he worried about students who were colleagues of Matt Eisenfeld and studying that year in Jerusalem. So he caught a flight to Israel soon after Matt's burial in Connecticut. Before he left, he made a promise to his wife: In Jerusalem, Lebeau would take no buses. So this morning, he opted to walk across Jerusalem and through the Valley of the Cross to the Schechter Institute.

Then he heard the bomb's hollow thud and felt the ground shake. The King Solomon Hotel was less than half a mile from Jaffa Road. Lebeau knew another bomb had exploded. He thought briefly of walking toward the explosion, then stopped. He had come to Jerusalem to offer comfort for the friends of Sara and Matt, many of whom would be gathering this same hour at Schechter. Surely, they heard the bomb's thud, too, and perhaps saw the column of smoke rising from Jaffa Road. Lebeau wondered how the students would react.

Lebeau turned and walked toward Schechter. An hour later he stood at a podium in the first-floor study hall. He called Sara and Matt "two gentle souls." He said "their bodies were shattered by an act of inhumanity but their souls escaped the carnage without scar or blemish." He noted that "violence was the antithesis of their lives" but that "the deaths of Matt and Sara captured the world's attention. Violence always captures attention but people were drawn to this tragedy sensing something special in their deaths."

He turned his attention to the students and faculty members before him. He saw Edward Bernstein, who had spoken of Sara and Matt on Israeli television. He noticed Matt's former roommate, Matt Berkowitz, and Michael Bernstein, who invited Sara and Matt to the apartment he shared with his wife to talk about marriage, and Avigal Young, who hosted Sara and Matt for lunch on the Saturday before they died.

Almost everyone had mentioned to him how the deaths of Sara and Matt had unsettled them, freezing them in a newfound fear of taking buses or even entering any sort of unprotected public space where a suicide bomber might be lurking. Several spoke of leaving Jerusalem and returning to America. Others were angry—with the Palestinians, with Israel, with the endless conflict.

"Essential to the process of comforting is the need to talk about the lives of Matt and Sara and the experiences we shared with them," Lebeau said. "Our recollections have been painful, but the endurance of that pain is necessary for us to better comprehend the meaningfulness of their lives. The more we speak and remember, the more we guarantee that the tragedy will not overwhelm our sense of their vitality and their accomplishments that we so cherish."

Lebeau mentioned their commitment to prayer, their resolute schedules of studying scriptures, even their attempt to help the homeless woman, Annie. In their short lives, Lebeau said, Sara and Matt had managed to blend their spirituality with action. "Imagine what the world might be like if we adopted their sense of urgency and intensity," LeBeau said. "For this reason, we must emulate them."

On the following day, another bomb exploded in Tel Aviv. Thirteen more Israelis died and 130 were injured. It was the fourth suicide attack in nine days. The death toll for all the attacks exceeded sixty.

The only difference between this latest bombing and the others was the Palestinian who planned it. Hassan Salameh was not involved. The Tel Aviv bombing was carried out by Hamas's terrorist brother, Palestinian Islamic Jihad—the same group that orchestrated the bombing in April 1995 that killed Alisa Flatow.

Several days later, Sara's cousin, Rivkah Fishman, walked into Jerusalem's police station, a block away from the bus stop where Majdi Abu Wardah boarded the Number 18 bus with his duffle bag. For Fishman, Sara's brutal murder was still fresh and painful. But after the funerals, memorial services, and burial, and the long days of greeting guests during shiva, someone had to retrieve the personal items that Sara and Matt carried that last day.

Fishman identified herself to a police officer, then was handed two packages. She found Sara's watch—still ticking. And Sara's rings, her credit cards, and wallet and money.

She reached for Matt's package. Fishman pulled out three books—two burgundy-colored volumes of the Talmud and a smaller book of Jewish prayers. The books smelled of fire and smoke, with a faint aroma of the chemicals that Jerusalem's fire fighters sprayed on the Number 18 to douse the flames. Otherwise, they were intact. The flames had not damaged any of the pages or, for that matter, the covers.

Fishman fell silent and studied the books. Then a thought came to her. She remembered a line from the Book of Deuteronomy: "From his right hand came a fiery law for them."

For years, Fishman had struggled with the meaning of that line. But now, as she held the books that had survived the bombing and the fire, she understood the words in a new context. Yes, Sara and Matt had perished in a terrible explosion and fire, brought on by a lawless act. But she felt the law would ultimately provide an answer to this tragedy.

Fishman mailed Sara's watch and rings to Arline Duker in Teaneck and sent the books to the Connecticut home of Matt's parents. Several days later, Len Eisenfeld found a package at his door. He opened it and pulled out Matt's Talmud volumes.

Then Len noticed Matt's prayer book. As Len held the book in his hands, it seemed to open on its own to a page that featured a prayer for peace.

The page had a reddish stain that did not belong there. Len looked closer.

It was a drop of blood.

# PART II

# ASH

# CHAPTER 5

On a Wednesday morning in April, about eight weeks after Sara and Matt were killed, Arline Duker walked through the gates of the White House with Len and Vicki Eisenfeld. Their arrival was not unexpected. The parents of Sara and Matt had been invited to watch President Bill Clinton sign into law a new bill that was supposed to punish terrorists.

Arline, Len, and Vicki passed through a security checkpoint and were led to the South Lawn, a rolling expanse of lush, seemingly weed-free greenery that flows like a soft carpet all the way to Constitution Avenue and then up a hill to the Washington Monument. The South Lawn, with its perimeter of magnolia, maple, elm, and oak trees seems to offer a barrier to the harried, sometimes frenzied realm of Washington politics. It had been a sheep pasture when Woodrow Wilson was president during World War I, but by the last decades of the twentieth century, the lawn had become a pastoral setting for the pomp, power, and pageantry of the presidency.

The president's helicopter, Marine One, lands and departs from the South Lawn. Kings, queens, and foreign presidents are fetted there, including, in 1993, Israeli Prime Minister Yitzhak Rabin and Palestinian leader Yasser Arafat for the ceremonial signing of the Oslo Peace Accords. Each spring, children frolic on the grass during the White House Easter egg roll. And on almost any evening when the weather is warm, the lawn could be the setting for all manner of White House political dinners or parties.

On this day, the ceremony was not meant to be lighthearted or celebratory. The law that the president was signing was actually the culmination of several years of painstaking efforts by his administration and Congressional leaders from both political parties to toughen up America's antiterrorism statutes, including a provision to limit appeals for terrorists who had been sentenced to death and another provision that blocked suspected terrorists from access to classified evidence during their deportation hearings.

The so-called Antiterrorism and Effective Death Penalty Act, or AEDPA, was not without its share of opponents, though. Much like the Patriot Act, which would be signed into law after the 9/11 attacks in 2001, the AEDPA had been roundly criticized by civil libertarians for giving law enforcement too much power. The executive director of the American Civil Liberties Union, Ira Glasser, was especially caustic: "It is a sad day for all Americans when the President of the United States chooses political expediency over the Bill of Rights."

Adding to the politics that had been part of the law's journey through Congress and not passing up an opportunity to blame Republicans, even President Clinton had some harsh words about the new law he was signing. But Clinton's assessment, in what was viewed as an attempt to appeal to conservative voters, was far different from the ACLU's.

In a statement that ran on for more than 1,400 words, Clinton said the law was not strong enough. "I asked that law enforcement be given increased access to hotel, phone, and other records in terrorism cases. I asked for a mandatory penalty for those who knowingly transfer a firearm for use in a violent felony. I asked for a longer statute of limitations to allow law enforcement more time to prosecute terrorists who use weapons such as machine guns, sawed-off shotguns, and explosive devices. But the Congress stripped each of these provisions out of the bill. And when I asked for a ban on cop-killer bullets, the Congress delivered only a study, which will delay real action to protect our nation's police officers."

Nonetheless, Clinton called the new law "a real step in the right direction" that "provides valuable tools" for combating terrorism. "It stands as a tribute to the victims of terrorism and to the men and women in law enforcement who dedicate their lives to protecting all of us from the scourge of terrorist activity," he said.

Clinton's statement, along with the critiques from others, underscored how much the law had been debated and amended. Almost every sentence had been argued over numerous times.

Yet one provision seemed strangely immune from public praise or criticism. Deep in the bill was a seemingly nondescript paragraph that allowed relatives of American victims of terrorist attacks that occurred overseas to file lawsuits in US courts and to seek some measure of financial compensation—much as a victim in an auto accident could file suit against the driver of another car, citing negligence, carelessness, or some level of disregard for human life.

Arline Duker and Len and Vicki Eisenfeld did not know it, but that single paragraph would dominate their lives in the coming years.

The paragraph was an amendment. The provision allowing lawsuits against terrorists was actually a major change in a previously sacrosanct federal law that set strict limits on how much sway US courts—and Americans themselves—had over the activities of foreign governments.

Named the Foreign Sovereign Immunities Act, the law spelled out a set of rules that blocked US citizens from filing lawsuits against foreign governments, except in very specific instances, such as certain business transactions. For example, if a business owned by a foreign government, say a Chinese government steel mill, failed to fulfill a contract to deliver an order of reinforced beams to build US highway bridges, then a US company would be allowed to file a lawsuit and possibly collect damages.

The notion of offering immunity to foreign governments had been a cornerstone of international diplomacy for almost two centuries, though the concept was born thousands of years before, as governments and tribes across the world tried to fashion methods for handling disputes. The modern notion of immunity between nations was an attempt to establish a worldwide system—a concept of understanding—in which foreign governments would not be dragged into all manner of legal proceedings.

The amendment, which had been inserted into the legislation, offered a new legal twist on the concept of foreign immunity, however. If US citizens were killed or injured overseas, or even within the United States, by a foreign terrorist, lawsuits could be filed in their name in US federal courts to collect damages. But the new legal provision set limits on what nations could be sued. After months of legal and political wrangling, Congress decided to allow lawsuits to be filed only against nations that had been listed by the US State Department as state sponsors of terrorism. In 1996, this list had just seven names: Cuba, Iraq, Libya, North Korea, Sudan, Syria, and Iran. A State Department assessment, however, singled out Iran for special attention. In its 1996 report entitled "Patterns of Global Terrorism," the State Department described Iran as "the premier state sponsor of terrorism" and the "most active."

The report listed a wide array of Iranian-sponsored terrorist activities, ranging from weapons smuggling and plotting assassinations to offering safe haven in Iran to terrorists from other countries and even ordering the death of the popular author Salman Rushdie. But one notation in the report would become especially significant, even provocative: a finding that Iran had offered money and training to terrorists who could disrupt the Middle East peace process by staging attacks in Israel. Three Middle East terrorist groups were named in the report as receiving Iran's money and training—Hezbollah in Lebanon and Hamas and Palestinian Islamic Jihad in the West Bank and the Gaza Strip.

Arline Duker and Len and Vicki Eisenfeld did not know about the State Department's report on terrorism when they walked onto the South Lawn of the White House to watch President Clinton sign the Antiter-rorism and Effective Death Penalty Act. They harbored only a vague idea of what sorts of powers were contained in the Act and how they might be affected.

The AEDPA was something of a hybrid legal stew that had been sim-mering for years after being tinkered with by many cooks. Most experts agreed that the seeds for the Act were sown in a singular event that turned out to be the equivalent of a diplomatic earthquake—the seizure of the US Embassy in Tehran in November 1979 by Iranian dissidents who then held fifty-two Americans as hostages for 444 days. What came to be known as the "Iran Hostage Crisis" was a transformative moment, not just in US politics but in how America understood its ability to use power.

Throughout the crisis, the powerful US military seemed impotent. What's more, established rules of international diplomacy suddenly seemed uncertain, even irrelevant. The Iranian dissidents who leaped over the embassy walls and captured US Foreign Service workers and Marine guards had the overt support of Iran's revolutionary government and its leader, Ayatollah Ruhollah Khomeini. And yet, the Iranian government not only declined to negotiate; it ignored accepted international customs that a nation's embassy and its diplomats had special protection and even immunity from the host nation's internal politics.

During the 1980s, attacks by a variety of Middle East terrorist groups increased against unprotected civilians, not only in Israel but also beyond. A TWA jetliner was hijacked in June 1985 by operatives affiliated with the Lebanese-based Hezbollah party, and a US Navy sailor, Robert Stethem, was shot to death. In October 1985, an Italian-based cruise ship, the *Achille Lauro*, was seized by Palestinian gunmen and a wheelchair-bound Jewish-American tourist, Leon Klinghoffer, was murdered—his body and wheelchair dumped overboard into the Mediterranean as his wife looked on in horror. Then, in December 1985, the ticket counter at Rome's airport was riddled with machine-gunfire by gunmen affiliated with the pro-Palestinian Abu Nidal group. Sixteen people were killed and ninety-nine were wounded, including a US diplomat.

By the mid-1980s, the discordant politics of Lebanon had made that nation a terrorists' breeding ground. Once again, Iran was in the forefront, notably by supporting the attack by Iranian-backed operatives on the US Marine headquarters at Beirut's airport. Later, in the 1980s, Iranian-backed members of the Hezbollah terrorist group—and other fringe groups that had tacit Iranian support—began seizing westerners in Beirut and holding them captive. The hostages ranged from the Associated Press's Beirut bureau chief, Terry Anderson, to a Marine officer, a CIA station chief, American college professors, and even a British church official who had volunteered to try to convince the hostage takers to release their prisoners.

As aggravating and exasperating as these events were, three more events proved to be the most significant in pushing Congress to pass new antiterrorism legislation. On a night in December 1988, only days before Christmas, a bomb, planted by Libyan agents in a suitcase, blew apart a commercial jetliner in flight to America over Lockerbie, Scotland. The bombing of Pan Am Flight 103 was the most devastating terrorist attack on civilians in decades. All 243 passengers and sixteen crew members were killed along with eleven Lockerbie residents who died from falling debris. Many of the passengers were US college students on the way home from Europe after a semester of studies.

Pan Am 103—or, as it became known, "the Lockerbie bombing"—sparked a movement that had not emerged even after the numerous terrorist attacks of the 1970s by Iranian, Palestinian and other Middle East operatives. Within a few months of the explosion, relatives of Pan Am 103 victims arrived in Washington, staging protests at the gates of the White House and Congress and demanding answers—and a plan of retaliation.

Until then, the US government had seemed reluctant to use its massive military might to respond to acts of terrorism. After the 1983 bombing of the Marine encampment in Beirut, President Ronald Reagan did not order any retaliatory strikes against terrorist camps in Lebanon. Even when France, which lost fifty-eight paratroopers in a similar bombing of its Beirut barracks on the same day as the Marines attack, sent jet fighters to attack terrorist camps, Reagan declined to follow suit. Three years later, Reagan changed his mind. After Libyan agents set off a pipe bomb in a Berlin disco and killed two US soldiers, Reagan ordered US Navy jets aboard an aircraft carrier in the Mediterranean Sea to attack several targets in the Libyan capital of Tripoli. The attack was criticized for not striking any significant targets.

In the wake of the Pan Am 103 bombing, the US military seemed equally hamstrung. No retaliatory attack was launched. The jetliner bombing became an FBI criminal investigation. Meanwhile, relatives of victims began to call lawyers, asking if they could file a lawsuit seeking compensation for their loss. The idea, while perhaps logical and even noble, had a key problem. US laws did not allow American citizens to sue foreign nations for acts of terrorism.

Congress took up the debate. A variety of laws were proposed and languished. The problem was not so much a lack of support in the US Senate or House but a formidable opponent in the form of the US State Department.

US diplomats feared that if laws were changed to allow Americans to file lawsuits against foreign governments, and perhaps to seize assets in the US such as foreign bank accounts or even foreign-owned businesses or other properties, that American assets overseas might be seized in retaliation.

Then two more terrorist attacks took place. In February 1993, Islamic militants, who had been living in the United States and had come under the influence of a blind Egyptian cleric who openly called for America's destruction—even though he had been granted political asylum in the US—set off a massive fertilizer bomb in the parking garage of New York's World Trade Center. Only six people died but the attack was seen as yet another warning sign about the growth of terrorism.

No laws were changed, however. It would take yet another terrorist attack to do that.

On April 19, 1995, a disgruntled former US Army soldier, who harbored deep resentment against the US government, set off a fertilizer bomb outside the federal building in Oklahoma City and killed 168 people, including more than a dozen children in the building's day-care center operated for the parents who worked there. The bomber, Timothy McVeigh, was not an Islamic jihadist; he proclaimed himself to be a Christian. But the attack on the Oklahoma City federal building seemed to send a clear message not only to Congress but to the White House that key laws needed to be changed to protect America from terrorist attacks.

Within a month of the Oklahoma City attack, a proposed antiterrorism bill was drawn up by Senator Robert Dole, the Republican majority leader who was considered a frontrunner for his party's nomination to run against Clinton in 1996. Dole's bill worked its way through various committees. The result was a series of provisions that included limits on death penalty appeals by convicted terrorists as well as streamlined proceedings in deportation hearings of suspected foreign terrorists who were caught inside the US. In what seemed like a footnote, Senator Arlen Specter, the Pennsylvania Republican and former prosecutor, slipped a provision into Dole's bill that allowed US citizens to file civil lawsuits against foreign nations where Americans had been killed in terrorist attacks.

State Department lawyers worked feverishly behind the scenes to cancel out Specter's provision. One concern by State Department lawyers was that allowing a blanket freedom to file lawsuits could result in court cases against some nations who were considered US allies but had nonetheless been accused of terrorism or of allowing terrorists to operate within their boundaries. But Spector, who was supported now by lawyers for families who lost relatives in the bombing of Pan Am 103, held firm. So the State Department proposed a compromise. Instead of allowing US citizens to sue any foreign government where an alleged terrorist act took place, why not allow lawsuits only against foreign nations that were singled out by the State Department as state sponsors of terrorism? Specter and his allies agreed. And when President Clinton stepped onto the South Lawn of the White House on April 24, 1996, to sign the Antiterrorism and Effective Death Penalty Act, the provision allowing for lawsuits applied to just the seven nations listed by the State Department, including Iran.

It was one thing to create a new law that permitted lawsuits against foreign sponsors of terrorism, such as Iran. Like any lawsuit, the key to any legal action against a nation like Iran would come down to basic evidence that could withstand the scrutiny of a US court. If anyone harbored such concerns on that South Lawn April morning, however, they were not voiced. Despite the grim underpinnings of the legislation, this was considered a triumphant day by the Clinton administration. White House publicists presented the passage and signing of the AEDPA as evidence of a different sort—namely, that Democrats and Republicans had found common ground in combating terrorism.

For Democrats—in particular, the Clinton administration—the passage of antiterrorism legislation offered a chance to counter mounting Republican criticism that Democrats and the White House were not tough enough on terrorism. In elections only two years earlier, amid a withering storm of accusations from conservative Republicans led by Rep. Newt Gingrich, Democrats lost control of the Senate and the House of Representatives. For Democrats, the loss of the House was especially significant. It was the first time since 1952 that Republicans managed to gain a majority of seats in the 435-member House. And now, in less than seven months, President Clinton would face his own battle for reelection against Bob Dole.

Despite Dole's role in shaping the antiterror legislation, Clinton still claimed victory. The president considered himself to be an early supporter of tougher new antiterror standards, especially after the bombing of the Oklahoma City federal building.

After the Florida-based Brothers to the Rescue pilots had been shot down over international waters by the Cuban Air Force the day before Sara Duker and Matthew Eisenfeld had been killed, Clinton voiced support for an expanded proposal to allow the pilots' relatives to seek compensation from Cuban assets that had been withheld by the US government since the Castro revolution. That proposal now had been broadened in the new antiterror law to allow US citizens to go to court to claim access to assets not only from Cuba but other nations labeled as state sponsors of terrorism. Such provisions in the new law, combined with Clinton's 1,400-word accompanying statement that the legislation should have been even tougher, gave the president an opening to claim that he was certainly not soft on terrorism.

As he stepped to a podium that morning, Clinton seemed to sense some measure of victory. He clearly seemed pleased with the scene before him. Not only was Bob Dole looking on, but the White House had invited several dozen people who had been touched in some way by foreign and domestic terrorism. Besides Arline Duker and Len and Vicki Eisenfeld, the audience on the South Lawn that morning included the daughters of Leon Klinghoffer; relatives of the pilots shot down by the Cuban Air Force; the parents of murdered US Navy sailor Robert Stethem; twenty-two survivors of the Oklahoma City bombing; seven office workers who escaped from the World Trade Center's twin towers after the 1993 bombing; and four relatives of victims who had been killed aboard Pan Am Flight 103.

Clinton called the new law a "mighty blow" to terrorists who would attack US citizens. "America will never tolerate terrorism," Clinton said. "America will never abide terrorists."

❧

As they watched the president that morning from seats in the crowd on the South Lawn, Arline Duker and Len and Vicki Eisenfeld were still in mourning. Looking back, they remember feeling engulfed by emotional numbness and shock at their fresh loss only two months before. At the same time they felt intensely curious about the new law that the president was signing and that Congressional leaders from both parties seemed to embrace.

How would this change their lives, though? Certainly, tough new antiterror safeguards—if they were tough—would not bring back Sara and Matt. Also, the notion of gaining some form of compensation from terrorist sponsors seemed vague and distant.

Two months after their children's murders, Arline, Len, and Vicki knew only that Hamas had claimed responsibility for the Jaffa Road bus bombing. They had no idea of the complexity of the bomb plot. Nor had they heard the name of the plot's organizer and bomb-maker, Hassan Salameh.

Five weeks before the White House bill signing, Clinton visited northern New Jersey. The president was on the way to Egypt for an antiterror summit conference with a variety of Middle East leaders, including Israeli Prime Minister Shimon Peres and Palestinian President Yasser Arafat. But the day before he left, Clinton spoke on the campus of Fairleigh Dickinson University in Hackensack, New Jersey, about the need for America to continue to pursue a peaceful settlement to the Israeli-Palestinian conflict.

Arline Duker sat in the FDU audience that day along with Stephen Flatow as invited guests. Much like the remarks he would deliver at the White House in April, Clinton's speech addresssed in broad terms how terrorism had become such a dangerous force to be reckoned with. He vowed not to let terrorists derail the ongoing Middle East peace process, even though he also acknowledged that terrorism had a personal cost in the lives of those who lost loved ones. Pausing in the midst of his remarks, Clinton singled out the Duker and Flatow families "for their incalculable sacrifice and their continued devotion" to the peace process.

It was a comforting moment. But Arline Duker, as well as Len and Vicki Eisenfeld, who did not come to the FDU speech, had grown increasingly uncomfortable with the new spotlight that had illuminated their lives.

A death changes family dynamics. But murder causes all manner of emotional fissures to open up, psychologists say. A murder of someone by an act of political or religious terrorism opens even deeper wounds. "This is an unfamiliar place. It feels very surreal to us," Duker told news reporters covering the president's speech at Fairleigh Dickinson. "It feels like we have been taken out of our lives."

Stephen Flatow had already felt removed from his old life and had decided to spend more time drawing attention to the dangers of terrorism. Soon after Flatow's daughter, Alisa, was killed, he was asked to speak to a group that was raising money for Israel. Flatow reluctantly agreed. As he spoke, though, he felt a cathartic sense of relief. In stepping to a microphone and telling the story of why his daughter had grown to love Israel and how she died there, Flatow felt he was doing something constructive against the horrors of terrorism. "It's my form of therapy," he told friends.

Arline Duker felt no relief in those first weeks, even though she had offered remarks after Sara's funeral and tried to make herself available when the news media knocked on her door. She was not shy with strangers. Duker was, after all, a therapist. Nor was she unaccustomed to speaking in front a group. She had been a teacher. But at times Duker found herself trapped in a back-and-forth wrestling match with her feelings—what one of her psychological colleagues called "pendulating." During portions of her day, Duker was able to meticulously arrange time to make statements to the news media or even to finalize decisions about Sara's death, including how to arrange for her personal belongings to be shipped home. Then Duker felt pulled in another direction, sometimes even voicing the shockingly obvious: "Oh, my God, my daughter is dead."

She found that she could not cope well if she was alone for long periods. Nor could she tolerate long car rides without some major distraction. She continually reviewed in her head what she knew about that final Sunday morning, imagining how Sara got up and caught the bus with Matthew and what Sara and Matthew were doing the moment they died.

More often than not, Arline wondered why she did not try to call Sara on that final day. Perhaps a phone call would have delayed Sara long enough so she would miss the Number 18 bus that was blown up. Who knew? Still, the possibility haunted Arline.

The hardest part was falling asleep. In those early weeks, Arline was overwhelmed with insomnia. She discovered that she did not fear sleep as much as waking up. When she awoke, even after a rare restful sleep, Arline found that her thoughts immediately returned to that February Sunday when the telephone rang and she learned that Sara was dead—killed by a terrorist's bomb, on a bus. "When you are awake, you can manage the horror of what happened," she said. "But when you fall asleep, you relive the whole phone call again."

In Connecticut, Vicki and Len Eisenfeld battled similar emotional tides. In the first weeks, the business of planning a funeral and welcoming friends and relatives to their home offered some measure of consolation and helped to fill the time. But by mid-March, the anguish over their son's murder—and the dashed hopes of a joyful marriage to Sara—deepened in an even more painful way.

Len went back to work at the hospital, trying to rely on his doctor's habits and routines to get him through the day. Often he found that the habitual process of visiting with patients, consulting with other physicians, filling out reports and conducting tests offered a respite from his grief. But at some point in the day, Len found himself with no patients to see, no colleagues to speak with, no reports or tests to complete. He was alone, and sometimes he found himself retreating to the men's bathroom where he would open the door of a stall and weep.

Likewise, Vicki battled the grief trapped inside her mind. Hour after hour, she found herself thinking about what had happened to Matthew. Much like Arline Duker, Vicki went over Matthew's movements on that Sunday morning—the bus ride with Sara, the bomber, the explosion, the phone call. Then, she thought of Hamas. What, if anything, could be done to hold someone accountable?

A week after the bombing, Palestinian police on the West Bank arrested Mohammad Wardeh and charged him with helping Hassan Salameh to recruit his cousin, Majdi Abu Wardeh, as the suicide bomber aboard the Number 18 bus. A day after his arrest, Mohammad Wardeh was sentenced to life in prison by a Palestinian court. No US officials were at Wardeh's trial. Nor were any Israeli officials there. As for a prison sentence, Palestinian officials released no details about where Wardeh would serve his life sentence.

The following week, Israeli soldiers arrived at the al-Fawwar refugee camp where Majdi, grew up with five brothers and five sisters. The soldiers ordered the camp's residents to leave their homes and walk to a nearby hillside. The soldiers went to the home where Majdi's family lived, a concrete block structure that stood on a narrow alley-like street. The soldiers placed explosive charges on the first and second floors, pushed a button, and blew up the house. The Wardeh family—the parents and the remaining ten children—moved into a Red Cross tent.

Neither Arline nor Vicki or Len were immediately told about the arrest and trial of Mohammad Wardeh or the destruction of the home of Majdi Wardeh's family at the al-Fawwar camp. That news came months later.

The tide of thoughts and random stories about what was taking place in the Middle East and in the United States—or what was not taking place—began to wear Vicki down. Each day seemed to bring a new set of concerns and issues. After weeks of this, Vicki was exhausted. "I can't stand what's in my head," Vicki said.

As with Arline, falling asleep was difficult. Whatever sleep Vicki managed to get turned out to be mostly restless. So Vicki turned to replacing the angry, mournful, and confused noise in her head with another noise. She started listening to books on tape. "I could turn on a story and be somewhere else," she said.

On many nights, those stories put Vicki to sleep.

—◦—

After President Clinton finished his remarks on the South Lawn of the White House on that April morning, he picked up a pen and signed the new antiterrorism law. Arline, Len, and Vicki rose from their seats and walked into the White House. A presidential aide guided them toward the West Wing. One of the president's aides opened a door to the Roosevelt Room, a conference and meeting space dominated by a long wooden table with chairs, already filled with people who had been sitting near Arline, Len, and Vicki as Clinton signed the bill outside. The president's staff had arranged for an expert to speak to the group about the bill and the specifics of launching some sort of lawsuit against terrorist organizations.

Arline, Len, and Vicki found seats at the table. A man and a woman seated nearby introduced themselves as the parents of Navy sailor Robert Stethem. Across the table sat several relatives of the Brothers to the Rescue pilots. At another seat was the wife of a CIA worker who was shot to death in January 1993 by a disgruntled Pakistani-born Muslim as he waited in traffic at a stoplight outside CIA headquarters in Virginia.

Someone asked Arline, Vicki, and Len to introduce themselves.

"I'm the father of Matthew Eisenfeld," Len said. "He and Sara Duker were killed on a bus in Jerusalem in February."

From around the table, Len, Vicki, and Arline heard people gasp.

Len was stunned. He thought of all the people seated around the table and how each had suffered a loss. Yet so many seemed to be shocked at the deaths of Matt and Sara. The gasps he heard were not so much uttered in shock but in sympathy. Len sensed that this was a group who knew from personal experience what Arline, Len, and Vicki were going through—why they couldn't sleep, why they sometimes broke down in tears, why they carried an uneasy anger that mixed with a sense of helplessness at what had taken place in their lives and what had been taken from them.

A woman turned to Vicki.

"Oh God," she said. "You're just babies at this."

The woman's remark was meant to be sympathetic. But it hinted at something deeper, to a harder, painful, and longer path that these other families had been following.

Arline, Vicki, and Len had read about many of the people in the room and how their lives had been torn apart by terrorism. But they had never met them and certainly did not know about the years of torment some of them had endured. From their own experiences, Arline, Vicki, and Len already knew how anger and depression had suddenly become recurring strong currents running through their lives. They also knew how much their idle thoughts had become dominated by all manner of concerns about whether they could have done something to stop their children from stepping onto the Number 18 bus. Beyond that, Arline, Vicki, and Len had almost no sense of what lay before them. This—the vague and undefined concept that the woman mentioned—seemed as mysterious as outer space, and as deep and formless a void.

When it came to terrorism and its impact on the lives of ordinary people, the primary reference point for Arline, Vicki, and Len was Stephen Flatow. But Flatow was not at the White House to watch President Clinton sign the new antiterrorism law. He had been invited, but he stayed home.

"I wasn't going to dignify the ceremony," he said.

Flatow was not bitter or even angry as much as frustrated and emotionally flattened. A year had passed since Alisa's murder. While Flatow tried to busy himself with fund-raising speeches on behalf of pro-Israel groups, his personal sadness deepened in recent weeks as the first anniversary of Alisa's death loomed. As Arline, Vicki, and Len were beginning to confront, Flatow felt the heaviness of a parent's grief from the death of a child and how that grief does not easily subside with the passage of time. Flatow thought of Alisa constantly—at work, in the car, at home. He had begun to feel, as psychologists generally point out, that the grief over a child lost to a willful, planned murder—in this case, an act of terrorism—can be even more profound than a child lost to a lengthy illness or even in a car accident.

Flatow knew that although her killers had not targeted Alisa, her murder was no accident. Flatow had come to believe that his daughter's bus was singled out for an attack because it was filled with Jews, many of them young students or Israeli soldiers. As he often said, "She died because she was Jewish and because she wanted to live in the land of Israel."

To reach such a conclusion had left a deep emotional wound in Flatow. It confirmed for him his worst possible fears: that the bombing was an act of hatred. But what to do about it? A year of speaking about Israel and his daughter's death had left him feeling helpless. Adding to this pain was the slow realization that the most powerful nation in the world seemed incapable, or unwilling, to track down his daughter's killers.

Flatow searched hard to find comfort. He rarely turned down a chance to talk about Alisa's death, viewing his speeches to Jewish groups or appearances on TV programs as giving him strength. But what of Alisa's killers?

In October 1995, Flatow received a telephone call from Colette Avital, Israel's consul general in New York. She told him that the leader of Palestinian Islamic Jihad, the shadowy group that claimed responsibility for the bombing that killed Alisa, had been shot to death in Malta.

The killing of Fathi Shaqaqi, a Jerusalem doctor who founded the Palestinian branch of Islamic Jihad and was among those credited with promoting suicide bombing as a form of terrorism against Israelis, seemed like a plot from a spy novel. Shaqaqi traveled under a false name, Dr. Ibrahim Ali Shawesh. He stopped in Malta for a few days before heading to Tripoli where he hoped to meet with Libyan leader, Muammar al-Gaddafi, who reportedly promised to help finance Palestinian Islamic Jihad's activities.

Shaqaqi never made it to Tripoli. As he walked to his hotel in the Maltese coastal town of Sliema on October 26, 1995, a man on a motorcycle pulled up and drew a semiautomatic pistol equipped with a silencer and a special attachment to catch spent cartridges so they could not be found by police investigators and traced. The man on the motorcycle fired three shots into Shaqaqi's head then sped away.

The killing, which had the earmarks of a professional execution, was believed to be the work of Israel's top-secret international spy agency, the Mossad. But when Avital phoned Flatow several days later, she made a point of saying that Israel was not taking credit for Shaqaqi's death.

Flatow hung up the phone. He understood that tracking down and catching suspected terrorists was not easy and that punishing them was even more difficult. But the street shooting of a leader of a terrorist group did not strike Flatow as much of an accomplishment. The problem of terrorism was much more complex. The terror bombing that killed Alisa went far beyond the control of this Palestinian doctor gunned down on the sidewalk outside a hotel in Malta.

"I wasn't dancing in the streets," Flatow said. He nevertheless wondered where the investigation into his daughter's death might lead—if a thorough investigation was actually taking place.

As a lawyer, Flatow had been trained to see most events as following a logical progression. And yet, the investigation of his daughter's killing seemed to have no clear pathway. Various political figures in the United States and in Israel—even in the Palestinian government—had promised a full investigation. But, aside from the killing of Fathi Shaqaqi, there was little to show for their efforts. Now, a full year after he buried his daughter, Flatow wondered if any significant effort had been made to catch the actual bombers in Gaza or whether all the principled statements by various leaders in Israel and in the US about the rule of law and the need for accountability had been set aside in the name of politics, diplomacy, and the desire to sculpt a peaceful settlement to the Israeli-Palestinian conflict.

What Flatow did not know was that one of the Palestinian operatives who planted the bomb that killed Alisa was a member of a Hamas cell linked to Yahya Ayyash, the so-called "Engineer" whose killing by Israeli agents had been later cited as a reason for the bombing of the Number 18 bus in Jerusalem. As Ayyash was teaching bomb-making to members of the group responsible for the Alisa Flatow's bus, another of his protégés, Hassan Salameh, was at work on his first bomb, this one also for a target in Gaza.

A month after Alisa's killing, Salameh placed a bomb aboard a donkey cart near Khan Yunis in the Gaza Strip. As the cart approached a bus stop, the driver pushed a button. Only the driver and donkey died. The incident barely made the news.

But Salameh learned a key lesson. When the bomb aboard the donkey cart detonated, it was not close enough to its target. The next time Salameh would make sure his bomber would be much closer.

Flatow had yet to hear of Salameh or even much about Ayyash. He held out little hope that his government—or other governments—were serious about catching his daughter's killers. Certainly he did not see how going to the White House to watch Clinton sign the antiterrorism bill would lift the haunting sadness that griped him and members of his family.

"We were just not up to it," Flatow said. "Emotionally, we couldn't do it."

Flatow felt deflated, unable to envison just yet what he might do to hold anyone accountable for Alisa's murder.

He would soon change his mind.

# CHAPTER 6

ALISA FLATOW WANTED TO SEE PETRA.

Just as Sara Duker and Matt Eisenfeld would hope to do ten months later, Alisa thought of taking a break from her studies in Jerusalem and riding a bus down the spine of Israel to the Negev desert, then crossing into Jordan at the port city of Eilat. From there, she would catch another bus along the eastern side of the Jordan River, a mostly treeless, rocky region of jagged peaks and meandering valleys that reach like veins and arteries along the Arabian Peninsula.

If she wanted, she could approach Petra just as the ancient Nabataeans had—by walking through a narrow canyon where the rocks seem to glow with the translucent hue of raw salmon. Then she could explore the ancient temple that had been cut into the rocks along with homes and burial vaults.

Israel was not entirely safe from terrorism. Yahya Ayyash had already become Israel's most wanted fugitive after he was implicated in a half-dozen suicide bombings during the previous two years. Ayyash's bombers mainly targeted buses or bus stops. In 1994, thirty-five Israelis had died—twenty-two of them in just one bus bombing in downtown Tel Aviv. For that attack, Ayyash introduced the deadly design that would later be adopted by Hassan Salameh: bombs made from Cold War–era explosives, antitank land mines that had been dug up in the desert along Egypt's border and packed in a duffle bag with shrapnel of nails, screws, and ball bearings.

In January 1995, Ayyash struck again. This time, Ayyash formed an alliance between his Hamas followers and Palestinian Islamic Jihad. If PIJ would supply the suicide bombers, Ayyash and Hamas would build the bombs.

A vulnerable target was selected—the busy Beit Lid junction on a highway north of Tel Aviv where soldiers frequently congregated on Sunday to catch buses that would take them to their bases after weekend visits with their families. The junction also had a symbolic value for Ayyash and Hamas. Near its southwest corner sat Ashmoret Prison, where Israel had jailed Sheik Ahmed Yassin, the wheelchair-bound founder of Hamas who had helped to promote a new Islamic theology that sanctioned suicide attacks against Israelis. For this attack, Ayyash assembled three bombs.

The first bomb was carried by a Palestinian operative wearing an Israeli military uniform. He walked into a knot of soldiers waiting for a bus at the junction and pushed a button. Three minutes later, as the wounded cried in pain and bystanders who had not been hurt ran to help, another Palestinian operative walked up, also disguised as a soldier and seeming to want to tend to the wounded. Instead, he pressed the button on his satchel and more soldiers went down. In all, twenty soldiers and one civilian died.

The third bomb was found amid the carnage at Beit Lid. Police speculate that it might have been designed to explode when Israeli officials and political figures visited the scene, as they usually did after a major attack. Prime Minister Yitzhak Rabin walked by the unexploded bomb when he toured the site, unaware of how close he was to death.

If Alisa was worried about suicide bombers on buses, she did not mention it.

Just as Sara and Matt would later embrace what they believed to be a newfound freedom to travel in the wake of the Oslo Peace Accords, so Alisa wanted to cross the border from Israel as a Jew and visit a formerly hostile and off-limits archeological site in Jordan.

But she never made it to Petra; her friends could not make the trip, and Alisa did not want to travel alone. She chose Gaza instead.

At the time, the Gaza Strip was home to approximately one million Palestinians. Along with the West Bank, where another 1.6 million Palestinians lived, the Gaza Strip was considered a key piece in what Palestinians hoped might one day become a new nation. The Gaza Strip, however, was also home to some 6,300 Israeli Jews who built a string of communities along the beaches. For Israel, Gaza's Jewish settlements had become an agricultural success, with all manner of vegetables grown, not just in the rich soil but inside expansive greenhouses too.

Alisa and two young women friends traveling with her were not interested in the farms. Gaza also had some of the most beautiful beaches along the Mediterranean, and, with Passover approaching and their schools on a short hiatus, Alisa and her friends decided to spend a few days swimming and soaking up the sun at the Gazan settlement of Gush Katif, which featured a hotel.

Just after dawn on the morning of April 9, 1995, a Sunday, Alisa picked up the telephone in her Jerusalem apartment and dialed the number for her parents' home in West Orange, New Jersey. Her father, Stephen, answered.

It was still Saturday night on the East Coast of the United States. Stephen looked at the clock—11:30 p.m. in West Orange, but around 6:30 a.m. in Jerusalem.

The timing of the call did not bother him. Stephen and his wife, Roslyn, had opted for a late dinner. The meal they had ordered from a local kosher Chinese restaurant had just arrived.

Stephen noticed his daughter seemed happy, excited.

"What are you doing up so early," he asked.

"Don't you remember I'm going on vacation?" Alisa said.

Stephen knew that Alisa had been planning a spring break. He just didn't know if she had selected a destination yet. He asked where she was going.

"Gush Katif," Alisa said.

Stephen drew a blank. He knew the name, but couldn't remember the location of Gush Katif.

"Where is that?" he asked.

"Gaza," said Alisa.

Stephen paused. He felt the worry building inside him and handed the phone to his wife.

Like many American Jews, Stephen Flatow encouraged his children to spend time in Israel, soaking up the culture and studying scriptures. But he insisted that his children follow several basic rules if they traveled anywhere within Israel: No hitchhiking; stick with buses or other forms of public transportation. Don't travel alone. And make sure to select a definite destination; no aimless wandering.

When he heard his daughter say she was going to the Gaza Strip, Stephen knew she would have to pass through several militant Palestinian areas. He tried to keep calm and not raise his voice.

He asked how Alisa planned to get to Gaza.

Alisa described a route with a first leg similar to one that Sara and Matt would take—a local Jerusalem bus to the city's central terminal. From there, a bus to Ashkelon, then another bus into the Gaza Strip. All the buses would be driven by Israelis, with the Israeli military keeping watch at checkpoints along the route.

He asked what was so special about the Gaza Strip that she would select it as a vacation spot. "She wanted to get a tan," he said years later, remembering the conversation.

Stephen and Roslyn chatted for a few seconds. Certainly Alisa was following the rules—traveling on a bus with friends to a specific destination. They decided their daughter would probably be safe.

Stephen reached for the phone again.

"Call us when you get back on Wednesday," he said, then hung up.

"You forgot to ask the name of the resort," Roslyn said. "What if something happens?"

"Don't worry," Stephen said. "If something happens, we'll definitely hear about it."

—⁓—

He slipped into a deep sleep that night. "Like a baby," Flatow recalled. When he awoke on Sunday morning, Flatow dressed quickly and headed out the door for the short drive to a synagogue where he usually joined a handful of other men for traditional morning prayers.

Alisa's red Toyota Corolla sat in the driveway. Flatow opened the door and slipped behind the wheel. He turned the key in the ignition, then backed out and drove down his street. At the corner, he pushed a button to turn on the radio. Without Alisa around, Flatow kept the radio tuned to a New York City–based station that usually played nonstop rock and roll. But as Flatow turned at the corner to head to the synagogue, the steady diet of Elvis, the Beatles, and the Rolling Stones was interrupted by a news report of Palestinian terrorists attacking a bus in the Gaza Strip.

Flatow felt sickened. "I knew right then and there," he said. "I felt it inside me. I didn't hear the sound of the explosion. I didn't hear the sound of broken glass, but I knew that she was somehow involved. And I knew there was nothing I could do. She was in God's care."

Flatow drove to the synagogue, which was temporarily located in a residential house while a larger worship space was being constructed. As he walked in, he did not tell any of the other men about the radio report he had just heard. He wrapped the leather tefillin straps around one arm and his forehead, then draped his prayer shawl over his head as the men's voices filled the room with one of Judaism's oldest declarations of faith, the Shema.

"Hear, Israel, the Lord is our God. The Lord is one. Blessed be the name of his glorious kingdom for ever and ever . . ."

Flatow had selected a seat at the end of a row of chairs. As the men finished the Shema and began to recite a series of blessings known as the Shemoneh Esrei, Flatow heard a phone ring in the kitchen.

"I knew it was for me," he said.

He left his seat, walked into the kitchen and grabbed the phone. It was Roslyn.

She had just received a call from the father of one of the women traveling to Gaza with Alisa. A bomb had exploded near the bus, and the father said his daughter and another young woman were back in Jerusalem—safe. Alisa was still at the scene, however. She may have been injured. The caller did not know.

Flatow told Roslyn he was coming home.

He walked back to his chair, and removed his prayer shawl and tefillin. "I've got to go," he whispered to a friend.

—◦—

Alisa grabbed the window seat just behind the driver in Ashkelon for the final leg of her trek to the beach hotel at Gush Katif.

Another woman who was traveling with her, Kesari Rusa, a student in Jerusalem, sat next to Alisa on the aisle. The third woman in their group, Chavi Levine, who was one of Alisa's roommates in Jersusalem, grabbed a seat across the aisle. The three American women were among only a handful of female passengers. Most of the other seats were filled with Israeli soldiers, heading back to their bases in Gaza.

On the outskirts of Ashkelon, where the land flattens out, the bus turned onto a two-lane, southerly road and approached the Israeli checkpoint known as the Erez Crossing. Just south of Erez, the road takes a slight easterly course through alfalfa fields and past olive groves and away from Gaza City with its crowded Palestinian neighborhoods.

Only twenty-five miles long and no more than seven miles wide, the Gaza Strip looks like a sandy finger stretching along the Mediterranean Coast between Israel and Egypt.

On the southern end, a series of small Israeli farm communities dotted the landscape. Known as the Gush Katif block, the enclaves were protected by Israeli military units who guarded checkpoints to make sure that Palestinians did not attack Jewish residents. Getting to those checkpoints, however, meant that Israeli buses had to pass through neighboring Palestinian villages.

Just after noon on Sunday, April 9, 1995, Alisa's bus approached the Israeli community of Kfar Darom, whose sixty families mostly tended fruit orchards. Just north of town a pickup truck, loaded with explosives, parked on the side of the road. As Alisa's bus passed, the truck pulled onto the road and followed. After several minutes, the truck sped up, pulled alongside the bus and the driver pressed a button.

— ◆ —

Kesari Rusa thought someone had thrown a rock at the bus. It was not uncommon for Palestinian residents of the West Bank or the Gaza Strip to demonstrate their opposition to Israelis by showering cars or buses with stones.

Rusa heard what she later told authorities sounded like a "dull sort of loud noise." She looked to her left. The bus window had shattered.

Alisa fell into Rusa. Alisa's eyes were open but blank, unblinking. Alisa's hands had curled into balls.

The bus kept moving for another hundred meters, then rolled to a stop. In the rear of the bus, seven Israeli soldiers were slumped across their seats, dead. Fifty-two others were injured. Blood streamed from the faces and heads of many.

Several Israeli residents from Kfar Darom, including a man with a video camera, pried open the bus door. They pulled the living passengers off, then put Alisa on a stretcher. Several paramedics arrived and cut off Alisa's blue denim skirt and white blouse. A medical helicopter landed. Alisa was placed on board for a ten-minute flight to Soroka Medical Center in Beersheba.

She had not spoken a word since the explosion, but she was breathing.

—~—

The drive from the synagogue took less than five minutes. As soon as Stephen Flatow walked in the door of his home, he reached for the phone and dialed the Israeli Consulate in New York City.

He got a busy signal.

Flatow found a telephone book and opened to the blue-colored pages that listed contact information for a variety of state and federal government offices. He scanned a column for federal agencies and found a Washington, DC, phone number for the US State Department.

A State Department operator answered. Flatow quickly ran through what he had heard—that there had been an attack on a bus in the Gaza Strip, that Alisa's friends were allowed to return to Jerusalem but Alisa was kept at the scene, that he did not know his daughter's condition and needed help finding information.

The operator switched Flatow to the State Department crisis center. A man answered. He took down the number of Alisa's US passport and her Jerusalem address, then promised to call back.

Flatow looked at his watch. It was just nine o'clock in the morning in New Jersey—four o'clock in the afternoon in Israel. Surely someone must know something definitive about Alisa.

Other friends began to call, asking why Flatow had suddenly left morning prayers at the synagogue after taking a phone call. Flatow explained what he knew—which wasn't much. One friend promised to call his contacts in the Israeli Defense Ministry. Another promised to call friends involved in Jewish social services in Israel.

Flatow took out a legal pad and started writing down names and numbers he had called. He was trying to be logical—a lawyer framing out the dimensions of a potential problem to solve, not a father wrestling with sketchy information and wondering whether his daughter had been injured in a dangerous spot almost six thousand miles away.

"I was focused and directed," he said. "I was someplace else."

Flatow's family—Roslyn, his son, Etan, and daughters, Francine, Ilana, and Gail—were now awake and trying to stay calm. "They didn't know what to do. They were upset," Flatow said.

The phone rang. It was 10:30 a.m. The man from the State Department was on the line. He had no new information but asked Flatow to stand by the phone and wait for a call from the US Embassy in Tel Aviv.

Thirty minutes passed. The phone rang again. An embassy staffer in Tel Aviv confirmed that Alisa had been taken to Soroka Medical Center in Beersheba. Other staffers from the embassy were driving there now and would call as soon as they arrived.

Another thirty minutes passed.

The phone rang again. Flatow recognized the Israeli accent of the man on the phone. It was a doctor at Soroka Medical Center.

The doctor started to explain Alisa's condition, but Flatow cut in. The doctor's command of the English language was so poor that Flatow could not understand what he was saying. Flatow asked for someone else to speak to. A woman picked up the line and offered to translate.

What Flatow heard was not much help, though. Surgeons at the hospital operated on Alisa and she was now in the hospital's intensive care unit. Flatow's mind raced with questions.

What kind of operation? And what were Alisa's injuries?

The doctor would not say.

Flatow hung up. Shortly, the phone rang again. It was another man from the hospital. He asked Flatow to come to Israel right away.

Flatow noticed that no one from the State Department or the US Embassy or the hospital had yet told him much about Alisa's injuries. Flatow assumed that his daughter had been struck by shrapnel. But how? And what part of her body?

"Where was she injured?" Flatow asked.

"In the head," the man from the hospital said.

Flatow paused.

"What's her prognosis?" he asked, still trying to maintain his lawyer's logical methodology of chronicling information.

Flatow sensed the man on the phone seemed uneasy.

"You should come right away," the man said.

Flatow hung up.

A friend, Paul Wolf, booked two tickets for a flight on the Israeli airline, El Al—for himself and Flatow. But the flight was leaving at 1 p.m. from John F. Kennedy International Airport, some twenty-five miles away on the edge of the New York City borough of Queens. Flatow threw some clothes in a bag.

It was now after 11:30 a.m.

The phone rang again. It was New Jersey's US Senator Frank Lautenberg. He was in Israel and heard from the American ambassador, Martin Indyk, that Alisa had been injured. Could he do anything?

Flatow rattled off what little information he knew, mentioned he was catching a flight to Israel, thanked Lautenberg and hung up.

The phone rang again. A rabbi was on the line. He heard that Alisa had been in injured and that Flatow was flying to Israel. The rabbi had a suggestion for how Flatow could pass the time on the ten-hour flight: Read the psalms and promise to make charitable pledges.

Flatow thanked the rabbi, hung up and ran out the door. An hour later, he boarded an El Al 747 jetliner. As the giant plane headed across the Atlantic, Flatow tried to read the psalms. He tried to sleep.

But he could not relax.

"What the hell am I doing?" he thought to himself.

He stared at the video screen on the back of the seat in front him and turned on a channel that charted the flight route to Israel.

"My mind was a blank," Flatow said. "I didn't know what I was thinking."

He was still wearing the same clothes he wore to the synagogue that morning.

~~~

The 747 touched down at Ben Gurion International Airport just after 7:30 a.m. on Monday, April 10. Flatow looked out the window and noticed a white Chevrolet suburban waiting on the tarmac beside two Israeli police cruisers. A flight attendant came to his seat.

Flatow would be the first off the plane.

Two US Embassy staffers guided him to the Chevy Suburban. Flatow settled into the back seat with Paul Wolf, now joined by Wolf's son, Daniel, who had flown in from London and spoke fluent Hebrew.

The Suburban quieted. The embassy staffers were not talking. Flatow sensed the need to break the ice.

He turned to Wolf's son.

"Daniel, so who do we sue in this situation?"

It was a poor attempt at a joke. But Flatow felt hollow. It had been more than twenty-four hours since the attack on the bus in Kfar Darom and he still had no idea of his daughter's condition—only that she had been injured in the head.

The drive from the airport to the hospital in Beersheba took almost two hours. A doctor guided Flatow to the intensive care unit and into a room with four beds.

Alisa was in the corner bed. Her eyes were closed and her face was slightly puffy. Her shoulder-length hair had not been cut, but Flatow noticed the bandage on the back of her head.

A ventilator purred. A tube had been placed in Alisa's mouth. Her arm was connected to an IV.

Flatow reached for Alisa's hand. It felt warm. He then leaned toward his daughter's head, his mouth near her ear. "Everything's going to be okay," he said. "Daddy's here."

Flatow straightened up and paused for a second or two, then let go of Alisa's hand.

It dropped to the bed.

Minutes later, in a small conference room, Flatow sipped a bottle of orange soda and officially learned from a hospital surgeon what he already suspected.

Alisa was brain-dead.

The room fell silent. Thirty seconds passed. Then the surgeon said, "We have a question for you."

Flatow sensed what the doctor was about to say.

"You want her organs for donation, don't you?" Flatow said.

The doctor nodded. "Yes," the doctor said. "Would you help?"

Flatow phoned Roslyn. Then he called two rabbis for advice, one of whom was a pediatric neurologist.

Then he agreed that surgeons at the hospital could remove Alisa's organs. First, however, Flatow asked if he could see his daughter one last time.

He walked back to Alisa's bedside. Flatow had not slept in more than twenty-five hours but he wanted time alone with Alisa.

He sat on the bed, listening to the ventilator, then whispered again to her.

"Wake up now," he said. "Show them that they are wrong."

Alisa did not move.

Flatow sat in silence studying his daughter's face. After an hour, he got up and walked into another room, where he signed the papers to donate Alisa's heart, lungs, kidneys, and other major organs to needy patients in Israel.

The embassy staffers drove him to the Hilton Hotel in Tel Aviv. An hour after he settled into his room, the phone rang.

President Bill Clinton was on the line.

"Mister Flatow," the president began. "My wife and I were sitting here this morning talking. We don't know if we could handle it the way you are handling it if something happened to our daughter. You are a brave man."

"Mister President," Flatow said. "You'd do anything for your daughter, correct?"

"Yes," Clinton said.

"Just because my daughter isn't with me doesn't mean I stop being her father," Flatow said.

"God bless you," Clinton said.

Flatow thanked the president, then hung up.

━ ⁓ ━

A year passed.

Then two more months.

It was now June 1996. Sara Duker and Matthew Eisenfeld had been killed. Congress had passed the Antiterrorism and Effective Death

Penalty Act and Clinton had signed it into law during a White House ceremony that Flatow had skipped.

Flatow spoke briefly to Clinton again—when the president visited with the Duker and Flatow families before a speech he gave at Fairleigh Dickinson University in New Jersey before heading to an antiterror conference in Egypt. The conference had been hastily arranged in the wake of a wave of bombings, one of which had killed Sara and Matt. Flatow wanted no part of politics. But in their meeting at Fairleigh Dickinson, Flatow urged Clinton to pressure Yasser Arafat to crack down on Hamas and Islamic Jihad. Clinton nodded and Flatow remembers him saying that Arafat was a key factor in curtailing terrorism. But Flatow did not believe that any special effort would be made in the near future to hold terrorists accountable, even those who murdered Alisa.

Flatow knew that the new law that Clinton signed contained a special clause that gave permission for victims of terrorism and their families to file lawsuits. Flatow was disheartened, though. The possibility of filing a lawsuit seemed remote—at best.

Then, several weeks later, the phone rang.

A rabbi in New York who had been involved in the campaign to crack down on Palestinian terrorism wanted Flatow to meet an attorney who might be interested in taking his case to court.

Flatow asked who the attorney was. The rabbi mentioned a name—Steven Perles.

Flatow had never heard of him.

The rabbi explained that Perles had played a key role in winning a judgment in a long-disputed war reparations case on behalf of Hugo Princz, a Jewish-American citizen in Europe who was imprisoned as a teenager by the Nazis during World War II and was now living in Highland Park, New Jersey. Flatow had never met Princz, but certainly knew his story, which had become a cause célèbre within New Jersey's tight-knit Jewish community.

Princz was born in Czechoslovakia in 1922. His mother was a Czech-born Jew. But his father who was also Jewish, had been born in the United States and was an American citizen. This meant that Hugo Princz was automatically considered to be a US citizen too, even though the family continued to live in Czechoslovakia.

By the time World War II erupted, Princz's father, Herman, had established a successful business that leased harvesting equipment to Czech farmers. Herman and his wife, Gisella, who had become a US citizen, now had a daughter and two other sons besides seventeen-year-old Hugo, and elected to stay in Czechoslovakia even though they had heard that Jews in other countries invaded by the Nazis had lost their homes and were being shipped off to concentration camps. The United States had not entered the war yet and Herman and Gisella figured their US citizenships would give their family a neutral, protected status. They were wrong.

By December 1941, the United States had declared war on Germany, which had annexed Czechoslovakia and begun to implement the same anti-Jewish policies that the Princzes had heard about in Europe's other occupied countries. Without warning, in March 1942, Herman, Gisella, and their children were arrested by Slovak police. The police then turned the Princz family over to the Nazi SS.

Each member of the Princz family had an American passport. But Czechoslovakia's Nazi government refused to allow the family to return to the United States as part of a civilian citizen exchange that had been supervised by the Red Cross. Instead, the Princzes were dispatched to a series of concentration camps with other Jews.

Herman, Gisella, and their daughter were sent to the Treblinka death camp where they died, according to court records. Hugo Princz and two younger brothers ended up at Auschwitz, then were assigned to the Birkenau camp where they were forced to work at a nearby I.G. Farben chemical plant as slave laborers. Princz's brothers were injured on the job, removed from their work gangs, and starved to death. Princz managed to live.

After laboring as a bricklayer at I.G. Farben, he was forced to work at a factory that built Messerschmitt fighters and bombers for the German Luftwaffe. By the spring of 1945, as US forces neared, Princz was forced to board a freight car jammed with other prisoners and sent to another concentration camp to be killed. But American soldiers stopped the train.

Noticing the "USA" that the Nazis had stitched on his camp uniform, the soldiers pulled Princz out of the group of other prisoners and sent him to an American military hospital for treatment.

For the first time in three years, Princz was not only a free man but he was officially recognized as an American citizen. After recovering in the hospital, he moved to New Jersey, got married, and eventually settled into a job as a butcher at a supermarket. He was the only member of his family to survive the war.

In 1955, Princz applied for compensation as part of a postwar reparations agreement in which the new Federal Republic of Germany—then known as West Germany—offered monthly financial payments to Holocaust survivors. But Princz's application was turned down. The West German government determined that Princz was neither a German citizen at the time of his arrest, nor a refugee as defined by the Geneva Convention after World War II. A court later determined that Princz might have qualified for reparations when the German government changed its eligibility rules in 1965. But Princz missed the deadline to apply before the statute of limitations for war reparations expired in 1969.

Another fifteen years passed. By 1984, Princz embarked on a new strategy to draw attention to his story.

With the help of US Senator Bill Bradley of New Jersey, Princz convinced the US State Department to send a series of requests to the German government and to the US subsidiaries of I.G. Farben, which included BASF and Bayer, to pay some sort of financial reparation to him or to establish a pension fund.

Once again, every request was denied, along with additional overtures from officials in the Bush and Clinton administrations—including even a personal attempt by President Clinton to convince German Chancellor Helmut Kohl to settle the matter on basic moral grounds.

Frustrated and running out of options, Princz decided to find a lawyer. One evening, while attending a large banquet, he happened to be seated at a table with a New Jersey bank president and his wife.

When the banker's wife heard that Princz had been at Auchwitz, she mentioned that she, too, was a Holocaust survivor. But rather than being confined to a concentration camp, she said that she had been hidden throughout the war by a Christian family and spent much of her time confined to small hiding places, including a space under a farmer's haystack.

As the woman finished her story, she mentioned that she had applied to the German government for a war reparation as a Holocaust survivor and was receiving more than $1,000 a month. She then turned to Princz and asked what amount of financial restitution he was receiving.

Slowly, Princz began to tell his story to the woman and her husband—how his entire family had been lost, how he had worked as a slave laborer, and how his application for war reparations had been denied on a technicality about his citizenship and refugee status, then denied again because he missed a filing deadline.

As Princz finished, the woman's husband mentioned that he had just won a multimillion-dollar judgment in a bank fraud case in Costa Rica. It had been a complicated case, he said. But he had managed to find a lawyer in Washington, DC, who knew how to navigate the nuances of international law and politics, then find the most persuasive legal threads to help stitch together a successful case.

The banker mentioned a name: Steven Perles.

Perles was born on the first day of summer in 1951 in Boston. But after graduating law school at the Virginia's College of William and Mary in 1975, he became a fixture in Washington.

Initially, Perles's legal expertise was not focused on courtrooms or even in legal briefs. For six years after law school, he helped to shape and shepherd legislation through Congress as a legal counsel and legislative aide to Alaska's powerful Republican senator, Ted Stevens. How the outspoken Alaskan senator and the bookish young lawyer from Boston connected was a bit of an accident. In law school, Perles had developed an interest in environmental law. In the mid-1970s, as federal clean-air regulations were just beginning to be written, Alaska had several unique problems. One of the most notable was the way the state's severe weather patterns tended to affect air pollution, which perhaps would violate the new, national regulations. Perles wrote a law school research paper on Alaska's dilemma. Stevens read the paper and hired Perles for his staff.

After six years on Capitol Hill, Perles was ready to strike out on his own. He was just turning thirty, and he wanted to establish a law practice that specialized in international law. For the next six years, Perles handled a wide variety of cases, including one that reached the US Supreme Court involving Japanese whaling firms.

Perles had never had a client like Hugo Princz, though. After Princz left a message at Perles's Washington office, Perles waited several days to return the call. It wasn't that Perles was avoiding the case. Perles's wife was giving birth to their first child, a son. After his wife and newborn boy were resting comfortably, Perles found a hospital pay phone and dialed Princz's number.

The Princz case was steeped in politics. Perles knew that. He also knew that Princz had a strong moral anchor to his case—namely, that he was a Holocaust victim and had been denied just compensation because of a technicality. But Perles sensed that simply having moral righteousness on your side was not always enough to win a satisfactory judgment. Sometimes you needed to play a strong political hand, especially if the case involved international law.

As he listened to Princz's story of his last application being rejected by German authorities because he missed a deadline for filing, Perles remembered a lesson he learned several years earlier while working with Ted Stevens on similarly frustrating issues with foreign governments. "Most of these governments do what is in their perceived national interest, whether we think it's right or wrong," Perles said. "My job is to create an environment, either by carrot or stick, where they believe that what I want them to do is in their perceived national interest."

So began almost seven more years of political lobbying, culminating in a landmark federal lawsuit in which Princz filed suit against the German government for a series of charges that hardly seemed connected to something as momentous as the Holocaust. Princz's suit accused Germany of false imprisonment, assault and battery, negligent and intentional infliction of emotional distress, and a failure to pay proper wages for work at the I.G. Farben and Messerschmitt plants.

The case may have emerged from a complicated story of citizenship and Nazi war atrocities. But Perles turned it into a straightforward argument over the kinds of basic legal issues that are dealt with on a daily basis in almost any court in the United States.

Not surprisingly, Princz—and Perles—won the first round of their lawsuit in US district court. But they lost when Germany took the case to a US federal appeals court, claiming that it was protected by America's Foreign Sovereign Immunities Act. The Act listed specific instances in which US citizens could file legal claims against a foreign government—and false imprisonment, assault, battery, emotional distress and a lack of proper payment for work did not qualify, according to the appellate judges.

By now, Princz and Perles had also drawn the attention of lawyers for the US State Department, who argued that American citizens should not be given wide permission to file lawsuits—and to collect damages—from foreign governments. The State Department lawyers feared drastic repercussions if such suits were allowed to multiply.

It would not be the last time Perles confronted such an argument. Perles had done a masterful job of drawing attention to the plight of Hugo Princz. What had been an uncertain legal case, with all manner of arcane nuances involving the immunity of foreign governments and the payment of war reparations, became a clear and powerful moral cause. Now in his late sixties, Princz was portrayed as a long-suffering victim who had lost not only his family in the Holocaust but had been denied even a fraction of the compensation that other concentration camp survivors had received years before from Germany. Even though the US appellate court blocked Princz from collecting a judgment against Germany, the German government suddenly changed its mind and began negotiating with Perles for a settlement.

Princz ended up sharing a portion of a $2.1 million settlement from Germany with 11 other Holocaust survivors. His case also helped another 235 survivors to collect portions of an additional $18.5 million settlement. Finally, Princz collected an undisclosed amount of money from German firms who used prisoners for slave labor during World War II, including the modern subsidiaries of I.G. Farben and Messerschmitt.

On a June morning in 1996, barely two months after President Clinton signed the Antiterrorism and Effective Death Penalty Act, Stephen Flatow walked into the Washington office of Steven Perles.

The telephone call from the rabbi several weeks earlier had persuaded Flatow to seriously consider a legal case, though he felt he had little chance of succeeding. On the other hand, such a case might be a first step in testing the new clause in the antiterrorism legislation that allowed Americans to pursue foreign terrorists in the same way that accident victims would file claims against bad drivers.

Flatow felt such a case was risky. Yet, aside from paying for his traveling expenses from New Jersey to Washington and perhaps some additional costs to file court papers, the case would not drain his bank account. What's more, the idea gave him energy. He was tired of feeling melancholy. Yes, he was still deeply sad over the loss of Alisa and he knew that he and the other members of his family would never be the same again—no amount of money in a legal judgment would change that. His daughter had been murdered by a man who believed he was acting on God's behalf.

It was hardly a case of negligent death. It was a case of murder, pure and simple. But in place of a homicide case, Flatow decided he would accept a civil case—if he could get into court and present evidence to a judge that proved who the killers were.

Flatow liked Perles in a way that surprised him. Perles seemed to see the big picture, not only what it would take to win in a federal court, but he understood the kind of research and money the case would require. Flatow already knew about the successful judgment Perles had won for Hugo Princz. But Flatow was not looking just for money. He also wanted an official court ruling that pointed a legal finger at his daughter's killers.

Flatow sat down at a conference table in Perles's Washington office. Perles took a seat on the other side, then leaned back in his chair and put his feet on the table.

Flatow sensed that Perles had confidence. Already Perles had studied the new law that Clinton had signed. He had also studied Alisa's murder.

Perles looked up. There was a problem, he said.

Whom would Flatow actually sue? Islamic Jihad claimed to have detonated the bomb that killed Alisa. But the new antiterrorism law specifically said that only seven countries—Iran, Iraq, Syria, North Korea, Cuba, Libya, and Sudan—could be sued. Many intelligence experts had long felt that Islamic Jihad had close ties to Iran and that its operations were even financed by the Iranians. But what kind of proof could be submitted in court? Premonitions were one thing; hard evidence that could pass muster with a federal judge was something else entirely.

And one more thing: The new law merely gave permission to sue. It cited no specific cause, no process—none of the important legal roadmap pointers that experienced lawyers need when they assemble a case.

Perles felt that the ballyhooed antiterror legislation that Bill Clinton signed, which gave victims the right to take terrorists to court in civil lawsuits, would not have passed muster in a first-year law school class.

Perles looked at Flatow. The law had to be changed.

Photo of Alisa Flatow,
hanging on wall of
Stephen Flatow's office
COURTESY OF STEPHEN FLATOW

Matt and Sara relax
on a beach shortly
before leaving for
Jerusalem.
COURTESY OF ARLINE
DUKER

Matt and Sara on
an apartment ter-
race in Jerusalem
shortly before they
were killed
COURTESY OF DUKER/
EISENFELD FAMILIES

Bus stop in Jerusalem where
Matt and Sara boarded the
Number 18 bus
PHOTO BY MIKE KELLY

Jaffa Road in 2012
PHOTO BY MIKE KELLY

Hassan Salameh,
who orchestrated
the plot to bomb
the Number 18 bus,
during prison
interview with author
© 2006 JAMES W. ANNESS/
NORTHJERSEY.COM

"Martyr photo" of
suicide bomber Majdi
Abu Wardeh, created
by Hamas after he
detonated the bomb
on the Number 18
bus on Jaffa Road
PHOTO BY MIKE KELLY

Shrapnel taken from bodies of bomb victims by trauma
surgeon Dr. Avi Rivkind
PHOTO BY MIKE KELLY

Coffins with bodies of Sara Duker and Matthew Eisenfeld are carried to
side-by-side graves in an Avon, Connecticut, cemetery.
PHOTO BY STEVE DUNN, *THE HARTFORD COURANT*

Muhammed Abu Wardeh, father of suicide bomber Majdi Abu Wardeh, at his home in al-Fawwar refugee camp
PHOTO BY MIKE KELLY

Rubble on lot at al-Fawwar refugee camp where home of suicide bomber Majdi Abu Wardeh once stood. The home was destroyed by Israeli soldiers as punishment for Wardeh's bombing of the Number 18 bus on Jaffa Road.
PHOTO BY MIKE KELLY

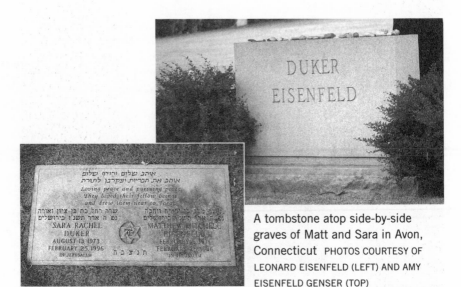

A tombstone atop side-by-side graves of Matt and Sara in Avon, Connecticut PHOTOS COURTESY OF LEONARD EISENFELD (LEFT) AND AMY EISENFELD GENSER (TOP)

Dr. Aharon Oren, who supervised the Hebrew University biology lab where Sara worked before her death, points to her name on a memorial to terror victims at the campus in Jerusalem.   PHOTO BY MIKE KELLY

Former Shin Bet chief Ami Ayalon
PHOTO BY MIKE KELLY

Former Shin Bet official Avi Dichter
PHOTO BY MIKE KELLY

Dr. Avi Rivkind in his office at Hadassah Ein Kerem Medical Center, Jerusalem
PHOTO BY MIKE KELLY

Dr. Yehuda Hiss, chief forensic pathologist, standing outside Israel's Institute of Forensic Medicine, pointing to area where relatives waited for news on fate of Jaffa Road bombing victims
PHOTO BY MIKE KELLY

Former Shin Bet official Yisrael Hasson at his office at the Israeli Knesset
PHOTO BY MIKE KELLY

Former Palestinian Security Chief Jibril Rajoub
PHOTO BY MIKE KELLY

# CHAPTER 7

THE CAR ROLLED SLOWLY ALONG THE NARROW, TWISTING ROADS THAT
cut through the rocky hills and valleys south of Jerusalem. A Palestinian
man steered. Another Palestinian man sat in the front passenger seat.
Israeli police would later say that nothing about the car or its occupants
seemed unusual. To other motorists—and to dozens of police and undercover agents searching for potential Hamas terrorists—the two men
seemed like dozens of other commuters, trying to rush home from a job
or school.

It was Friday evening, May 17, 1996. Almost a month had passed
since Arline Duker joined Len and Vicki Eisenfeld at the White House
to watch President Clinton sign the new antiterrorism law that opened
the door to possible lawsuits by them and other American families victimized by foreign terrorist attacks. It would be several more weeks before
Stephen Flatow and Steve Perles discovered that mounting a legal case
using Clinton's new law against Alisa Flatow's killers was no easy task.

In Israel, a raucous and caustic election campaign was winding down,
with polls showing that support had slipped dramatically for Shimon
Peres, the embattled prime minister. Peres was still slightly ahead of challenger Benjamin Netanyahu in most surveys, but the margin seemed to
shrink each day. Fearing that more terrorist attacks might drain voters'
confidence in his ability to protect Israelis and sink his chances for victory against Netanyahu, Peres ordered Israel's military and counterterror
apparatus to high alert. With voters scheduled to head to the polls in
twelve days, the last thing Peres needed was another bus bombing.

The car cruised past tiny vegetable farms, olive groves, vineyards, and
fields where teenage boys tended herds of sheep. It passed stone houses
abandoned decades ago and other stone homes adorned with TV anten-
nas and driveways filled with rusty, decade-old cars. It passed factories
that made bricks, small wooden roadside stands that sold vegetables, cafes
where tired men drank coffee at patio tables, and hamlets with minarets

rising above small mosques. Not far from the al-Fawwar refugee camp, where Majdi Abu Wardeh lived before detonating the bomb aboard the Jaffa Road commuter bus, the car turned onto a road that led over a steep hill and into the ancient city of Hebron. It was just after 7 p.m. Dusk.

By the spring of 1996, Hebron had become a volatile nexus in the Israeli-Palestinian conflict, as well as a nettlesome and equally symbolic stumbling block to peace negotiations. Sprawling across a series of hills deep within the West Bank, Hebron was founded more than four thousand years ago by the Biblical patriarch, Abraham, who is also honored by Muslims as a prophet. In 1996, Hebron was home to more than 120,000 Palestinians and several hundred Jewish settlers who had braved regular sniper attacks to maintain a tiny colony while nursing a deep distrust of the Oslo peace process.

Both sides viewed the city as an important cornerstone of their respective faiths. Hebron was home to the Cave of the Patriarchs—or, as many Israelis called it, the Cave of Machpelah. As the reputed burial spot of Abraham, the cave was sacred to Jews and Muslims. Given the history of animosity between Jews and Muslims on the West Bank, both sides had divided the cave for visitors from their separate faiths—Muslims in one spot, Jews in another. And both viewed their portions as bastions to protect, even to the point of death.

The murders of twenty-nine Palestinian worshippers at the cave two years earlier by Baruch Goldstein were still fresh in the minds of those on both sides. Goldstein's February 1994 rampage raised tensions inside Hebron and was seen as a warning of how fragile the Oslo process had become. In recent weeks, many Israeli intelligence analysts had come to believe that the bombing of the Number 18 bus on Jaffa Road on the second anniversary of the Goldstein murders was a form of symbolic retribution. By May 1996, however, those analysts had greater reason to worry about Hebron.

Since the bombings in Jerusalem and other cities several months earlier, Shin Bet agents and Israeli military intelligence officers felt that Hebron had become home to a growing number of Hamas activists intent on plotting future attacks. Adding to the concern, Israel, as part of the Oslo peace process, had agreed to turn over control of a portion of Hebron in the spring of 1996 to Yasser Arafat's Palestinian Authority security forces, led by Jibril Rajoub, a former Palestinian militant who had been jailed by the Israelis years before. Even before the February-March bombing campaign, Shin Bet and the Israeli army did not trust Arafat or Rajoub to monitor Hamas closely. After those bombings, and with Peres running for reelection, Israeli officials postponed the turnover of power in Hebron.

In the three months since the wave of bombings, Shin Bet agents had picked up a series of reports indicating that Arafat had given tacit approval for Hamas to stage the February and March attacks. Or as Shin Bet's Jerusalem chief, Yisrael Hasson noted, "We know Arafat gave permission. But what does it mean?"

That question would bother Hasson and other Israeli officials for years. Hasson felt that Arafat did not sign off on the specific plans, locations, or dates of the bombings. But Hasson was confident that Arafat generally approved of some sort of attack by Hamas to avenge the killing of Yahya Ayyash. "The problem is not whether Hamas wanted to do it," Hasson said. "Hamas wanted to bomb every day. The key problem was Arafat."

Neither Hasson nor other Shin Bet officials knew at that time that Norwegian diplomat Terje Roed-Larsen shared similar concerns after Arafat's emphatic, yet vague, warning to steer clear of Jerusalem on February 25. Like Hasson, Larsen had become convinced that Arafat was playing a delicate and diplomatically dangerous game of trying to keep his distance from Hamas bombings yet remaining aware of them and offering some measure of approval.

Such suspicions by Hasson and Larsen hardly mattered now. The bombings confirmed what many Israeli officials and even such diplomats as Larsen and high-ranking Americans privately feared, that Arafat was not serious about stopping terrorist attacks.

Shimon Peres's advisors, especially Chief of Staff Avi Gill, had come to believe that Arafat's lack of effort to stop Hamas was deliberate. In Gill's mind, Arafat wanted to depict himself to the Israelis as a more palatable alternative to the Hamas radicals. So while the Israelis—and others such as Terje Roed-Larsen and the Americans involved in the Oslo negotiations—disliked Arafat and his slippery style of diplomacy, they viewed him as the least dangerous of all Palestinian options.

"Arafat always felt that having an active, violent threat against Israel was helpful for his bargaining with Israel," said Gill. "Not that he was in direct collaboration with Hamas, but that all the time, he was able to hint at the alternative."

By the spring of 1996, Peres and his advisors also became aware of a startling development. Israeli intelligence had amassed solid evidence that Iran had been urging Hamas to step up its terrorist attacks in Israel, confirming to some degree what US Ambassador Martin Indyk suspected.

"We knew that the Iranians were pushing Hamas," said Gill. But, as with Arafat, Israel faced a similar dilemma with Iran. It was one thing to know the larger context of the bombings and that perhaps Iran was trying to exert its influence in the Middle East power struggle by using Hamas terrorism to derail the Oslo peace process. But what was to be done about it?

Israel—backed by the Americans and others—was trying to hold onto some semblance of the Oslo process, according to Gill. While Israel and others sensed that Arafat was the wrong man to rely on, they did not want to cut their ties with him and viewed him as the least dangerous choice among Palestinian leaders who seemed capable of honoring a peace agreement. "On one hand," said Gill, "we wanted Arafat to crack down on Hamas. But we also wanted to preserve our relationship with him."

Nonetheless, Gill and others in Peres's circle came to believe that Arafat was not as smart and wily as others thought him to be. Eventually, Gill felt that Arafat had no idea how detrimental the bombings of February and March would be to the Oslo process. He also doubted that Arafat understood what impact Iranians might have on Palestinian attempts to form their own nation. "Arafat did not realize the magnitude that this terrorist campaign would have," said Gill.

In the meantime, Shin Bet investigators were trying to solve a crime— actually, a mass murder. In various West Bank towns, Shin Bet agents had already arrested several key figures in the Jaffa Road bus bombing. But the most sought-after Hamas operative, Hasson Salameh, had managed to stay hidden. It was now almost three months since those bombings yet Shin Bet still had no firm idea of Salameh's whereabouts or what his next plan might be.

———

As the car entered the outskirts of Hebron and wound through a series of narrow, twisting streets, it approached an unexpected and decidedly unwanted obstacle. Israeli solders, urged on by Shin Bet intelligence analysts who hoped to keep Hamas operatives off guard, had set up a temporary checkpoint and were searching all vehicles.

The car slowed, then stopped. As Israeli soldiers asked the driver for his ID card, the Palestinian man in the passenger side opened the door and started to run away.

A soldier yelled at the man to stop. Standing nearby, the sergeant in charge of the roadblock, had already cocked his rifle because he suspected trouble. As it turned out the sergeant was right. The Palestinian man drew a pistol from his belt. Before the Palestinian could pull the trigger, the sergeant fired. The Palestinian man kept running and disappeared down an alley.

An hour later, Israeli soldiers, after mounting a citywide manhunt, found the man at Hebron's al-Alia Hospital, where doctors were treating him for a painful bullet wound in his buttocks. The soldiers, meanwhile, searched the car and found several land mines, grenades, and a box of rifles and pistols. They also identified the other Palestinian who was driving the car, Rizzek Rajoub, a cousin of Yasser Arafat's security chief, Jibril Rajoub.

The arrest of a Hamas operative with family ties to a high-ranking Palestinian official, who was supposedly helping Shin Bet to monitor terrorism, was unsettling but not surprising to Israelis. Since the signing of the Oslo accords, Israeli counterterrorism authorities said they tried to find ways to build a cooperative partnership with the Palestinian police, a relationship that was, at best, framed more by a sense of pragmatic skepticism than trust.

While Shin Bet officials had been monitoring intelligence reports that more Hamas squads were trying to infiltrate Israel from their bases in the Gaza Strip, by the spring of 1996 Shin Bet had little confidence that Palestinian authorities would notify them of an impending attack. So Israel police and Shin Bet agents embraced a middle-ground policy; they attempted to share information with the Palestinians (and glean some information too) while remaining on full alert. Now, hearing that one of the men arrested at the Hebron checkpoint was related to the chief of Palestinian security, Israeli officials felt as if they were on their own in battling potential terror plots.

"We had an alert that there was going to be a terror attack leaving Gaza to Israel," said Shin Bet's Avi Dichter. "We had to turn over those pieces of information to the Palestinians. After a while, we understood that we were sharing information, not with a partner. I wouldn't say an enemy, but someone who doesn't try to stop terrorists. That made it very difficult to be from outside the Gaza Strip."

As Shin Bet's commander who oversaw the agency's operations in the Gaza Strip, Avi Dichter played a key role in the killing of Yahya Ayyash with the exploding cell phone in January 1996. But Dichter was not satisfied. Even years later, he would have preferred to capture Ayyash alive so Shin Bet's agents could have questioned him about future attacks. Dichter was sure that, before Ayyash died, he had managed to pass on some of his bomb-making expertise to other Hamas members. One of those, said Dichter, was a new operative whose name had recently surfaced in intelligence reports: Hassan Salameh.

From his home at a kibbutz north of Tel Aviv, Shin Bet's Yisrael Hasson heard the report of the suspicious bomb-laden car in Hebron, the fugitive with the bullet in his buttocks, and the familiar name of the driver. It was Friday, the Sabbath. Hasson was about to eat dinner with his family, but the brief encounter at the checkpoint in Hebron had piqued his curiosity. Who was the other Palestinian who ran away? Now that Israeli soldiers had captured that man and were holding him at a hospital in Hebron, Hasson needed to get to the scene.

"We didn't know who this was," Hasson said of the wounded suspect at al-Alia Hospital. "But I felt that this was very, very important."

Since the bus bombing on February 25 in Jerusalem—and the bombing of another Number 18 bus on Jaffa Road a week later—Hasson had devoted most of his time to tracking down the Hamas operatives involved. What concerned him most was whether Hamas was planning other attacks. With the discovery of a car filled with land mines—the same kind of explosives used in the Jaffa Road bus bombings—and the capture of a man who was desperate enough to leap from a car surrounded by heavily armed soldiers and run away, Hasson felt his investigators might have the break they were searching for all these weeks.

Hasson picked up the phone and called al-Alia Hospital and asked to speak to the doctor who treated the man. The doctor said the man was still sleeping from the anesthesia he had been given during surgery to remove the bullet from his buttocks.

Hasson asked when the man would wake up.

The doctor estimated at least another hour.

"Good," Hasson thought. He asked the doctor to let the man sleep a little longer if possible.

Hasson hung up. Within minutes he was in his car, speeding toward Hebron.

An hour later, Hasson walked into the man's hospital room. The man was groggy but awake. Hasson paused for a second or two by the door to the room to study the man's features. He was short, stocky, with a receding hairline, a patchy beard, and a protruding nose.

Hasson did not recognize the man. He was, as Hasson later concluded, a new operative who had never been photographed by Shin Bet.

Hasson stepped closer to the bed. Like many Shin Bet veterans who had devoted their careers to tracking down suspected terrorists in the Palestinian villages of the West Bank and throughout the Gaza Strip, Hasson spoke fluent Arabic.

"Shoo issmak?" Hasson asked.

"What is your name?"

The man did not hesitate to answer.

"Hassan Salameh."

❦

Salameh writhed in the hospital bed as his anesthesia wore off and the stinging pain returned. Doctors placed an oxygen mask over his mouth and nose. Salameh shook his head from side to side and seemed in no mood to say anything more than his name. Yisrael Hasson was not worried. A longer interrogation could wait until Salameh felt better. For now, he had what he needed—a name.

And what a name it was. The most wanted man in Israel, who masterminded the most devastating terror attacks in more than a generation, had been captured—by accident.

For the first time in more than two months Israeli authorities felt they had been blessed by luck. This was a major break in a case that not only had confounded them but also had been the focus on an intense investigation and accompanying fear that another suicide bombing was being planned. They had already arrested other Hamas followers who had participated in the bombings on Jaffa Road and in Ashkelon. But Salameh was the ringleader, the bomb-maker, and the deputy commander of Hamas's military wing—the al-Qassam brigade. Based on the fact that Israeli soldiers found other explosives and guns in Salameh's car, Shin Bet's investigators felt relieved that they had probably prevented yet another bombing from taking place.

Because of the Sabbath, which began around 8 p.m. on Friday—roughly an hour after Salameh was arrested at the hospital—and extended to sunset on Saturday, Israeli authorities were in a bind. They had major news to proclaim and wanted a large TV audience. But they did not want to interrupt the Sabbath. So they waited twenty-four hours to announce Salameh's capture.

Just after the Sabbath concluded at 8 p.m. on Saturday, Israeli Major General Uzi Dayan called a press conference to announce that Salameh had been arrested. "We've settled the blood feud," Dayan said.

In hindsight, Dayan's comment seems exaggerated. The larger conflict between Israelis and Palestinians was far from settled. But Dayan's words underscored the fact that Israeli military leaders and Shin Bet counterterrorism teams felt an immense sense of relief that a temporary checkpoint on the streets of Hebron and a random search of a car resulted in the capture of such a high-ranking Hamas operative. "We were in a long run after Hassan Salameh," Dayan said. "We do know that he was planning other terror activities when we captured him."

As he spoke to journalists, Dayan stood in front of maps and aerial photographs of Hebron and its narrow streets. He said the army had no prior intelligence that Salameh was planning to drive into Hebron. "Salameh's capture was achieved because of our massive, twenty-four-hour-a-day security activity," Dayan said. Asked if Salameh's wound was serious, Dayan said: "All I care about is whether or not he can talk."

Regardless of whether Salameh would provide helpful information to counterterrorism investigators, his arrest was already being trumpeted as a political victory. For months, Israeli political polls showed a diminishing lack of trust among voters that Prime Minister Shimon Peres's support of the Oslo peace process would actually bring peace between Israelis and Palestinians. With national elections scheduled for May 29 and with Peres's once-commanding lead over challenger Benjamin Netanyahu reduced to single digits, the capture of Hassan Salameh was viewed by the Peres campaign as a possible boost for the embattled prime minister and a welcome response to critics who said his administration was not taking the terrorist threat seriously.

Certainly Peres seemed delighted. "This relieves the pressure," Peres said of Salameh's capture. "This man really was a ticking time bomb."

Hamas did not hesitate to respond and attempt to dilute Israel's sense of victory. Soon after General Dayan and Prime Minister Peres spoke, Salameh's colleagues in Hamas's al-Qassam military wing vowed revenge for the capture of their deputy commander. "The Qassam brigades will not hesitate to carry out the strongest revenge against the cowardly Zionists for this ugly crime," Hamas announced in a leaflet.

With dozens of Israeli soldiers on the streets outside, Salameh remained at al-Alia Hospital in Hebron for another day. But he needed more surgery to repair the bullet wound to his buttocks by a more experienced surgeon who had dealt with his share of bullet wounds. So under heavy guard and while most people in Israel and on the West Bank were asleep, Salameh was transferred to Hadassah University Hospital Ein Kerem in Jerusalem. It was after 2 a.m. when Salameh was wheeled into Hadassah, where his new surgeon would be the same man who had patched the wounds of the victims of Salameh's bloody handiwork on the Number 18 bus on Jaffa Road almost three months earlier, Dr. Avi Rivkind.

That Israeli's top trauma surgeon would be asked to operate on Israel's most wanted terrorist was no surprise. Hadassah Medical Center had long prided itself on treating patients without paying attention to religion or nationality. When he walked into the operating room and examined the Palestinian man who had just been brought from the hospital in Hebron, Rivkind had no idea of Salameh's notoriety.

"I did not know it was Hassan Salameh. No one told me," Rivkind said later. "I didn't pay attention. We work and then we ask the questions. I didn't ask who it was."

Salameh didn't talk either.

During his career, Rivkind had come to expect patients to question him, with the questions ranging from "Will I survive?" to "Can someone call my boss?" But what surprised Rivkind about the Palestinian man lying on the gurney was his silence. Rivkind knew some basic Arabic words that he often used in treating Palestinian patients. He asked Salameh to breathe deeply, for example. Salameh took a deep breath. But other than following a few fundamental commands, Salameh never spoke.

"He did not speak one word," Rivkind said. "Nothing. It's not the relationship I'm used to with my patients."

Nevertheless Rivkind quickly diagnosed Salameh's problem. Salameh's colon had been torn by the single rifle bullet that had passed through his buttocks. Rivkind donned a surgeon's gown and walked into the operating room and, over several hours, he delicately repaired Salameh's colon.

After the surgery, Salameh was wheeled to a private room. Two Shin Bet agents kept watch inside the room and another guarded the door from the hallway as Hassan Salameh slept.

Three days later, he talked.

—◆—

On Tuesday morning, May 21, 1996, Sergeant Major Yosy Ohayon of the Israeli police, walked into Salameh's hospital room. As with many law enforcement agencies across the world, the Israeli police have established a set of protocols for interrogating prisoners.

Sergeant Ohayon first identified himself then read an eighty-four-word statement to Salameh in Arabic, summarizing the charges against him—namely, that he was "suspected of being a member" of the al-Qassam Brigade and that Israeli authorities were now accusing him "of sending people who committed suicide terrorist attacks" in which forty-six people were killed. As if that were not enough, Sergeant Ohayon added a not-so-small postscript: Salameh had also been charged with illegal possession of weapons and explosives.

"You do not have to say a word unless you wish to," Ohayon told Salameh. "However, anything you say will be written by me and may be used as evidence."

And so, Salameh began to tell his story.

Israeli police records indicate that Salameh participated in four interviews—the first on May 21, 1996, with Sergeant Ohayon at Hadassah University Hospital Ein Kerem, and others in July, August, and December of 1996 at other locations. There is no hint in the transcripts that Salameh paused or asked for time to ponder Ohayon's instructions or asked to contact an attorney, or even whether he felt he needed an attorney. Taken together, the transcripts, along with his public statements during subsequent court appearances, and in a 1997 TV interview and a later interview with this author, show him not only willing to talk about his work as a Hamas operative and bomb-maker but occasionally seeming to brag about his various missions and how he trained for them. He spoke easily and concisely, his thoughts connecting from one episode to the next without the halting, clipped phrasing or one- or two-word answers of a man who was being forced to talk or was merely going through the motions of answering questions.

At times, he seemed arrogant and self-congratulatory, enthusiastic about his record of bloodletting. But mostly he was chillingly pedantic in his matter-of-fact recitation of details, from the names of other Hamas operatives who worked with him, the types of cars that transported him to meetings to discuss "operations," to his own cold-blooded explanations of how he built his bombs and recruited young men to carry them aboard buses and kill themselves while killing others.

In that initial session with Sergeant Ohayon, Salameh did not begin with a recounting of the bombings on Jaffa Road, which had dominated debate in Israel's election campaign and cast doubt on the future of the

Oslo peace process. Salameh started his story before Oslo had even been signed, as if he wanted the full story and its context to be known before he described the bombings.

It was 1992, in the dusty Khan Yunis refugee camp about twenty miles south of Gaza City on the Gaza Strip where Salameh's family lived after fleeing a Palestinian village near Ashkelon after Israel declared its independence four decades earlier. Salameh had just turned twenty-one. He was unmarried, with only a few college credits earned in classes at Gaza's Islamic University. He decided to drop out and make a career change. He joined the Islamic Resistance Movement, or Hamas.

The decision hardly seemed out of character for Salameh. His first venture into the complicated social, spiritual, economic, and political quicksand of the Israeli-Palestinian conflict began several years before. It was December 1987 and across the Gaza Strip and the West Bank, Palestinians revolted against two decades of Israeli occupation in what became known as "the Intifada," or the uprising. Eventually, thousands of Palestinians would join in a variety of violent and nonviolent strikes, armed confrontations and other forms of protest against Israelis across the West Bank and the Gaza Strip. From its initial stirrings in December 1987, the Intifada continued another six years, until just before the Oslo accords were signed. (A "Second Intifada" erupted in 1998 and lasted until 2004.)

Some Palestinians attacked with bombs, guns, or knives. But most reached to the ground around them and picked up rocks to throw. Rock throwing at Israelis, especially by Palestinian teenagers, grew into a near-daily activity and became the most common method of protest. Palestinians tossed rocks at Israeli cars, buses, schools, army convoys, police checkpoints, homes, and synagogues—almost any target imaginable.

When the Intifada erupted, Hassan Salameh was sixteen. His hometown of Khan Yunis, which had about thirty-five thousand residents at the time, was only a few miles from Israel's Gush Katif beach settlements, including the community of Kfar Darom, where Alisa Flatow was heading when she was killed. On many days, Salameh and other Palestinian youths would make their way to spots along the roads leading to Gush Katif to throw stones, especially near the Kissufim Junction.

Salameh's family said he was frequently arrested by Israeli authorities and even shot in the pelvis by an Israeli solider during a rock-throwing protest in 1988. When he spoke to Sergeant Ohayon or to other Israeli interrogators, Salameh was hardly shy about his exploits as a Palestinian street protestor or, later, in more violent operations supported by Hamas. But none of the transcripts indicate that Salameh had been shot or arrested by the Israelis before he was wounded and apprehended in Hebron.

By late 1992, the Intifada had reached a pinnacle—perhaps a break-ing point for Israelis. Protests had become noticeably more violent. After six Israeli security officers were killed in a series of confrontations in early December 1992, Prime Minister Yitzhak Rabin embarked on one of the most drastic security measures since the founding of Israel more than forty years before. Israeli authorities had already begun to arrest Pales-tinian protestors—and suspects—and place them in camps that were surrounded by barbed-wire fences and guard towers manned by Israeli soldiers. But beginning on December 16, Israeli authorities designated more than four hundred Hamas supporters in the West Bank and Gaza Strip as "inciters" who "endanger human lives by their activities."

The four hundred were not processed through Israel's courts or even formally charged with crimes. They were simply put on buses and driven north toward Lebanon. Israeli human rights activists were aghast, as were Palestinian leaders. After court challenges failed to stop the caravans, the buses crossed into Lebanon and ordered the four hundred Hamas mem-bers off, then headed back to Israel.

The Hamas deportees were told to stay put. Israeli border guards had orders to stop them from returning to the West Bank or to the Gaza Strip. The Lebanese government, meanwhile, refused to admit them. But Lebanon's Hezbollah party accepted them and brought them into a vari-ety of camps and villages that dotted the border between Lebanon and Israel.

What happened in those camps during the next two years would eventually affect the Israeli-Palestinian peace process in profound ways.

The Hezbollah hosts and the Hamas guests were Muslims, but from two distinct Islamic traditions. Most Hezbollah members were Shiites and followed many of the religious dictates of Islamic clerics in Iran;

most Hamas members were Sunni Muslims and were more closely afflli-ated with the theology embraced by Egypt's Muslim Brotherhood. Both opposed the existence of the State of Israel. But the two groups differed in modes of Islamic worship and in some aspects of Islamic theology, notably the Islamic definitions of martyrdom and suicide.

In Lebanon, Hamas Sunnis learned of a new form of warfare that had long been embraced by the Hezbollah Shiites—suicide attacks against so-called infidels. A decade earlier, Hezbollah had carried out the suicide truck bombing of the US Marine encampment in Beirut. Other suicide operations followed.

What is significant about those attacks is how the Hezbollah opera-tives who blew themselves up were honored for their suicides. They were not merely labeled valiant soldiers, willing to sacrifice themselves. They were called martyrs—*shaheeds*.

While the link between suicide and martyrdom had a centuries-long tradition within the Shiite branch of Islam, Sunni members of Hamas and Palestinian Islamic Jihad in the West Bank and the Gaza Strip had been reluctant to embrace the idea of suicide. Simply put, the Koran banned suicide.

When it came to suicide attacks, however, Hezbollah's Shiite clerics embraced a different Koranic theology. Hezbollah equated any sort of attack against infidels—even if the so-called infidels were unarmed—as the equivalent of martyrdom. While Islamic attackers might deliberately kill themselves as a way of killing infidels, as the Hezbollah driver of a bomb-laden truck had done in the attack on the Marines in Beirut, their deaths were seen as a form of martyrdom worthy of the highest honors in Islam.

There is no reliable account of whether Hamas members engaged in theological discussions about martyrdom and suicide with their Hezbol-lah hosts in Lebanon. However, one of Hamas's founders and theological leaders, Sheik Ahmed Yassin, embraced this new concept of martyrdom and played a major role in promoting a theology that reclassified Hamas suicide bombers as shaheeds, or martyrs who die for the sake of Allah. In Islamic tradition, suicide is not only forbidden but is considered one of the worst sins a Muslim can commit. By contrast, a shaheed was given an exalted status in Paradise. The theological shift, promoted by Yassin and others, was no small endeavor, as Israelis and others would soon discover.

In mid-December 1996—almost ten months after the Number 18 bus attack on Jaffa Road—an Israeli researcher gained permission to interview Sheik Yassin in his prison cell. What emerged in the interview by Dr. Anat Berko was a succinct and fearsome explanation of the new theology of martyrdom being embraced by Hamas. After beginning her interview by discussing the meaning of justice, self-defense of one's homeland, freedom of religion, the interpretation of peace treaties between Israel, Egypt, and Jordan, and the Islamic concept of Jihad, Berko, who was researching her doctoral thesis on suicide bombers, shifted gears.

"What makes Muslims want to commit suicide for the sake of a certain goal?" she asked Yassin.

"Here your understanding is wrong," Yassin replied. "The person who kills himself in (one of) many ways by shooting or taking drugs or to escape from life and its problems, because of personal distress, that is suicide, but the person who goes to fight an enemy, who fights him who took his land, his country or who took his property, fights him and is killed, such a person is considered a shaheed and not someone who committed suicide."

Berko asked about the death of a shaheed and what it means.

"It is not a question of 'dead' since the shaheed is not dead," Yassin answered. "He is alive with Allah. First and foremost, the faith of a Muslim, of an Arab, is that he believes that anyone who is with Allah is in better circumstances than if he were in this world."

Most Palestinians did not initially embrace this new theology. In March 1996, a month after the Number 18 bus bombing on Jaffa Road, a poll conducted by the Palestinian Center for Policy and Survey Research in Ramallah found that only 21.1 percent of Palestinians living in the West Bank or the Gaza Strip expressed support for suicide bombings. A year later, another poll found that 32.7 percent of Palestinians supported suicide attacks. By October 2003, 74.5 percent of Palestinians—three out of four—looked favorably on suicide attacks.

Sheik Yassin was not among the four hundred Hamas operatives transported to Lebanon. He was in jail in Israel during that deportation.

But from his prison cell, Yassin issued a series of proclamations to his Sunni followers in support of suicide martyrdom that had previously been embraced only by Shiites. In later research on this theological and tactical change in warfare, a number of academics concluded that Yassin, along with several other Islamic clerics—notably the Egyptian-born Sheik Yusuf al-Qaradawi—had formed the foundation for what would be a devastating terror campaign against Israel that would last more than a decade.

That campaign began on an April afternoon in 1993, at a dusty roadside cafe in the Jordan Valley, just north of the ancient city of Jericho. Hamas, in what some reports claim was an alliance with Islamic Jihad, staged its first suicide attack with a homemade bomb designed by one of its first converts to the new theology of suicide martyrdom—Yahya Ayyash.

A Hamas operative parked a truck next to a tourist bus and detonated the bomb. Although only the driver died, Ayyash learned from the attack how to build bigger, more powerful bombs. That first bombing was only the beginning.

Among the four hundred suspected Hamas loyalists rounded up by Israeli security forces and deported to Lebanon were two of Salameh's brothers—or so Salameh said. He told his Israeli interrogator in that first interview at the hospital that both brothers had been arrested before and were living in a camp run by Hezbollah.

In early 1993, Salameh said he left the Gaza Strip on a journey to visit his brothers. According to this account, Salameh said he embarked on almost two years of traveling, though this was not just a personal journey to find his brothers. Salameh visited several Hamas offices.

What is missing from Salameh's story is whether he had been ordered by the Hamas leadership in the Gaza Strip to visit his brothers or other Palestinians he saw during his travels across the Middle East in 1993 and 1994. It seems unlikely that Salameh simply floated in and out of various Hamas offices without a plan or orders.

But Salameh never explained the decision-making behind his travels or made it clear that he was asked. Nor did he say who financed his travels. He worked several jobs during that two-year period of traveling, but not the kind of work that would allow him to cover airfare, meals, and lodging. It's likely that Salameh's journey was financed by Hamas.

"In early 1993, I left Gaza and crossed Allenby Bridge to Jordan," he told Sergeant Ohayon. "I stayed for one week and then left for Sudan."

In Sudan, Salameh said he contacted the head of the Hamas office and was hired as "the night guard." After eight months, he traveled to Syria. "In Damascus, I went to the Hamas office," he said. The director of the Hamas office in Damascus then drove him to Marj al-Zohour, a Lebanese town near the Israeli border where many of the four hundred Hamas deportees were living. Salameh said he stayed there a month, then returned to Damascus and moved in with a relative whom he did not name. He did not say if he actually saw his brothers.

What is noteworthy about Salameh's life in Damascus after he returned from Lebanon is that he did not get a job as he had done in Sudan. "I did not work but I underwent military training," he told Sergeant Ohayon.

Salameh said his instructors were from the Democratic Front for the Liberation of Palestine, a group that dabbled in Leninist-Marxist ideology while also focusing on strategies to attack Israelis. "They trained me in assembling and disassembling weapons and in preparing both small and large demolition charges," he said. "I was in training every day in Syria"—which was about twelve months, according to the transcript of his interrogation by Sergeant Ohayon.

Salameh offered few other details about his training. And there is no indication that Sergeant Ohayon pressed him for those details. For example, Salameh did not reveal names of his instructors and only said "the trainers were Palestinians." He also did not describe the types of weapons he trained with or what sorts of explosives he was using. Finally, he said nothing about whether he spoke to anyone in Sudan, Syria, or Lebanon about the new strategy of suicide bombing that Hamas has embraced.

As it turned out, he was not telling the whole truth.

Salameh said he returned to the Gaza Strip in December 1994. But as he crossed the border into Gaza from Egypt, he was arrested by Yasser Arafat's security forces. He spent the next six months in jail.

As with his training in Syria, the details of Salameh's arrest and imprisonment are scant. He does not describe what crime he was charged with. Nor does he say where he was imprisoned. No independent account or set of records are available to corroborate Salameh's story of his arrest. The transcript of Salameh's interrogation indicates, however, that he may have been carrying a rifle or a pistol when he tried to cross into the Gaza Strip. Again he does not describe what sort of firearm he carried, only that he wanted to keep it after he left prison. "After my release," he told Sergeant Ohayon, "I applied to the Palestinian Authority, along with all the other Hamas activists, for a license for my weapon."

By the mid-1990s, the Gaza Strip had become a furnace of Palestinian dissent and nationalism, and Salameh saw his future as a Hamas operative. His return to the Gaza Strip also coincided with the return of one of Hamas's most notorious leaders, Yahya Ayyash.

Unlike Salameh, who tried to enter the Gaza Strip from Egypt and was reportedly apprehended, Ayyash successfully sneaked across the Gaza border from the West Bank and avoided Israeli Shin Bet agents. Ayyash's elusiveness and bomb-making skills were becoming legendary. And while Ayyash had been born on the West Bank, Shin Bet intelligence analysts had long assumed that he would try to make his way to Gaza. Ayyash's wife and son were living on the Gaza Strip, along with other members of his family. By the spring of 1995, as Hassan Salameh was finishing his prison sentence in a Palestinian jail, Shin Bet agents had already begun to piece together Ayyash's whereabouts in the Gaza Strip.

It's not clear from that first interview at Hadassah Ein Kerem Medical Center whether Salameh met with Ayyash. Salameh does not describe a meeting. But Ayyash's assassination on January 5, 1996, was a turning point for Salameh in the story he told to Sergeant Ohayon. Ayyash had been a key figure in the al-Qassam brigade, the military wing of Hamas. After Ayyash died, he was replaced by bomb-making protégé Mohammed Deif, who grew up in Khan Yunis, the same Gaza Strip community as Salameh's.

Deif was born in 1960 and was eleven years older than Salameh. In his interview with Sergeant Ohayon, Salameh did not say whether he knew Deif during his boyhood in Khan Yunis. But after Salameh's release from prison in June 1995, he linked up with Deif. The two, after all, seemed to be on the same path within Hamas's military wing—both as bomb-makers, with Deif learning his trade directly from Ayyash.

After Ayyash's death, Salameh said Deif asked for his help. "I was contacted by Mohammed Deif who told me that because Yahya Ayyash was killed, we would commit terrorist attacks," Salameh said.

Until this point in the interview, Salameh had offered only sketchy details about his exploits from 1992 to 1996. That tone changed, however, with the mention of Mohammed Deif and the plan to stage terrorist attacks to avenge Ayyash's death.

For several hours, Salameh outlined the plot that led to the suicide bombings on February 25, 1996, of the Number 18 bus on Jaffa Road, then at the bus stop in Ashkelon, and a week later the suicide bombing aboard another Number 18 bus on Jaffa Road. He described how Deif ordered a "squad" of Hamas operatives to infiltrate Israel from the Gaza Strip and how Salameh followed "through the same break in the fence." He mentioned the rendezvous with the Hamas squad in an orange grove near the port city of Ashdod and the explosives he carried—"three suitcases with thirteen kilograms of TNT explosives in each," a total of almost ninety pounds. He also shed light on some of the financing of the bomb plot, explaining that Deif initially gave him "1,520 Jordanian dinars," or approximately $2,200.

Salameh described how he linked up with Hamas members in the Jerusalem area, how he tried to assume the identity of a college student at Birzeit University in the Palestinian city of Ramallah, and how he recruited "three youths for committing suicide attacks."

He talked of traveling from Jerusalem to Ramallah, to Hebron, and back to Jerusalem. He mentioned that he spent at least one night in a college dormitory—and how he linked up with a Hamas contact on campus by using a password, "fanhales." He described how he scouted the locations for the bombings "where a lot of Jews would die," how he eventually befriended Mohammad Abu Wardeh, who helped Hassan Salameh to recruit his cousin, Majdi, and another teenager from the al-Fawwar refugee camp as the first suicide bombers. He even outlined how he was able to obtain more money from Hamas. Each Friday, a messenger from

Mohammed Deif would make his way to the prayer services at the al-Aqsa mosque atop the Temple Mount in Jerusalem. The messenger would then pass money and other written messages to Hamas couriers who would then contact Salameh at one of his hideouts. "I do not know the name of that messenger," Salameh told Sergeant Ohayon. "Through this messenger, Mohammed Deif forwarded letters and funds to me."

It also seems that Salameh was able to communicate back to Deif by passing messages to the Hamas courier who came to the al-Aqsa mosque. Salameh told Sergeant Ohayon that he even took the risk of notifying Deif of the impending suicide bombings—which may offer a hint of how Arafat learned that an attack was planned and why he urged Terje Roed-Larsen to avoid Jerusalem on Sunday, February 25, 1996. Whether Salameh communicated in a code is not clear. "Prior to that first attack I notified Mohammed Deif in a letter about the attacks that were scheduled for Sunday," he admitted.

In the days leading up to that fateful Sunday, Salameh described how he met with the bombers at a mosque in Ramallah and again at a safe house in the East Jerusalem neighborhood of Abu Dis. He explained how he built the bombs—in particular, how he "wrapped the explosives with large and small nails," and how Majdi Abu Wardeh was "dressed in new civilian clothes" to blend in with the students and commuters who joined Matthew Eisenfeld and Sara Duker on the Number 18 bus.

Finally, Salameh mentioned how he heard that the bombs he had assembled had been detonated. He had gone to Ramallah. "On Sunday morning," he told Sergeant Ohayon, "I heard on the radio about the attacks that had taken place." He did not say if he felt exhilarated or sad or even whether he knew of the high death toll.

After radio report of the attacks, he reached out for Mohammad Abu Wardeh and arranged another meeting at a mosque in Ramallah. "I told him that I wanted one more guy for committing an additional attack," he said of a bombing that would take place the following Sunday aboard another Number 18 bus on Jaffa Road. He also found a new hiding spot for his stash of explosives—in the home of Rizzek Rajoub.

As with his meetings with the other suicide bombers, he did not describe how long he counseled the young men, whether they asked any questions about their fate or whether they demonstrated any reluctance. Salameh offered only a matter-of-fact synopsis of the conversation that, in retrospect, seemed more akin to a mundane business transaction than a mission that would result in the death of the bomber and many others. "We met near the mosque," Salameh said. "I proposed to him to commit a suicide bombing attack, and he agreed."

After the third bombing on March 3, 1996, Salameh shifted strategy. "There was an order from the Hamas headquarters to stop committing suicide terrorist attacks and begin kidnapping soldiers," he told his interrogator.

At the same time, Salameh was also aware that he and other Hamas operatives who carried out the bombings were the subject of one of the largest manhunts in Israeli history. He told Sergeant Ohayon how he narrowly escaped arrest on several occasions during the three months he was on the run in the West Bank. He also described the series of homes where he hid—including supplying the names of Palestinians who offered him refuge and the false name he adopted. "Throughout that whole time I had a nickname," Salameh said. "I was not called 'Hassan' but only 'Abu Hasar.'"

Salameh added, however: "Everyone knew that I was Hassan Salameh."

The kidnapping of a soldier never took place. Salameh described at least one attempt—in Jerusalem—that was "unsuccessful." But he offered no details—nor is it clear if Sergeant Ohayon asked for any. When he drove to Hebron with Rizzek Rajoub on that Friday evening in May and was stopped at a checkpoint, Salameh said he was attempting to pull together another plan to capture an Israeli soldier and was on his way to a meeting at a mosque in Hebron to talk to other Hamas operatives.

"A soldier stopped us and fired at me," he said.

Salameh's story at this point seemed credible. He listed places he visited, names of his hosts, jobs he held, and a schedule of his travels. In that first interview at the hospital, Salameh stopped twice to take naps, once for a nurse to tend to his wounds, and one more time for a physiotherapist to check on his overall condition. What is notable about that interview, however, is the length. The session with Sergeant Ohayon concluded with Salameh confirming the translation of his statement and signing his name in Arabic. It was 5:50 in the evening, more than seven hours after Sergeant Ohayon walked into his hospital room and announced to him, "You do not have to say a word unless you wish to."

⁓

Six weeks later, Salameh talked again.

His second interview, on July 2, 1996, began with two questions that had not been asked in the initial session at Hadassah Hospital.

"Is the testimony you gave from the hospital true? And were you conscious of what you said?" the Israeli interrogator asked.

"Yes, what I said was true," Salameh answered, then quickly added: "Maybe I forgot a few things. I was pretty frightened when I testified."

What Salameh "forgot" to mention in that first interrogation on May 21 at Hadassah Ein Kerem Medical Center was hardly inconsequential. Besides traveling to Jordan, Lebanon, Syria, and Sudan, he made one more stop before returning to the Gaza Strip to formulate plans for his bombing campaign: He went to Iran.

# CHAPTER 8

WHEN A MURDER OCCURS, POLICE OFTEN FORGE LONG AND DEEPLY INTI-
mate relationships with families of victims. Many experienced investigators routinely reach out to relatives for help in sorting through leads to
track down a suspected murderer. Sometimes hard-driving detectives and
beat cops view these connections with victims' families as an opportunity
to offer comfort. Occasionally, they even look to families for support and
inspiration for themselves as they encounter the inevitable pitfalls and frustrating dead ends that are part of almost every complicated investigation.

Whatever the case, the relationship between cops and victims' families is understandable and inevitable, say psychologists. Relatives of murder victims suddenly find themselves in painfully vulnerable positions,
with few confidants other than police officers with whom they can share
their sorrow, anger, and pain.

That relationship takes on more profound dimension when police
finally catch a killer. After an arrest, cops often notify the victim's family
before calling a press conference. For many officers, it is a matter of pride
to tell families that a killer has been caught. It's also an opportunity for
cops, steeped in the routine of dealing with crooks and collecting evidence,
to help a family bring closure and context to its grief. Many relatives of
victims—especially the parents of murdered children—say they feel relief
knowing that a killer has finally been captured and is facing justice.

None of this happened after the deaths of Matt Eisenfeld and Sara
Duker or, for that matter, when Alisa Flatow was killed. In each case, a
variety of Palestinian operatives were captured by Israeli and Palestinian
security forces.

The suspects included Hassan Salameh. But the Duker and Eisenfeld
families heard nothing about him during that first year.

The Flatow family found itself in a similar predicament. There had
been a telephone call to Stephen Flatow in the fall of 1995 from the New

York–based Israeli Consul General Colette Avital about the assassination of a Palestinian leader in Malta who was linked to Alisa's murder. But what sort of link was it? As Flatow hung up the phone after Avital's call, he considered this new information vague and imprecise. The killing seemed like the work of Israel's Mossad spy service, but the Israelis were not admitting involvement. Meanwhile, the dead man, Fathi Shaqaqi, was a well-known leader of Palestinian Islamic Jihad, which had taken responsibility for the bombing that killed Alisa. But had Shaqaqi actually planned the bombing or recruited the bombers, or built the bomb? What about the actual bomber and the others who participated in the plot?

Flatow had no idea. In the ensuing months, he heard little more. He had no inkling, for example, that Israeli police had already arrested several members of Palestinian Islamic Jihad in the bombing. The same was true with information not shared with the Duker and Eisenfeld families. In addition to Salameh, other Hamas operatives had been apprehended, including Mohammad Abu Wardeh, who encouraged his cousin Majdi to be the suicide bomber. But that news never reached the Dukers or Eisenfelds.

Salameh's arrest in Israel was covered by Israeli's media. But the American press barely mentioned it and instead focused most of its attention on Israel's new prime minister, Benjamin Netanyahu, who had defeated Shimon Peres in an election in late May by a margin of 1 percent—about thirty thousand votes.

Two more years would pass before Arline Duker and Len and Vicki Eisenfeld would discover the true story behind Hassan Salameh.

—⁓—

Six months after Hassan Salameh was captured, Len and Vicki Eisenfeld walked into the headquarters of the Federal Bureau of Investigation in Washington, DC. It was Tuesday, December 3, 1996. A month earlier, President Clinton had defeated his Republican challenger, Kansas Senator Robert Dole, and won a second term. The comfortable margin of victory—almost ten points over Dole—was not just an electoral triumph for Clinton. It was a none-too-subtle confirmation that he was able to fight off criticism, largely from conservatives, that he was not tough enough to crack down on the growing problem of international and domestic terrorism.

In the months since they had watched Clinton sign the Antiterrorism and Effective Death Penalty Act into law, the Eisenfelds and Arline Duker began to ponder how they might pursue a lawsuit. But as Vicki Eisenfeld first voiced in the days after she buried her son, how could either family file a lawsuit against Hamas? As both families quickly learned, Hamas was a shadowy organization, with few recognizable assets that could be claimed in a lawsuit. What about Iran, though?

Stephen Flatow was moving ahead with his own lawsuit, although he had still not filed court papers. While Flatow and his lawyer, Steven Perles, had managed to lobby Congress to strengthen the AEDPA, they still faced the problem of who could actually be targeted in a lawsuit.

It was hardly a small concern. Lawsuits cost money. Perles had already signaled that a major antiterrorism lawsuit, in a federal court and under the untested provisions of the AEDPA, might cost as much as $100,000 just to collect evidence from the Middle East and other sources and to hire expert witnesses. But without a clear target that could provide compensation to reimburse the families and the lawyers for their expenses, why move forward?

Not surprisingly, the Eisenfelds and Dukers each had different worries about what a lawsuit meant, though they shared a common bond in the deaths of Matt and Sara and the hopes both families nurtured for them. For the Dukers and Eisenfelds, that bond would become especially tight. The hoped-for wedding of Sara and Matt that would have formally joined both families would never take place, but in a tragic way both families were joined nonetheless.

After burying Matt and Sara, Len had gathered Vicki and Amy along with Arline and her two remaining daughters and declared that he hoped the two families would remain united.

"We used to be a family of four," Len said. "Now we are a family of six."

In contemplating a lawsuit, however, one of Arline's primary concerns was money. As a single mother, she still had two daughters to put through college. She had some savings. But a lawsuit to pursue an international terrorist organization could drain them. In the end, what would she win? A judgment that merely blamed Hamas for the bombing that killed Sara and Matt offered little satisfaction. Hamas had already admitted that its operatives were involved in the bomb plot.

Vicki and Len shared similar concerns. Would a lawsuit achieve anything? But as Arline, Vicki, and Len discussed their next steps, they had no idea that they were missing crucial pieces of information about Iran and its connection to the Jaffa Road bombing.

Stephen Flatow faced a similar predicament. Largely with the help of Perles, Flatow learned that American intelligence officials had long felt that Iran played a behind-the-scenes role in the growth of Palestinian terrorist groups such as Hamas and Palestinian Islamic Jihad. But in strategizing for his lawsuit, Flatow and Perles wrestled with a difficult question: If Flatow filed suit against Iran, what sort of proof could he offer that Iran was actually involved?

That concern was on the mind of Len and Vicki Eisenfeld when they conferred with FBI officials on that Tuesday in December 1996. Was Iran actually involved in the Jaffa Road attack? With its designation by the US State Department as a state sponsor of terrorism, Iran could be sued under the provisions of the AEDPA. But lawsuits require proof. As they left the FBI offices and headed for another meeting at the Department of State, the Eisenfelds still had no answers.

Less than a week after Matt and Sara had been killed, the FBI announced it was entering the case. But the FBI had not really mounted much of an investigation at that point, and instead trusted Israeli authorities to collect evidence and interrogate suspects. If FBI officials learned anything from their Israeli counterparts, they did not share it that day with the Eisenfelds.

After meeting with the FBI, Vicki sensed that the bureau wanted to mount an investigation. Yet Vicki also left with the "sense that everyone is trying to cover their asses" and that no substantial analysis of evidence had taken place.

Len had already spoken to a lawyer at the Justice Department. Like Vicki, he felt his family was in a state of legal limbo. The murder of an American citizen in another country was considered a crime; US authorities could, if necessary, extradite a suspected murderer for a trial on American soil. But Len had the impression that the Justice Department had not even been given a list of suspects by Israeli authorities—nor was it rushing to obtain such a list. For now, the FBI and Justice Department officials said they were satisfied that the Israelis were taking the lead in catching the Hamas operatives who bombed the Number 18 bus. "They were willing to let the Israelis do their thing," Len said of American investigators. "They were not planning to do anything. They were just collecting information and would keep us informed."

After leaving the FBI, Len and Vicki traveled across town to meet with Kenneth R. McKune, the acting coordinator for counterterrorism at the US Department of State. Like their discussion with the FBI, the Eisenfelds' meeting with McKune seemed uneventful. Thinking about it later, Len rated the conversation with McKune as "somewhere between a five and a six on a scale of ten." Len found McKune to be guarded and not all that forthcoming, especially with information about Hamas and how its operatives had managed to pull together such a sophisticated bombing.

Len and Vicki both felt uneasy. Why was their government not jumping to their side to help?

As he left that day Len asked McKune if he could stay in touch. A few days later, Len telephoned McKune to thank him for the meeting. And on December 22, 1996, McKune followed up with a letter.

As he read McKune's words, Len was stunned—and elated. The guardedness that Len felt from his meeting with McKune three weeks earlier was gone. "On a scale of one to ten," Len said, "this letter was an eight."

"Per your request," McKune wrote, "I am including in this letter some thoughts on responsibility for the bombing which killed your son and Sara Duker in Jerusalem on February 25, 1996."

McKune enumerated some facts that Len and Vicki already knew: That a suicide bomber blew up the Number 18 commuter bus on Jaffa Road; that Hamas claimed responsibility; that three US citizens had died. (Forty-nine days after the bombing, Ira Weinstein, a fifty-three-year-old butcher who had moved to Israel with his family a decade earlier and held dual American and Israeli citizenships, died from severe burns.)

McKune wrote that the "Department of State believes that the Izz al-Din al-Qassam Brigades, the military arm of Hamas, carried out this bombing." Then, he added one more morsel of insight: "We also believe that Iran provides training and financial assistance to Hamas."

McKune cited a State Department report that had been released only weeks after Matt and Sara were killed. "Tehran currently provides Hamas with weapons and explosives training and occasional financial assistance," the report said. "Tehran also provides the groups with monetary assistance, which we estimate averages $2–3 million per year."

Len and Vicki studied the letter carefully. For months they had been battling two powerful emotions—their grief and their desire to find out who killed Sara and Matt. It had been difficult to focus. Or, as Len later said, "We were just so fresh in our grief."

Now, in December 1996, Len and Vicki had what they believed to be their first solid proof that Iran might have been involved in the bombing. They were not shocked; Stephen Flatow had already heard similar statements from State Department officials. Vicki said years later that "it was like the pieces of a puzzle were falling into place little by little. We thought it was just Hamas. We weren't thinking of it in the broader sense."

Still, it was one thing to be told that Iran was linked to the bombings and another thing to obtain evidence of such a link. McKune's letter, with its reference to the State Department's report about Iran's support of terrorist groups, was significant. But even the report, backed up by a letter written by a key figure in America's counterterrorism efforts, was lacking the solid confirmation that would be indisputable in a court case. Steven Perles, who was already advising the Dukers and Eisenfelds about a possible lawsuit, felt he needed to establish a more definitive connection between Iran and Palestinian terrorism. But by the end of 1996, it was not easy finding a government official in Washington, DC, who had a deeper knowledge of Iran's terrorist strategies and who would share that insight in a courtroom. The obvious choices were the US intelligence agencies and their legions of analysts. But in general, those officials were off-limits to private lawyers looking to support a lawsuit against a foreign government.

Perles decided to look elsewhere.

In Israel, Hassan Salameh had changed his story dramatically. In his second interview with Israeli interrogators on July 2, 1996, Salameh conceded that he journeyed to Iran to learn how to build the bomb that killed Sara and Matt and the others aboard the Number 18 bus. In his first interrogation seven weeks earlier at Hadassah Ein Kerem Medical Center, Salameh had not even hinted about his Iranian training. Why did he change his story?

Salameh dropped this revelation into the tale he told to Israeli interrogators in his second interview as subtly as he might ask for a glass of water. His Iranian trip was well funded, well organized, and included special training in tactics, weapons, and explosives at a special camp that had been built by Iranian officials. It was also not a brief visit. "We stayed three months in Iran," Salameh told interrogators.

Israel officials seemed instantly to understand the importance of what Salameh was saying. They viewed the disclosure of his Iranian trip not just as a breakthrough in a police investigation, but as information that had military and strategic value to Israeli's intelligence services and to Israel's diplomatic and defense planning. And because of what they perceived to be the larger value of Salameh's disclosures, Israeli officials labeled Salameh's confessions top-secret and classified. Israel did not even notify US authorities at the time what it had learned from Salameh.

Why Salameh did not mention Iran in his first interrogation at Hadassah Ein Kerem Medical Center remains a mystery. Experienced police detectives say that it often takes several conversations to convince a suspected killer to reveal all aspects of a murder. But it's difficult to decipher why Salameh did not disclose anything about his Iranian trip in that initial interview and why he opted to discuss it so openly in the second.

Did he have a change of heart? Did he merely want to brag—as Shin Bet's Yisrael Hasson predicted he would? Was Salameh really telling the truth when he said he was "pretty frightened" during that initial interrogation and that "maybe I forgot a few things"? Or had he undergone what Israeli authorities describe as "intensive" questioning that can include punching, slapping, sleep deprivation and isolation? Such techniques, which were occasionally used by Israeli investigators investigating terrorist incidents, had been heavily criticized in Israel and elsewhere by human rights advocates, while Israeli officials defended their use as necessary to obtain information to prevent other attacks.

Whatever the case, Salameh has never explained his change—not even when interviewed years later by this author. Nor have his Israeli interrogators offered any insight.

The transcript of Salameh's second interview on July 2, 1996 offers no clues about why he suddenly decided to talk about his Iranian training, other than an admission that he was afraid during that initial interrogation and omitted several key details. But the differences between the first and second interviews are striking.

In that first interrogation at the hospital, Salameh said he left the Gaza Strip in early 1993 and embarked on a journey of almost two years that took him to Jordan, Sudan, Syria, and Lebanon, including attempts to visit his brothers in Lebanon and training for an unspecified period with weapons and explosives in Syria by the Democratic Front for the Liberation of Palestine.

In his second interview, Salameh said his military training did not end in Syria. Before returning to the Gaza Strip in late 1994, he said he took a flight to Iran with a cadre of other Hamas activists where he embarked on intensive training.

In that second interrogation, Salameh mentioned Iran with the same matter-of-fact speaking style that was apparent in his first interview at Hadassah Ein Kerem Medical Center when he described how he recruited Majdi Abu Wardeh as the suicide bomber who boarded the Number 18 bus with Matt and Sara. But in addition to referring to his three-month sojourn to Iran, Salameh disclosed another secret about himself: The bombing of the Number 18 bus on Jaffa Road was not his first murder.

"Now let me tell you what happened in 1992," he began.

Salameh said that he was recruited into Hamas in 1992 by Jamil Wadi, a leader of the group's al-Qassam military wing who was killed the following year in a gun battle with Israeli soldiers. Wadi had a specific job for Salameh—to recruit other young Palestinian men. Salameh said he found five others, all from Khan Yunis. Together, they formed a cell. "I was the head of the cell," Salameh said.

Salameh's cell had nothing to do with attacking the Israeli military or promoting Hamas's political strategies. Nor did Salameh and his compatriots seem to engage in the myriad social service projects that made Hamas so popular among poor Palestinians, especially those living in the crowded refugee camps in the Gaza Strip.

Salameh was an enforcer. The primary focus of his cell, he said, was to hunt down and punish Palestinians who were believed to collaborate with the Israelis in the Gaza Strip.

Labeling someone as a collaborator did not involve a court or other independent legal authority. Often, the accusation was based on rumors and sometimes fueled by personal grudges and jealousies.

With their large network of contacts on the West Bank and in the Gaza Strip, Israel's Shin Bet intelligence agents often looked to ordinary Palestinians for information about upcoming Hamas activities, including protests, possible attacks and the whereabouts of reputed terrorist leaders and bomb-makers. In some cases, ordinary Palestinians were suspected of being collaborators if they merely sold property to Israelis or formed the most basic of business deals or partnerships with Jews.

One of Salameh's first targets was a Khan Yunis resident named Rabi al-Saadi. Salameh said that "in the course of our mission," his cell members "interrogated" al-Saadi. Salameh does not describe why al-Saadi was singled out as a collaborator. But the man was punished nevertheless. "We beat him with pipes and cut him with knives," Salameh said. "I had a knife and cut him. They beat him with chains and pipes. Eventually, we killed him."

Salameh's cell members "beat other suspects but none of them died," he claimed. At least two of the suspected collaborators were women—or as Salameh described them, "a girl from the Abu Moussa family" and "a girl from the Abu Sharat family."

"We visited them and threatened them with knives and axes," he said.

In 1993, Israeli police arrested one of Salameh's cell members. "I knew he would identify me," Salameh said.

Fearing he might be arrested by the Israelis, Salameh said he left Khan Yunis and "escaped to Jordan." By his own account, Salameh simply crossed the Jordan River from the Israeli-controlled West Bank into Jordan via the the Allenby Bridge.

In his second interrogation, Salameh essentially confirmed what he said during the first session when he described the early portion of his journeys. He stayed a week in Jordan with relatives, then traveled to Sudan where he worked for three months as a guard at the Hamas office. From there, he journeyed to Syria for weapons training with the Democratic Front for the Liberation of Palestine.

Salameh's story offers not only a look into his life as a Hamas operative but was considered by Israeli authorities at the time to be one of the most extensive descriptions of how Hamas was able to connect with other militant groups throughout the Middle East.

While in Sudan, he met a group of eighteen Hamas "fugitives" who after escaping from the Gaza Strip traveled through Egypt, where they were arrested and imprisoned. After their release, the eighteen operatives made their way to Sudan. According to the transcript, Salameh provided his Israeli interrogator with the names of each of the eighteen Hamas operatives.

"They asked to be trained in military procedures by Hamas," Salameh said. "They were sent by Hamas to Iran for training."

Whether Salameh traveled to Iran with this group or with another is unclear. But shortly after arriving in Sudan, Salameh left for Iran. "First we took a Sudanese plane to Syria," he said. "We met Iranians there who got us an Iranian flight to Tehran."

In Iran, he said he met Osama Hamdan, whom he described as the "head of Hamas in Iran." Hamadan would go on to become a key figure in Hamas, eventually ending up in Lebanon where he was regarded as the group's representative there. Whether Israeli authorities realized it or not at the time, Salameh's revelation that he met with such a high-ranking Hamas official in Iran—and that eighteen other Hamas operatives went to Iran, too—offers some measure of credence to the overall concern among Israeli and American intelligence officials of a strong connection between Palestinian militants and Iran.

In Tehran, Salameh said Iranians officials did not stamp his passport—a common technique to conceal a travel itinerary. From the airport, Salameh said he was taken to a military base where his training began in earnest.

He had ten instructors—"all Iranians," he said. Salameh learned how to assemble explosives, how to plant mines in the dirt, how to organize an ambush. His instructors taught him how to throw a grenade and operate a rocket-propelled grenade launcher. They took him regularly to a shooting range where he fired a wide variety of weapons including "Iranian rifles, Uzis, Russian Garinos, and large machine guns." They also taught him how to gather intelligence.

But what might be his most daunting morsel of information came at the end of his description of his Iranian sojourn. As something of a postscript, he added: "We learned how to take apart mines." Two years later, Salameh would use the explosives from a land mine that had been planted on the Egyptian-Israeli border to assemble the bomb that destroyed the Number 18 bus on Jaffa Road.

Salameh said he took a circuitous route back to the Gaza Strip, stopping in Malta, then Libya and then driving across Egypt. He did not pass through an official border checkpoint to return to the Gaza Strip. Carrying an AK-47 rifle, he set out on foot through the desert between Egypt and the Gaza Strip, looking for a secluded spot to cross into Gaza unnoticed. But he said Palestinian Authority police spotted Salameh and arrested him.

Despite his connections to Hamas or perhaps because of them, Salameh was sent to a Palestinian prison. It's not clear what crime he was charged with, though illegal border entry and weapons possession are two possibilities. When he was set free sometime in the spring of 1995—probably in the weeks after Alisa Flatow's killing—Salameh quickly reconnected with Hamas. As he described in his first interview, Salameh's link in Hamas was Mohammed Deif.

Unlike in that first interrogation at the hospital, Salameh was much more talkative in his second session in offering background on Deif. Salameh acknowledged that he had known Deif "from before" and that Deif "slept at my house." From the transcript, it appears that Salameh and Deif formed a loose-knit confederation of Hamas operatives in 1995. It's not clear at this point in the interrogations whether this group was in direct contact with Yahya Ayyash, who had also sneaked into the Gaza Strip around this period from the West Bank to visit his family. But Salameh left no doubt that his group was heavily influenced by Ayyash's call to organize more terrorist attacks.

In one portion of his second interrogation, Salameh indicated that a "Muhammed Ayesh" came to live with him for an undisclosed amount of time, along with another Hamas operative, Adnan al-Ghoul, who had been linked to Ayyash and to the April 1995 bombing that killed Alisa Flatow. But the different and somewhat confusing spellings of names in the transcript of the interrogation do not offer conclusive proof.

Ayyash had been hiding in a variety of homes in the Gaza Strip in the months after Salameh was released from prison. So it is possible Ayyash could have sought refuge with Salameh, especially in light of the fact that Ayyash's deputy commander, Mohammed Deif, was already hiding with Salameh.

Another factor is the desire by Deif and Salameh and others to learn more about bomb-making. Salameh, of course, had already received three months of explosives training in Iran. And with Ayyash now inside the Gaza Strip and trying to organize other bomb attacks against Israeli targets, it would not be unusual for all of these operatives to find a way to contact each other. But in that second interrogation, Salameh did not say whether he actually met Ayyash. The transcript does not indicate whether he learned anything from Ayyash, even indirectly. There is also no indication that Israeli interrogators asked him about it.

What seems apparent from the transcript is that Ayyash's assassination by Israeli counterterror agents greatly affected Salameh and his desire to organize attacks against Israelis. Just after Ayyash's death during the first week of January 1996, Salameh confirmed (again) what he disclosed to his interrogators in his first interview—that Mohammed Deif ordered him to mount a "major attack in revenge."

One piece of Salameh's story still remained missing in that second interrogation, however. After leaving the Palestinian jail in the spring of 1995, what did he do in the Gaza Strip for the next six or seven months before he left for Jerusalem and the bombing of the Number 18 bus on Jaffa Road?

Salameh said little about that period in his second interview—or in a third session in August 1996. What Salameh was holding back was a secret connection he had forged with Yahya Ayyash.

A day after Len and Vicki Eisenfeld met in Washington, DC, with FBI officials and with the State Department's counterterrorism chief, Kenneth McKune, Hassan Salameh spoke again with Israeli interrogators. It was December 4, 1996, Salameh's fourth interrogation session by police in Israel. Len and Vicki had no idea that Salameh was talking to his captors six thousand miles away as they tried to convince US officials to tell them more about the killers of Sara and Matt. They had still not been informed that Salameh had been arrested.

In that fourth interrogation on December 4, Sergeant David Cohen of the Israeli police repeated the same instructions to Salameh as he had heard from other interrogators. "You are not required to tell me anything unless it is your wish to do so," Cohen said. "However everything you say will be written down and used as testimony."

Salameh said he understood the statement and, after signing it, he began to talk about his life after he left the Palestinian jail in the spring of 1995.

Not long after his release from prison, Salameh said seven men visited him. Salameh said he already knew six of the men. All were from his hometown of Khan Yunis in the Gaza Strip. They included Mohammed Deif and Adnan al-Ghoul who had played a role two months earlier in the bombing of Alisa Flatow's bus. The seventh man was Yahya Ayyash.

Even though Samameh had mentioned Ayyash's name in previous interrogations, he had never disclosed that he actually met him. Now, in the fourth session, Salameh again changed his story—adding Ayyash's name to the Hamas operatives he became linked to.

Ayyash's arrival in the Gaza Strip was viewed by Israeli intelligence officials as a factor in helping to unify disparate elements of Hamas and Islamic Jihad. While the two Palestinian paramilitary groups had the same goal of attacking Israel, each considered the other a rival in the quest for ultimate power within Palestinian society, especially in the Gaza Strip where increasing numbers of operatives distrusted Yasser Arafat's Fatah Party. Ayyash had also begun to teach operatives such as Mohammed Deif and Adnan al-Ghoul how to assemble explosives, especially those used by suicide bombers.

With his Iranian training in weapons and explosives, Salameh was likely viewed as a new and valuable asset in the group of operatives that

Deif and Ayyash were organizing. Salameh told Sergeant Cohen that he was "repeatedly in contact" with Deif while he was serving his prison sentence. After his release, Deif approached Salameh with a question. Would Salameh "be interested in planning an attack" near Khan Yunis or in other coastal areas along the Gaza Strip that were still controlled by the Israelis?

Salameh agreed. The group soon selected a target—the Gush Katif "block" of Israeli settlements along the Gaza coast that included the community of Kfar Darom and the road where Alisa Flatow had been killed.

For this mission, Deif obtained the explosives from antitank mines. Salameh would extract the explosive materials from the mines and build a bomb. Salameh was also assigned the task of recruiting a suicide bomber.

The operation would turn out to be a rehearsal of sorts for the bombing of the Number 18 bus on Jaffa Road.

One of Deif's associates, a man named "Bara," obtained seven antitank mines. Using his Iranian training, Salameh dismantled the mines, extracted the explosive materials, and reassembled them into the kind of deadly bomb that could be carried by a suicide attacker.

Meanwhile, Salameh said he recruited several militants to spy on the comings and goings of Israeli soldiers to the Gush Katif settlement block. One militant, a fisherman named Omar, turned out to be especially helpful. Omar knew the area well and after scouting several potential targets told Salameh that a bus filled with soldiers usually drove into Gush Katif each day around one o'clock in the afternoon.

Salameh decided to attack the bus.

"Deif told us that he prefers to do the attack as a suicide bombing," Salameh said.

Deif showed Salameh where to hide the extra explosives that would not be used in the attack. Salameh then assembled the bomb.

"I took two mines to my house," Salameh said. He gave the five extra mines to Omar for use in later attacks. "I connected the two mines, back to back, glued them together," Salameh continued.

He attached two detonators and hooked up two, nine-volt batteries to the detonators. To finish the job and to make sure a suicide bomber could easily set off the explosion, Salameh attached another device. "Two switches to push, to cause an explosion," he said.

Then he put the bomb in a green suitcase.

"Where did you learn to make such explosives?" Sergeant Cohen asked.

"I learned in Iran," Salameh said.

Sergeant Cohen asked Salameh to draw a diagram of his bomb.

Salameh actually drew two diagrams on the handwritten report of his interrogation that he signed for the Israeli police. The first diagram looks like a doughnut with three arrows pointing outward from the center hole—wires from the detonator that he had inserted in a hole in the circular mine. The second diagram is much more detailed and shows how the wires connect to the trigger button. The diagram was virtually identical to the diagram he would later draw to describe how he assembled the bomb for the Number 18 bus.

After finishing the sketch, Salameh told Sergeant Cohen how he found a suicide bomber. Actually, Deif had already been working to find one, too. Deif received a note from a contact in Khan Yunis about two Palestinians in their early twenties who wanted to volunteer, said Salameh. As with the diagram of the bomb, the process of recruiting the bomber was hauntingly familiar to the one Salameh would later use in the Jaffa Road bus bombing.

Salameh brought one of the men to his home. Deif wrote a speech for the man to recite as part of a final videotape. Salameh found an Israeli-made Galil rifle and gave it to the bomber to hold as he spoke the words Deif wrote. Salameh handled the video camera.

"The speech included passages from the Koran," Salameh said.

Salameh did not mention Alisa Flatow or the bombing of her bus during his interrogations. But the plan that he conceived with Deif was remarkably similar in many ways to the attack that killed Alisa except for one key element: how the bomb would be delivered to its target. Instead of a pickup truck similar to one that blew up next to Alisa's bus, Salameh wanted the suicide attacker to place the bomb on a bicycle and to detonate it as he rode up to a bus carrying soldiers.

The suicide attacker had other ideas, though. Salameh said he "insisted on doing it with his brother's donkey and cart."

Salameh agreed. He selected June 25, 1995, as the date, less than three months after the suicide attack on Alisa Flatow's bus and just a month after another suicide attack with a donkey cart that killed the bomber and donkey and injured an Israeli soldier.

Around 11 a.m., Salameh's bomber drove a donkey cart to an intersection on a road near Gush Katif not far from the Israeli army headquarters for the region. To passersby, the cart would have been just another vegetable wagon pulled by a donkey—a common sight in the Gaza Strip. As an Israeli army jeep approached, the cart's driver pushed a button. The cart blew up, killing the driver and donkey and hurling vegetables across the landscape. Three soldiers who had been riding in the jeep were wounded.

"I heard an explosion at approximately 11 a.m.," Salameh said, adding ruefully: "I heard on the news that this bombing failed."

On January 20, 1997, President Clinton stood on the steps of the US Capitol to begin his second presidential term. With US Supreme Court Chief Justice William Rehnquist presiding, Clinton first recited the oath of office, then stepped to a podium and spoke for almost twenty-three minutes about his hopes for a second term.

Like most inaugural addresses, Clinton's did not offer a specific agenda as much as a set of goals as the nation looked to the twenty-first century. He said he hoped America's "old democracy" would remain "forever young" and "guided by the ancient vision of a promised land" with "our sights upon a land of new promise." He urged the nation "to shape the forces of the information age and the global society" and "to unleash the limitless potential of all our people, and yes, to form a more perfect union."

Clinton mentioned "terror" only twice in the 2,200 words that he spoke that day. The first reference was linked to racial prejudice; the second, to international terror—but only in an oblique way. "We will stand mighty for peace and freedom and maintain a strong defense against terror and destruction," he said.

On the next day, January 21, Kenneth McKune, wrote another letter to Len and Vicki Eisenfeld from his office at the State Department.

McKune explained that since he had last spoken with the Eisenfelds on December 3, 1996, and after writing a letter on December 21 in which he mentioned that Iran was a prime supporter of Palestinian terrorism, he "queried our embassy in Tel Aviv and our consulate general in Jerusalem regarding the status of the suspects associated with the terrorist bombing which killed your son and Sara Duker."

McKune mentioned a series of Palestinian names and offered a few sentences of description.

First on his list was Mohammed al-Deif, the Hamas military commander who "is believed to have been involved in providing logistical support to suicide bombers." McKune said that Deif "is believed to be at large in the West Bank or Gaza and is considered a fugitive by the Palestinian Authority."

After Deif, McKune cited four other Palestinians. Three were still fugitives. The fourth—Mohammad Abu Wardeh—was already known to the Eisenfelds as the man who helped to recruit his own cousin as the suicide bomber aboard the Number 18 bus.

Before signing off, McKune mentioned one more name. "Hassan Salamah has been imprisoned by Israel," he wrote, using an alternative spelling of Salameh's name.

McKune said nothing more about Salameh's significance—just those seven words in a single sentence, then signed off. "I hope you find this additional information useful," McKune wrote.

It was the first time that Len and Vicki Eisenfeld had seen the name, "Hassan Salameh."

As they read the letter, the mention of Hassan Salameh or that he had been arrested meant nothing to them. It was just a name of another Palestinian "imprisoned by Israel." With such a nondescript, matter-of-fact reference in McKune's letter, Len and Vicki assumed that Salameh was just a small player in the plot that killed Matthew and Sara. Almost twenty more months would pass before they discovered that Salameh played a far more significant role or that he had been telling Israeli authorities about his Iranian training.

—◦—

Five weeks after McKune's letter arrived at the Eisenfeld home, Stephen Flatow stepped before a bank of microphones in room HC-7 at the US

Capitol. It was noon. The Senate and the House of Representatives had recessed for lunch. Standing by Flatow's side was US Senator Frank Lautenberg, the liberal Democrat from New Jersey.

In the past year, Flatow and Lautenberg had grown to admire each other immensely. Both were Jewish and viewed themselves as ardent supporters of Israel. And both rose from working-class roots to different levels of success in the business world—Flatow as a lawyer who grew up in Queens and now ran a business that specialized in real estate title searches; Lautenberg, who escaped the harsh poverty of Paterson, New Jersey, during the Great Depression to build a multimillion-dollar data-processing firm before entering politics.

Like almost all members of the Senate and House of Representatives, Lautenberg supported the antiterrorism bill signed into law the previous year that allowed US citizens to file lawsuits against a select group of state sponsors of terrorism. But as Flatow and Steven Perles discovered, most legislators—and the White House, as well—did not realize that the clause allowing for the lawsuits was essentially toothless.

The AEDPA clearly allowed families to file lawsuits against state sponsors of terrorism such as Iran. But only small compensatory damages could be collected. Judges were barred from imposing large financial penalties on those nations—so-called punitive damages up to hundreds of millions of dollars that were viewed by legislators as a potential deterrent to terror-sponsoring nations. Lautenberg stepped in with a solution. He pushed through a new clause in the law, known as the "Flatow Amendment," which allowed victims to file for high punitive damages.

It was February 26, 1997—a year and one day since Sara and Matt had been killed. As he stood with Lautenberg before a group of journalists inside the US Capitol, Flatow sensed he was embarking on an uncharted legal path. Punishing terrorists was seen as a job for the police or the military. Now Flatow was asking a judge to treat the terrorist murder of his daughter as the equivalent of a negligent homicide, not unlike those cited in civil lawsuits argued each day in courtrooms across America.

Flatow knew his case was not easy. But he was willing to take the risk and wanted to be the first to test the new antiterrorism law and the amendment that carried his name. He also knew that other families of victims, including Arline Duker and Len and Vicki Eisenfeld, were considering lawsuits, and they would be paying close attention.

Lautenberg, who was joined by two New Jersey Republican congressmen at the press conference, James Saxton and Frank LoBiondo, said "there is no doubt that the funding spigot for international terrorism starts in Iran."

Then Steven Flatow stepped forward. He said he hoped he might collect $150 million in damages from Iran. But that figure was just an estimate. What Flatow most wanted was to send a message.

"When you lose a child, you want to pull the covers over your head and make the rest of the world disappear. But you can't do that," he said. "I am not a sovereign nation. I cannot wage war."

But he could go to an American court. And that's exactly what Stephen Flatow planned to do to hold his daughter's killers accountable.

# CHAPTER 9

THE ISRAELI COMMUNITY OF BEIT EL SITS ON A GENTLE HILLSIDE IN THE central West Bank, overlooking the Palestinian city of Ramallah and the mosque where Hassan Salameh asked Majdi Abu Wardeh to carry out the suicide bombing of the Number 18 bus on Jaffa Road. A marshy ribbon of flat fields separates Beit El ("house of God" in Hebrew) from Ramallah ("high place of Allah" in Arabic).

As the Olso peace process slowly toppled into disarray in the late 1990s after the bombings orchestrated by Hassan Salameh and others, Palestinian activists in Ramallah regularly marched along a narrow road that bisects those flatlands to demonstrate their disdain for the Israelis of Beit El. Often the marchers threw rocks at the Israeli soldiers who guarded Beit El. Sometimes they set fire to abandoned cars and discarded tires. Sometimes they fired guns.

After a few years, some of the activists devised an informal nickname for the road across those contentious flatlands that linked the two communities, especially after several Palestinians died in gun battles with Beit El's soldiers. They called the area "martyrs' crossroads."

On a Monday morning in June 1997, an armored convoy drove a shackled Hassan Salameh through the intersection near "martyr's crossroads" and led him into a military courtroom in Beit El. Salameh faced almost four dozen murder charges—for the men, women, and children his bombs killed a year earlier, including Matthew Eisenfeld and Sara Duker. But Salameh had come with his own message. He wanted to die, a martyr, sentenced to death.

Salameh's murder trial was not a galvanizing event in Israel. Journalists did not ignore it, but in a nation where terrorist bombings are a regular occurrence and bomb scenes are quickly cleaned up, the trial of one of Hamas's most deadly bomb-makers seemed relatively low-key. Almost none of the families of the forty-six people who died in the three suicide bombing attacks that Salameh orchestrated during ten days of mayhem in late February and early March of 1996 attended, in part because traveling to Beit El was not an easy trip for many Israelis. Also, many families were still too emotionally distraught to face the man behind one of the most devastating bombing campaigns in long history of the Israeli-Palestinian conflict.

The Eisenfelds and the Dukers did not come to Beit El. But their absence had nothing to do with the grief they endured. Arline, Len and Vicki had not been fully told about Salameh's role in the bombing, much less that he was on trial for murder. Likewise, Israeli investigators had not notified Stephen Flatow about the identities of Palestinian operatives involved in Alisa's death. Nor had anyone told Flatow about the suspected links between Salameh's circle of Hamas operatives—notably Yahya Ayyash, Mohammed Deif, and Adnan al-Ghoul—and the Islamic Jihad militants who carried out the bombing attack on the bus with Alisa. It was as if Salameh was a lone wolf and that his trial was an isolated event even though he was arguably one of the deadliest mass murderers in Israel's history.

Salameh's appearance in Beit El was not his first court appearance. Two months earlier, he was brought to another military court near the Gaza Strip, where he learned of the charges against him. Salameh was not silent and offered a strong hint regarding his motive for his killing spree—a motive he would repeat in Beit El. Turning to several reporters in the court that day, he said: "I believe what I did is a legitimate right my religion and all the world gave me, the right to defend my land, my country, and myself as a Palestinian."

As Salameh sat in the courtroom in Beit El with a lawyer who had been appointed to serve as his defense counsel, Israeli Army Colonel Ilan Katz studied him. Katz was not a combat officer but a military lawyer. After serving in the Israeli Army's judge advocate corps as a prosecutor for more than a decade, he had been promoted to judge. While American military judges spend most of their careers with cases involving soldiers charged with crimes that range from assault, drunkeness, and robbery to rape and murder, Katz had focused a large portion of his time on cases involving Palestinians who had been charged in terrorist attacks against Israeli targets. For Salameh's trial, Katz was not alone as the judge. A lieutenant colonel and a major joined him to form a three-judge panel.

Like many judges, Katz looked for a sign of fear or even mild appre-hension in the short, stocky Palestininan man now in his courtroom. But he found none. "He was strong," Katz said years later of Salameh. "He was very arrogant."

Salameh's demeanor did not surprise Katz. Five weeks earlier Salameh had already pleaded guilty to the forty-six murders he was charged with. For this trial, there would be no witnesses, no arguing between lawyers over admissibility of crime scene photos, chemical analysis of the bomb material found on the bus or even eyewitnesses' testimony. "The defendant admitted the offenses attributed to him," Katz announced as he began the proceeding. "According to the confession, we convict the defendant."

Before going ahead with arguments by the prosecutor and defense attorney on what sort of sentence the judges should impose on Salameh, Katz outlined the evidence. The judge noted that the defendant did not object to the evidence against him. "This abstention," said Katz, "consti-tutes a strengthening of the evidence that was filed by the prosecution."

Katz began with the February 25, 1996 bombing of the Number 18 bus. He pointed to Salameh's admission during his interrogation by Israeli police a year earlier of how he met with Hamas operatives on the West Bank, how Majdi Abu Wardeh was recruited as the suicide bomber, how the bomb was assembled, and how Salameh gave precise instructions for blowing up the bus. Katz pointed out that autopsies of the victims showed that many had been struck by ball bearings and other shrapnel that had been packed around the bomb. He noted that Wardeh's body had been identified through DNA samples taken from his parents by Israeli Shin Bet agents at the al-Fawwar refugee camp.

Katz then turned to the second attack that Salameh orchestrated on February 25, 1996—the bombing of the bus stop near Ashkelon—and his final attack a week later on another Number 18 bus on Jaffa Road.

The whole proceeding took an hour. Although the reading of the evi-dence against Salameh and the formal announcement that he was guilty were important, the real drama and key question before Katz and the two other judges was Salameh's punishment.

Katz wasted no time addressing that issue. After the verdict, he moved quickly to a discussion of the possible sentences that could be imposed.

Katz appointed an Israeli army sergeant as stenographer and another sergeant as interpreter, then turned to Lieutenant Colonel Avinoam Sharon, the military prosecutor, to speak first.

Sharon was one of Israel's most experienced and savvy military lawyers. He also became a liaison to the US Justice Department and a close advisor to Shin Bet officials who were shaping a counterterrorism strategy against Palestinian militants. Unknowingly, he also forged a unique connection to Matt Eisenfeld and Sara Duker. Sharon was almost two decades older than Matt and Sara. But he earned his undergraduate degree on the same college campus where Sara later earned hers—Columbia University—and just a block from Jewish Theological Seminary where Matthew had been enrolled. After studying law at Hebrew University, Shraron became a military prosecutor in Israel.

After years of laboring in military courtrooms, Sharon had become an administrator who assigned military prosecutors to different cases throughout the West Bank. He had not prosecuted a case for several years. But for the Salameh case, Sharon's commanding officer ordered him back into the courtroom. Sharon was considered Israel's best military prosecutor. Israel wanted to make sure nothing went wrong.

Sharon began his work months before. He assembled files on each victim and often spent his evenings studying autopsy reports and examining photos of the dead. It was gruesome work but Sharon felt he had to do it. Although the Salameh case obviously had an enormous political impact on the Oslo peace process, Sharon did not want to lose track of the fact that Salameh's bombs had killed forty-six people. Sharon vowed that he would mention each victim's name and offer a short description of who they were, no matter how ordinary their lives.

When he opened the files for Sara and Matt, Sharon noted that many of their friends had told Israeli police that they planned to marry. Sharon placed Sara's and Matt's files together. When it came time to talk about them, he vowed to speak of them as a couple—together.

As he prepared his prosecution strategy, Sharon anticipated that Salameh would plead not guilty and that his trial would be long and complicated, with numerous arguments over the small details of evidence. No matter. Sharon expected those sorts of arguments. But when Salameh pleaded guilty, Sharon feared that he would lose a chance to focus as much attention as possible on the victims and, in particular, the horrific nature of their deaths. As Judge Katz moved the trial to a discussion of possible punishments for Salameh, Sharon decided he would first speak of the people who died.

Sharon rose from his chair and began to read the names—first, the twenty-six victims from the Number 18 bus on Jaffa Road on Sunday, February 25, 1996, including Matt and Sara and Ira Weinstein, who died of burns six weeks later, then the name of the lone person who died at the bus stop in Ashkelon an hour later, and finally the nineteen additional victims on the Number 18 bus that was blown up by a suicide bomber on the following Sunday, March 3.

"May the Lord avenge their blood," Sharon said.

Sharon then turned his attention to Salameh and a legal argument that would not only set the tone for the proceedings but would affect Salameh's own life and his future.

"All of these individuals were murdered in cold blood by this defendant, who, in three attacks carried out forty-six murders," Sharon began. "This is not a matter of three offenses but forty-six separate acts of attacks against human life."

Even before presenting any evidence, Sharon wanted to emphasize what he described as the "particular nature and special circumstances of the offenses" and asked that the three judges before him convict Salameh of forty-six separate murders, then give forty-six separate and consecutive life sentences in prison so that Salameh would have little chance of being freed on parole.

"Our belief in the reverence of human life must also be expressed in the sentencing of an offender," Sharon said. "If the request of the prosecution sets a precedent, this is because the acts of the defendant form a precedent and require a precedent in response. This court must create and establish this precedent. This is the demand of the prosecution, the demand of the victims and our duty to the memory and honor of the forty-six victims."

Sharon's presentation was emotional and strategically erudite. As Judge Katz saw it, the mere reading of the names of forty-six people who had been killed by the bombs that had been made by Hassan Salameh was an effective way to demonstrate to the court the enormity of his crimes while also reminding the judges of how many innocent people had lost their lives.

Sharon was not through. He turned from the victims' deaths to Salameh and to a question that Israel's judges, prosecutors, defense attorneys, and political figures had wrestled with for years: What about the death penalty?

Since Israel's founding in 1948, its judicial system had executed only one prisoner, Adolf Eichmann, one of the key architects of the Nazi Holocaust. In 1960, after an international manhunt, Eichmann was tracked down in Argentina by Israel's Mossad spy service and captured. Without the Argentine government realizing what had taken place, a team of Mossad agents smuggled Eichmann back to Israel aboard an airplane. After a meticulous trial that attracted attention from around the world and galvanized Israel's citizens, Eichmann was found guilty of war crimes and hanged at an Israeli prison in 1962.

Since then, a variety of Israeli politicians, as well as journalists and lawyers, had argued for the death penalty in some especially brutal terrorist cases. Althouh Israeli judges always had the option of imposing the death penalty, no other execution had taken place in Israel since Eichmann's.

With Salameh's capture a year earlier, Israelis were reminded of the large number of his victims and the possibility of the death penalty was raised once again.

Sharon decided he needed to address the subject as straightforwardly as he could. He began by reminding the judges that the death penalty was hardly a "criminal theory" in Israel. Even though only one prisoner had been executed, the death penalty was still "a policy" in Israel and judges had the power to impose it. But Sharon noted—as if the judges did not already know—that "the considerations" in pondering whether to sentence a prisoner to death "are moral ones."

Sharon said he had already consulted with a variety of experts who guided him in shaping a proposal for sentencing Salameh if he was convicted. But before outlining his idea to the judges, Sharon cited a recent letter in an Israeli newspaper from the father of a young woman from Canada who had been killed by terrorists on a Tel Aviv beach.

The father argued against imposing the death penalty. He wrote that executing terrorists would fulfill a wish by many of them to be "identified as martyrs and heroes" and could prompt other Palestinian militants to "aspire for a martyr's death." Instead of hanging terrorists or executing them by some other method, the father suggested putting them in prison until they died there of natural causes. Such a punishment would not be viewed as martyrdom and was hardly the sort of glory that other potential terrorists might want to aspire to. Or as Sharon noted: "Nobody would be eager to rot in prison alone and forgotten, aged, and celibate."

Sharon made one more point. A life in prison, with forty-six consecutive life terms, is precisely the most effective and just sentence for Hassan Salameh and "what we request for the Court to do to the Defendant before us."

Salameh's court-appointed lawyer rose. He agreed with Sharon that the judges should not sentence Salameh to death. But he also said forty-six consecutive life sentences was unfair. "This is a question that belongs to the world of philosophy more than to the world of law," he said. "One sentence is certainly enough."

It was a brief and legally precise argument. Like any good defense attorney who represents a client who is guilty of a ghastly crime and has already pleaded guilty, Salameh's attorney was trying to convince the judges to impose the most lenient sentence. In this case, that would be a single sentence of life imprisonment for Salameh which, in the years to come, might offer him a better chance to be paroled.

Salameh had other ideas, however. As his attorney returned to his chair, Salameh rose to address the court. He turned first to the prosecutor "who considers me to be a murderer."

"I ask to make a distinction on the subject of murder," Salameh said. "There is a difference whether a person commits murder for the sake of murder and one who commits murder who is requesting a right." That right was the liberation of the Palestinian people, Salameh said, echoing the sentiments he had voiced at his previous court appearance.

Salameh turned to his own fate and to what the judges might decide.

"For my acts, I request that the death sentence be imposed and executed," he said.

⸙

Judge Katz and the two other military judges took another week to decide to send Salameh to prison or to the gallows.

On the following Monday, July 7, Katz again found himself looking at Salameh in the Beit El courtroom. Salameh's words the week before bothered Katz, especially his request for execution. To Katz, Salameh seemed to be daring his Israeli captors to kill him, even hinting that Katz and the other judges were afraid to sentence him to death because they feared an increase in Hamas terrorist attacks. On the other hand, Katz worried that keeping Salamah alive, even with a sentence of life in prison, left open the possibility that he might be turned loose one day in an exchange of prisoners between the Palestinians and the Israelis.

Alternatively, Katz had also been advised by the Shin Bet and the Mossad that executing Salameh could cause more harm in the future for Israelis by prompting more terrorist attacks, not only in Israel but in other nations too. Avinoam Sharon's own proposal as prosecutor to keep Salameh in prison for the rest of his life rather than executing him had been guided by that sort of advice from counterterror experts who feared reprisals if Salameh was killed. Sharon had spent many years watching criminals like Salameh. He knew that what they feared most was the loneliness of a prison cell.

Judge Katz, however, saw other problems with keeping Salameh in prison. Years later, as he reflected on the trial, Katz said he felt that Salameh's continued imprisonment could prompt Palestinian militants to kidnap an Israeli soldier and demand that Salameh be released in order for the soldier to be spared from death.

"The major question," Katz eventually decided, "is whether this punishment can reduce such acts of terror."

Katz's parents managed to escape the Holocaust during World War II and move to Israel where he was born. Katz never had to face the sort of evils that Nazism posed for Jews. Yet much of his life in Israel had been framed by the persistent danger of terrorist attacks. As a military prosecutor before becoming a judge, Katz had played a role in presenting evidence in dozens of terrorist cases. But as a judge, he felt a greater weight of responsibility to make sure he made a correct decision, not just for the accused terrorist standing before him in a courtroom, but for his nation as well.

"There are few things which are more difficult," he said. "First of all, you have to punish or hold a trial of the accused who is your enemy and you have to separate your own feelings and your own thoughts and try to make the trial as objective as you can. Sometimes you read the papers and see by your own eyes what those acts of terror cause. Also, you know that when you judge a simple criminal—let's say, someone who steals money or kills someone—you know that usually he doesn't aim his aggression against you. But when you judge a terrorist, you know that he aiming his violence against Israel as well as against you as a judge."

Then, there was Salameh himself. Katz looked for signs that Salameh felt any remorse for the forty-six lives he had taken in the three bombings. But Katz found no hint of regret or contrition. "Hassan Salameh was full of hate," he said. "I don't think he really cared whether he killed women or children. As long as he could kill as many Jews as he could, it was sufficient."

Katz began the sentencing hearing by summarizing the charges against Salameh; he pointed out that Salameh asked for the death penalty.

"There is no doubt that this is one of the most severe cases that has ever been brought before a judicial institution in the State of Israel," he said. He then mentioned another horrific attack years earlier in which thirty-four people had been killed. "Regrettably that record has been broken," Katz noted. "Forty-six persons lost their lives and let us not forget the many injured too. Every victim and every casualty is part of a family whose life has been changed and will never be as it was before the attack."

"The judges are unanimous that the acts of the defendant are very severe, lowly, repugnant and worthy of every condemnation and that the murderous conduct of the defendant, who is trying to add his own ideological pretext to the acts, is the behavior of a person that every human society must expel from within it."

Salameh's attacks were aimed specifically at Israel—and Jews, Katz continued. "Whoever aims to kill and massacre indiscriminately women, men, and children just because they are Jewish has excluded himself from man who was created in the shadow of God and cannot purport to be the protector of his people's rights."

But Katz also pointed out that not all of Salameh's victims were Israeli citizens or Jewish. "In the eyes of the defendant," Katz said, "the identity of the victims was of no consequence and, indeed in the attacks, foreign workers and an Arab resident also found their deaths."

Katz paused. While the judges agreed on Salameh's guilt and the horrific nature of his actions, they disagreed over how to punish him. Two judges favored a sentence of life in prison. A third judge called for the death penalty.

---

In Israel, when judges disagree on the type of sentence, they take a vote—and the majority wins. But they also take a vow: The judges do not disclose who favored the different sentencing options.

In the trial of Hassan Salameh, the identity of the lone judge who favored Salameh's execution has never been disclosed. Even after almost two decades, Katz declined to say how he voted or which of the three judges in Salameh's trial felt the death penalty was appropriate. "In our legal system," Katz said, "we are not supposed to tell which judge decided what kind of decision."

At the trial, Katz read the tribunal's majority opinion—that Salameh receive forty-six consecutive life sentences. But he did not want to end the proceeding without commenting on the death penalty that Salameh requested and that one of the judges wanted to impose.

"It is common after referring to the name of a victim of a murderous terrorist attack to add, 'May the Lord avenge his blood,'" Katz said. "This is no accident, as we believe that revenge and payback, in the sense of an eye for an eye and a tooth for a tooth, is divine retribution that exceeds the power of the mere mortal and [is] a matter for the Lord in heaven to deal with, while us meager humans try to express the extent of the atrocity, repulse, and condemnation of the acts of the defendant by sentencing him to life imprisonment for murdering each and every person who found his death in the attacks."

The hard task of judges, said Katz, was to distance themselves from "hot instinct and to adhere to cold discretion." He pointed out that Salameh's "greatest wish is to prevent the process of reconciliation between Israel and the Palestinians" by staging terrorist attacks. "What would be "fitting" would be for Salameh "to rot in prison until his last day and to see with his own eyes how his desire is cast into the wind and the process of reconciliation between the peoples slowly materializes."

Katz then began to recite a litany of victims' names and the sentence Salameh would receive for each death.

He began with Sergeant Yonatan Barnea, the twenty-year-old son of Israeli journalist Nahum Barnea. "Life imprisonment for causing the intentional death," Katz said. Next, he mentioned Arik Gaby, a sixteen-year-old cadet at the Israeli Air Force technical school. And Israeli Army Private Sharon Hanuka, twenty, who was scheduled to finish her military service in five months. And Army Corporal Merav Nachum, nineteen, who had enlisted only three months earlier. And a married couple, Jana Kushnirov, thirty-six, and her husband, Anatoli Kushnirov, thirty-seven, who emigrated from Ukraine three years before and left behind an eight-year-old son and a five-month-old daughter.

Katz pointed out that Boris Sharpolinsky, sixty-four, died on his way to work; that Peretz Gantz, sixty-two, had escaped from the Nazis as a boy during World War II; that Daniel Biton, forty-two, a gardner, was a father of three; that Masuda Amar, fifty-nine, was a grandmother of five; that Wael Jumah Kawasmeh, twenty-three, a Muslim from East Jerusalem, was due to marry in a month.

Then, Katz came to Matt Eisenfeld and Sara Duker. "Two cumulative life imprisonments for causing the intentional death" of Matt and Sara— "a Jewish couple from America who were about to marry, their tragic deaths uniting them forever."

———

Salameh did not speak. As Katz looked out on the court, Salameh showed no emotion as the names of the dead were read one by one, in each case preceded by the words, "life imprisonment." As he finished, Katz allowed the opinion of the dissenting judge to be read.

"I regret that in this case I cannot concur with the opinion of my learned colleagues," the anonymous judge wrote. "I believe that the abominable acts of the defendant necessitate in this case the imposition of the maximum sentence prescribed in the law, namely death."

"In the end there is no escaping asking the terrible but necessary question, which is: If this is not a case in which the death sentence is fitting, then what has to happen?"

The judges never answered that question. They were not required to.

Later that day, Hassan Salameh was taken to an Israeli prison. As he thought about Salameh later, Katz said he felt uneasy at what transpired in the courtroom in Beit El.

"I don't think Salameh will be rotting in jail," Katz said. "I think that there will come a day in which somebody will decide to release him."

Judge Katz was half right.

Hassan Salameh would stay behind bars. But he would neither rot nor keep silent.

# PART III

# RECOVERY

# CHAPTER 10

AT THE BASE OF CAPITOL HILL IN WASHINGTON, DC, THE US DISTRICT Courthouse stands as a silent, symbolic sentinel overlooking the intersection of two of the city's great thoroughfares, Constitution and Pennsylvania Avenues, which link Congress and the White House and the political and legislative tides that pass between them.

The federal judges inside the courthouse do not have the luxury of choosing their cases. Nor do they always know ahead of time whether a new law passed by Congress at one end of Constitution and Pennsylvania Avenues and signed by the president in the White House at the other end may be put to the test with a case inside one of their courtrooms. But in early 1997, as Israeli military Judge Ilan Katz prepared to preside over the murder trial of Hassan Salameh in the West Bank community of Beit El, an American judge at Washington's federal courthouse began to focus his attention on another terrorism case that would become the template for efforts by Arline Duker and Len and Vicki Eisenfeld to find out who killed their children.

US District Court Judge Royce C. Lamberth was less than thrilled to discover that he would be handling a lawsuit filed by Stephen Flatow against the Islamic Republic of Iran. Lamberth, a fifty-three-year-old Texan and former federal prosecutor who had been appointed to the federal judiciary a decade earlier by President Ronald Reagan, did not especially like the Flatow case and, in particular, what he viewed as its risky constitutional implications. As a constitutional scholar, Lamberth felt that the Antiterrorism and Effective Death Penalty Act, which was the basis for Flatow's case, contained fundamental flaws, especially its provision allowing US citizens to file lawsuits against nations that had been labeled as state sponsors of terrorism.

Lamberth certainly believed in maintaining a strong defense against terrorist attacks. A year earlier, US Supreme Court Chief Justice William Rehnquist appointed Lamberth as the presiding judge of the US

Foreign Intelligence Surveillance Court, the top-secret judicial body that issues search warrants on behalf of the National Security Agency and the FBI to monitor suspected spies or foreign terrorists. But Lamberth also believed that the US Constitution clearly stipulated that foreign affairs—and especially the government's response to the murders of Americans overseas by organized terrorist groups with ties to nations such as Iran—were the explicit domain of the president.

It was not the job of America's federal judges, Lamberth felt, to conduct foreign policy and punish other nations who orchestrated attacks on US citizens. Lamberth believed that job was clearly in the hands of the president—and with Congress if a formal declaration of war was proposed. "The Constitution gives the president great power in foreign affairs," Lamberth later said. "I don't want to infringe on his power."

What also concerned Lamberth was the possibility that, in a lawsuit against Iran or another nation that had been labeled a terrorist state, a ruling by him could later interfere with the president's ability to conduct diplomatic negotiations. "For a judge to get into the middle of that is very difficult," he said.

Lamberth was not alone in his concerns. As the Antiterrorism and Effective Death Penalty Act was debated in the US Senate and in the House of Representatives, lawyers from the State Department warned that the new law could impinge on all sorts of foreign diplomacy. But after watching the number of terrorist attacks against Americans increase during the 1980s, Congress had become fed up with the lack of a response by the White House, the State and Justice Departments, and even the US military. Perhaps multimillion-dollar lawsuits against Iran and other terrorist nations would send a more effective message.

Lamberth knew the politics well, in particular the interplay between the attempts by lawmakers in Congress to weave together solutions and the equally noteworthy concerns by officials in the State and Justice Departments to put them into practice. Even though he was born in San Antonio, Texas, and had earned his undergraduate and law degrees from the University of Texas, he had spent most of his professional career in Washington. After serving as a lawyer in the US Army's Judge Advocate Corps, including assignments in Vietnam and at the Pentagon, Lamberth worked as a federal prosecutor in Washington for more than a decade before donning his black judicial robes and taking his place at the US courthouse. Although he harbored lingering worries about the antiterrorism legislation and the possibility of more lawsuits like Stephen Flatow's, Lamberth also knew he had taken an oath to uphold all US federal laws, even if he did not like them. So, when the case file for Flatow's lawsuit against the Islamic Republic of Iran landed on his desk, he dove in and began to explore its complexities. It was the beginning of almost two decades of legal work by Lamberth on cases by US victims of overseas terrorism.

Tall and blessed with a laconic Texas drawl that made even his most difficult rulings sound comforting, Lamberth would come to realize that he was perfectly suited for the Flatow case despite his misgivings about the law it was based on. He was skeptical and thorough, as well as a careful listener who did not lose his patience easily, as some judges did. As Flatow and his chief lawyer, Perles, would soon discover, Lamberth would also prove to be surprisingly open to fresh legal ideas.

Perhaps Lamberth's most telling gift was rooted in his experience as a federal prosecutor years earlier. He knew firsthand the deep and longlasting pain of crime victims. Even before he met Flatow in his courtroom, Lamberth could sense how wounded he was by the loss of his daughter.

As Lamberth began routine meetings on the Flatow case in the spring of 1997, he discovered an unexpected problem. The target of Flatow's lawsuit, Iran, and a variety of its leaders named in the lawsuit, including Iran's Supreme Leader, Ayatollah Ali Hosseini Khamenei and its president, Ali Akbar Hashemi-Rafsanjani, had not acknowledged receiving a copy of the lawsuit. After filing the lawsuit at the federal courthouse in Washington, Perles tried to send a copy of the lawsuit to Iranian authorities—a standard courtesy that allows the target of the lawsuit to hire an attorney and file the necessary papers to answer and perhaps challenge the lawsuit.

With no American diplomats in Iran—the US Embassy in Tehran closed in 1979 and never reopened—Perles reached out to the Swiss government, which represents US interests in Iran. Eventually, a package containing a copy of the Flatow lawsuit was delivered to the Iranian government, Perles said. The envelope had been opened, then resealed, and the package was returned to Perles—with no message.

Weeks passed. Iran's government had not hired lawyers as it had done in previous, non-terrorism civil cases in the United States. Nor had it bothered to send even a brief message of protest to Judge Lamberth indicating that it would not show up in court. Lamberth found Iran's behavior to be highly unusual. In almost every instance, the target of a lawsuit hires an attorney or at least contacts the judge to ask for help finding an attorney or to complain about the unfairness of the lawsuit. None of that happened in the Flatow case. Iran simply ignored the lawsuit.

Flatow still faced another vexing problem with his case. Like Len and Vicki Eisenfeld and Arline Duker, Flatow, guided by Perles, had been searching for solid proof that would connect Iran to the bombing that killed Alisa. Several high-ranking US officials told them that Iran was linked to the attack. But how? Where was the evidence of such a link? Flatow and Perles knew that the Gaza-based militant group Palestinian Islamic Jihad had claimed responsibility for the suicide bombing of Alisa's bus. However, the new antiterror law signed by President Clinton stated clearly that the only targets of lawsuits could be a limited group of nations, including Iran.

Yet the opinions of intelligence experts about Iran's complicity, while certainly important to the policy strategists at the CIA, Congress, and the White House, did not provide the kind of conclusive proof needed to win a lawsuit. And without Iran even acknowledging the lawsuit, Flatow and Perles had little hope of questioning Iranian officials about their connection to Palestinian terrorist activities.

The State Department's acting counterterrorism chief, Kenneth McKune, had already been helpful. His letters to Len Eisenfeld, especially the one with a reference to the State Department's report about Iran's support of terrorist groups, was significant. But even the report, backed up by a letter written by such a key figure in America's counterterrorism efforts, lacked the kind of solid proof Flatow and Perles needed—and that Lamberth would surely demand.

Meanwhile, Arline Duker and Steven Flatow decided on another strategy to draw attention to the deaths of their children. Along with US Senator Frank Lautenberg of New Jersey, they signed a letter asking Palestinian Authority President Yasser Arafat to "stop the violence" that was growing in the Gaza Strip, throughout the West Bank and within Jerusalem itself and to cooperate with Israeli police in trying to stop terrorist attacks before they happen. The letter, delivered in person to Arafat by US Secretary of State Madeleine Albright, was never answered. Six weeks earlier, a suicide bombing orchestrated by Hamas militants in a downtown Jerusalem market near Jaffa Road killed sixteen people and injured another 178. A month after that, at another market near Jaffa Road, three suicide attackers recruited by Hamas set off bombs that killed five people and injured 181.

A few weeks after Flatow filed his lawsuit, Perles met with Leonard Eisenfeld at Reagan National Airport to discuss the pros and cons of going to court. In midsummer 1997, Flatow invited Arline Duker and the Eisenfelds to his home in West Orange, New Jersey, for a barbecue and more discussions about legal action. Besides the cost of mounting a legal challenge, Arline, Len, and Vicki worried about the results. Flatow painted a bleak picture: He did not expect a large windfall of cash from Iran in compensatory or punitive damages. He also did not expect a quick decision. "I expected it to be dragged out," Flatow said.

He couldn't have been more wrong.

—◦—

Just after 9 a.m. on the first Monday in March 1998, Stephen Flatow stepped off an elevator on the fourth floor of the US District Courthouse in Washington. His wife, Rosalyn, walked with him, along with his son, Etan, and his daughters, Gail and Ilana. (The Flatows' other daughter, Francine, was traveling in Israel on a study program before entering Brandeis University.) As instructed, the family followed the hallway to Courtroom 21.

For weeks, Flatow had nurtured two conflicting feelings about this moment—a numbing fear of the pain that might boil up inside him when reminded of Alisa's murder and the long-anticipated satisfaction that he might finally be able to hold her killers accountable in some way.

It was a courtroom without windows. And Flatow noticed as he walked through the bronze doors that the courtroom was virtually empty. Only a handful of spectators and journalists showed up. With

Washington's media focused on the brewing controversy over reports of President Clinton's sexual affair with a White House intern, the Flatow lawsuit against Iran had slipped off the radar screen.

Flatow walked with his family along a twenty-foot aisle of thick forest-green carpet in the center of the courtroom, past five rows of oak benches, then guided his family into the front row and sat down.

He thought of Alisa. When she was five years old, a neighbor accidentally drove a car over Alisa's foot. Flatow had been trying to take a nap inside the family's home in West Orange. But when he heard his daughter crying, he picked her up, put her in his car and drove to a hospital. In the backseat, Alisa moaned in pain, then stopped and asked her father, "Daddy why do these things always happen to me?"

Flatow remembered fumbling for a word or two to comfort his daughter. He told her that accidents happen and that you can't plan for them. Finally he said, "You just happened to be in the wrong place at the wrong time."

Since Alisa's death on the bus in Gaza, Flatow often found himself recalling that car ride to the hospital and his words to Alisa. He began to mention the story in speeches about her, often to Jewish audiences who were conducting fund-raisers for schools in America or in Israel. "I think back to that little five year old in the back seat of the car," he would say. "There will be times that things happen that you don't understand. But this much I know. Because you were in Israel, studying the religion that you love and the land that you love and the people that you love, this time you were in the right place. And we all find our right places."

The courtroom was quiet that morning as Flatow thought about his case. He figured he had already spent tens of thousands of dollars of his own savings on court filings and other expenses associated with the lawsuit, including dozens of trips to Washington to lobby Congress for counterterrorism legislation and to meet with Perles or government officials. He knew Perles had assembled a strong case. Perles had even brought in one of Washington's most experienced courtroom lawyers, Thomas Fortune Fay, to handle the opening and closing statements as well as question witnesses. Perles felt his skills were in shaping legal strategies and writing briefs; Fay was more adept at the verbal give and take during a trial.

Flatow admired Perles for seeing his own strengths and weakness and in finding someone like Tom Fay who could fill in. Fay also understood how Flatow's case was essentially not all that different from the kinds of personal injury lawsuits that are filed each day in courts throughout America. "It was a lot like any other lawsuit over a negligent death," Fay often said.

But it wasn't an ordinary lawsuit, as Flatow knew. Yes, Perles and Fay had developed what they believed to be a solid argument—that Iran was responsible because its funds were used to train bombers and to assemble lethal explosives that caused the unnecessary and negligent death of an innocent woman. And, yes, Perles and Fay had skillfully constructed their arguments in briefs and in Lamberth's court to parallel a standard personal injury case. But this was new legal territory. Six months earlier, the Cuban-American families of the Brothers to the Rescue pilots had been awarded $187 million in damages from frozen Cuban assets to compensate them for the deaths of their loved ones.

The Brothers to the Rescue lawsuit against Cuba was based on the same clause in the Antiterrorism and Effective Death Penalty Act that allowed Flatow to file a lawsuit against Iran. Both Cuba and Iran were listed by the US State Department as state sponsors of terrorism. The size of the judge's award—$187 million—seemed remarkable. But Flatow knew that being told by a judge they were entitled to the money was not the same as collecting it. The US government was already attempting to block the families of the Brothers to the Rescue victims from claiming some of Cuba's financial assets that had been frozen in US banks years earlier.

Flatow watched in silence as the lawyers studied their papers and Judge Lamberth settled into a chair behind the raised oak bench over which hung a large seal of the United States. For months, Flatow felt that the process of filing court papers and talking to his lawyer had been cathartic—an imperfect way to soothe his enduring pain over Alisa's death but nevertheless a process that helped him to channel his grief. He wondered if Judge Lamberth would offer another form of catharsis.

Just after 10 a.m., Lamberth's clerk announced, "Civil Action 97-396. Stephen M. Flatow versus Islamic Republic of Iran."

Judge Lamberth looked across the courtroom. "All right. Mr. Fay, are you ready to proceed?"

—◆—

Every trial has different phases. In many criminal trials in which a defendant is accused of a serious crime such as murder or robbery, the first step is for the defense and prosecution lawyers to agree on the composition of a jury. As the trial begins with opening statements by the opposing lawyers, the jury listens as the prosecution presents its evidence, after which the defense has an opportunity to respond. Even when a defendant forgoes a jury trial and chooses instead to allow a judge to hear all the evidence and reach a decision on guilt, both the prosecution and defense have opportunities to cross-examine witnesses and offer challenges on all manner of documents or other items offered as evidence.

The civil lawsuit by Stephen Flatow against Iran took a very different course. There was no jury—only Judge Lamberth would weigh the evidence and reach a decision. But what made the Flatow trial so uncommon was the refusal by the defendant—Iran—to come to court. As a result, Judge Lamberth and Flatow's attorneys knew ahead of time that there would be no challenges to the evidence, no cross-examining of witnesses. It was as if Judge Lamberth's courtroom was the stage for the Flatow family and its lawyers to tell its story and point an unchallenged finger of blame at Iran.

Lamberth was aware of how unusual the case would be. So were Perles and Fay. Iran's absence was worrisome to the judge and to Flatow's lawyers, not just from a legal perspective but also from the message the trial would send to the world. If America was putting Iran on trial for terrorism, shouldn't Iran be in court to answer the charge? That seemed only fair, and Lamberth hoped for that. He knew that Iran had hired American attorneys in the past when facing civil lawsuits in US courts over such questions as business deals that had not been completed. Lamberth also knew that he had the right to conduct a trial without Iran and that he could make a decision and have it upheld on appeal. Certainly, plenty of provisions and precedents in US law allowed for judges to make decisions even when one party in a lawsuit refused to participate. So after waiting months for Iran to respond, Lamberth decided to move forward with the trial. He declared that Iran had defaulted.

Tom Fay sensed the weight of the moment, and the global significance of the trial itself, as he rose from his chair to make an opening statement. He needed no reminder of Iran's absence; the oak table where Iran's lawyers would have sat was empty.

Fay began: "Your honor, we are here because on April 9th of 1995, Alisa Flatow, an American citizen, sustained what proved to be fatal injuries in an attack by a suicide bomber in the Gaza Strip area of Israel. The evidence will demonstrate that this went far beyond even the intentional killings that sometimes come before this court in murder cases. This was truly a slaughter of an innocent and others—I should say, innocents—to achieve a political end. . . ."

"As your honor knows," Fay continued, "this is truly an epochal case."

Minutes later, Stephen Flatow took the witness stand.

Fay began what what he considered a basic question: "Mr. Flatow, you were the father of Alisa Flatow?"

"No," Flatow answered.

Fay seemed dumbfounded. Then Flatow continued, "I'm still her father."

The brief exchange set the tone for what was to come. While emotional and deeply distressing, the first day's testimony with the Flatow family and others was actually some of the most effective for Fay and Perles to present. Flatow was the star witness whose testimony would not only help to frame the tragedy of Alisa's brutal death but underscore the continuing pain that had enveloped the entire family. As a lawyer, Flatow understood the significance of firsthand testimony. Equally important, he was comfortable sharing his feelings in court, especially how much he loved Alisa, and how painful it had been to him, his wife, and their children that she had died so violently.

On that first day, Fay called on one of Alisa's friends who had been with her on the bus to describe the shock of seeing her friend slump over, eyes wide open and her hands clenched. Fay also played a video, taken by an Israeli who lived near the Gaza Strip bomb scene, which showed paramedics trying to treat Alisa and placing her on a helicopter to be taken to a hospital. Finally, Fay called a forensic pathologist to the witness stand, who reviewed Alisa's autopsy reports and testified how shrapnel from the bomb had sliced into her brain.

But if any piece of testimony encapsulated the painful underpinnings of this case, it was Stephen Flatow's statement: "I'm still her father."

To Flatow, those were not empty words. He believed that his fatherly duty required him to pursue justice for his daughter and that her death had not ended his commitment to her.

As he listened that first day, Judge Lamberth felt tears come to his eyes several times. "Any judge is a human being first," he said later. "You cannot sit through that kind of testimony and not be drained at the end of the day."

But, as a father himself, Lamberth was especially drawn to Flatow's sentiments about Alisa. "It's tough to see that family suffer the way they did, with this young college girl who never did a thing wrong in her life. She could be my daughter or anybody's daughter," Lamberth said. "Nobody deserved to die in the awful way that she did die."

As important and moving as Flatow's testimony was in proving that Alisa had needlessly perished in a terrorist attack, Lamberth needed solid proof about Iran's possible connection. "There was no question about the injuries," Lamberth said years later. "The only question was whether Iran was behind it." Perles and Fay knew that too. If they were to convince Lamberth to hold Iran accountable, they had to present evidence that was compelling, convincing, and conclusive.

In shaping their legal strategy, Perles and Fay were not so much worried about whether Iran responded to the lawsuit. In this first legal test before Judge Lamberth, Perles and Fay knew they must show a definitive link between Iran and Palestinian terrorism. If Perles and Fay could not find that link, the entire lawsuit would collapse, no matter whether Iran's representatives showed up in court and no matter how emotional and tragic the testimony about Alisa Flatow's death was.

On the first day, amid the testimony of Stephen Flatow, Perles and Fay played a video recording of testimony by an Israeli expert, Reuven Paz, who was regarded as one of the best-informed experts on Palestinian terrorism. A former official with Shin Bet, Paz was one of the first to conclude that such militant groups as Hamas and Palestinian Islamic Jihad had strong ties to Iran.

But Perles and Fay needed something more.

⚊ ⚊

Washington is not just the epicenter of American politics. It is home to one of the greatest collections of news and information junkies in the nation, perhaps in the world. Besides thousands of journalists who cover every cul de sac of the sprawling federal government, there are swarms of media monitors, ranging from government officials and lobbyists to academics and researchers at think tanks, who spend hours each day consuming the steady torrent of information presented in all manner of newspapers, magazines, blogs, newsletters, and websites, as well as TV and radio programs. To outsiders, this world can seem insular, perhaps incestuous—a swarm of Washington-focused journalists producing a daily information buffet for a ravenous Washington audience of insiders. The sheer amount of statistics, budgetary figures, and assessments can seem so overwhelming that even important information is routinely over-looked. But sometimes what may seem to be the most inconsequential of tidbits suddenly leaps forth and sheds new light on a particular subject.

This is essentially what happened when Patrick Clawson, an econo-mist with a budding interest in how terrorists spend money, decided to study the annual budget for the Islamic Republic of Iran.

Even in Washington, with its diverse spectrum of experts on all man-ner of arcane subjects, Clawson was an anomaly. He was one of the few researchers in Washington (outside of the CIA and other intelligence agencies) who could read Farsi—the language of Iran, sometimes merely referred to as "Persian." Born in 1951 just over the Potomac River in Alexandria, Virginia, Clawson left the government-focused Washington area for college (Oberlin) and graduate school (the New School for Social Research in New York City). His specialty was not politics, but econom-ics. After teaching for several years at Seton Hall University in northern New Jersey, he returned to Washington in the 1980s as an economist at the International Monetary Fund, with a focus on the Middle East and a growing interest in the finances of terrorism.

Clawson had picked an important time to study Middle East terrorism. From Lebanon to Libya, barely a week passed without a new report of a terrorist attack. Palestinian attacks on Israeli civilian targets increased. Iran had begun to play a more active role. Only five years earlier, Iranian militants, spurred by an Islamic theology of revolution, had gained control of their own country, deposing the Shah and his corrupt, brutal regime and seizing the US Embassy and holding almost five dozen Americans hostage for more than a year.

Now those same spiritual and political militants actively sought to play a greater role in the entire Middle East, especially in Lebanon where Iranian-backed operatives affiliated with Hezbollah attacked the US Marine encampment in Beirut in 1983. Not only was Iran openly supporting Hezbollah, but American intelligence officials and others found proof later introduced in another lawsuit before Judge Lamberth, that Iran ordered the attack on the Marines.

In 1985, Clawson left the International Monetary Fund for a similar position at the World Bank. Later, he worked at the Foreign Policy Research Institute in Philadelphia, and at the National Defense University and the Institute for National Strategic Studies in Washington. By the early 1990s, Clawson joined the Washington-based Institute for Near East Policy, a think tank that monitored the political tidal flows in the Middle East and, in particular, the Israeli-Palestinian conflict. Clawson's primary interest was not necessarily Israel, though. He spent most of his time studying Iran and specifically the link between Iran's money and global terrorism.

Clawson made a practice of reading as many Iranian government documents he could get his hands on and even listening to radio coverage of debates within the Iranian parliament. Since 1983, he regularly read two Farsi-language newspapers each day. As an economist, he felt that if he could understand how the Iranian government spent its money, then he might have a better sense of what Iran's political and spiritual militants were thinking, especially when it came to Iran's overall strategy as a power player in the Middle East and financier of terrorism.

Clawson also made a point of studying the annual Iranian government budget. And in the course of reading the budget for the fiscal years of 1992–1993 and 1993–1994, he happened to notice what he felt were a series of suspicious expenditures. The Iranians openly listed figures for how much financial support they offered to Palestinian revolutionary organizations. That these expenditures were publicized at all was not especially shocking to Clawson. By the standards of other Middle East nations, Clawson found Iran to be far more open with information than many Western nations thought. In the course of monitoring Iranian newspapers and radio reports, for instance, Clawson discovered that Iranian officials—especially members of the Iranian Parliament—openly discussed allocations for various revolutionary causes. Beginning in 1992, Clawson decided to pay close attention to Iran's support for Palestinian Islamic Jihad—in particular the faction run by Fathi Shaqaqi.

Clawson started to connect the dots. Iran's government was dominated by Shiism, the Islamic branch that had embraced suicide bombing as a form of martyrdom. Until the 1990s, Palestinians, who largely adhered to the Sunni branch of Islam that banned suicide as a form of martyrdom, had not been involved in suicide attacks. But as the 1990s unfolded and especially after hundreds of Palestinian operatives from Hamas and Palestinian Islamic Jihad were deported to camps in Lebanon run by the Iranian-supported Hezbollah group and its Shiite followers, Clawson noticed a shift in terrorist tactics. More Palestinian militants were choosing to volunteer as suicide bombers. Was this linked to Iran and its Shiite theology of martydom?

Clawson figured the Iranians were playing some sort of role in this sharp change in Palestinian strategy. While other analysts figured the shift was largely theological—from a Sunni-based spirituality, which banned suicide as a form of martyrdom, to Shiism, which honored it—Clawson saw clear monetary connections. If Iran was making significant financial gifts each year to the cause of Palestinian liberation, would it be too much of a leap of logic to assume that Iran could be held responsible for Palestinian terrorism attacks?

Clawson felt such a link was not only logical but deeply dangerous, with profound potential consequences for the future of peace between the Israelis and Palestinians. If Iran was promoting suicide terrorism by Palestinians, surely that would loom as an impediment to the Oslo peace accords and the roadmap for peace.

By the mid-1990s, Clawson still had trouble finding a friendly audience for his concerns about Iran's meddling in the Israeli-Palestinian conflict. It's not that US and Israeli intelligence analysts were unaware of Iran and Shiite theology of martyrdom. Certainly, US Ambassador Martin Indyk felt that Iran was attempting to disrupt the Oslo process and even play a greater role in Palestinian strategy. And when called as an expert to testify before a variety of Congressional committees, Clawson found that he was invariably asked about the growing influence of Iran. But many officials in the US and in Israel still believed that the Palestinian leadership would steer clear of too much influence by Iran. After all, even the most radical elements of Hamas and Palestinian Islamic Jihad had deeper roots in Egypt's Muslim Brotherhood and its Sunni-based theology. And among Sunni Muslims, Iranian's Shiite-based politics was largely distrusted.

If that was the case, however, why would the Palestinians accept Iranian money for their "liberation"? Why would more Palestinian terrorists embrace the Shiite-based theology of suicide martyrdom?

Clawson discovered plenty of evidence in Iran's budget. Besides the expenditures specifically earmarked to the Palestinian revolution, Clawson found signs of a variety of other payments that were not as clearly defined. These included what Clawson assumed to be allocations to families of suicide bombers and the funding of the organizational infrastructure of the terror groups, including salaries for its members. Finally, Clawson found other funds that were given to Palestinian charitable groups with ties to the terror groups.

He was not satisfied. "We can assume that those figures may have been an understatement, that there were also secret accounts, what we call in the US government 'black accounts,'" Clawson later said.

Next, Clawson studied reports from other intelligence services, including the US, Israel, Egypt, Jordan, and Lebanon. What he found was a broad consensus of opinion that Iran was certainly contributing money to Palestinian terrorist groups.

Clawson came up with an estimate, or a range of amounts. But even his lowest estimate was far higher than the $2 million to $3 million cited by Kenneth McKune in his letter to Len Eisenfeld.

Clawson figured the Iranians were donating between $50 million and $100 million a year to all Palestinian revolutionary activities—with about $75 million earmarked directly for terrorism.

Despite his careful reasoning and meticulous research, Clawson had trouble gaining the attention of American and Israeli intelligence analysts or even the most anti-Iranian political figures in the federal government. In the mid-1990s, most of Israel's focus was on Yasser Arafat and the Palestinian Authority—the governmental power in the Gaza Strip and within the West Bank—with the belief that the Oslo peace process might finally resolve the Israeli-Palestinian conflict. Hamas and Palestinian Islamic Jihad, the primary groups receiving money from Iran, were considered dangerous, but certainly not as fearsome as they would become. Clawson discovered that even those American officials who distrusted Iran were not so alarmed at the growth of Iranian financial support in Palestinian affairs. "Why would they?" Clawson said. "If you shoved a complete and detailed report under the noses of many intelligence officials, they would have probably ignored it."

But Clawson found at least one person in Washington willing to pay attention to his concerns about Iran.

In early 1997, Steve Perles contacted Clawson and told him he was planning to file a lawsuit on behalf of Stephen Flatow against Iran, based on the newly enacted legislation signed by President Clinton.

Clawson did not like the new law. As a scholar, with a particular focus on international economics, he feared, as others did, that filing lawsuits against foreign governments could set off a chain of retributions against America and its overseas properties. In studying Iran, Clawson remembered all too well how the Iranian hostage crisis crippled the US government. Would the Iranians—or other foreign nations—seize other US property or even the private holdings of American citizens as retaliation against lawsuits?

Clawson preferred that international disputes, including questions of terrorism, be handled by diplomats or, in the worst cases, by military intervention. "Instruments of statecraft are more appropriate and effective than the courts," he said.

Nevertheless, Clawson agreed to help Perles.

Just after one o'clock in the afternoon of the second—and final—day of testimony in Flatow's lawsuit, Patrick Clawson took the witness seat in Judge Lamberth's courtroom. After guiding Clawson through his extensive academic credentials and the fact that he focused much of his attention on reading Iranian newspapers as well as almost any Iranian government document he can get his hands on, Tom Fay asked Judge Lamberth to accept Clawson as an expert on Iran's link to Palestinian terrorism.

Lamberth agreed.

Minutes later, Fay got to the heart of what he wanted Clawson to discuss. "Have you done a study also of the extent of Iranian financial support generally for terrorism during this 1995 period?" Fay asked.

"Yes, sir," Clawson said.

Clawson outlined the various pathways by which Iran funnels money to Palestinian groups. He then described his sources of information, which ranged from "the Iranians themselves" to statements made by terrorist groups and reports by a variety of intelligence agencies in the US, Israel, Egypt, Jordan, and Lebanon. Finally, he cited some numbers, the dollars that Iran contributes to terrorism.

On the low end, Clawson estimated "around $50 million a year." But because the contributions from Iran to terrorism often rose and fell with the ebbs and flows of the Iranian economy, Clawson said the figure was often higher. "I've never seen anything above $200 million," he cautioned. Within those high-low parameters, Clawson found that the "usual range of estimate that's given is $50 million to $100 million a year"—with an annual average of about $75 million.

Fay paused. On its face, this was an astonishingly high figure for the Iranians to contribute to the Palestinians. With his measured tone and precise style, Clawson had produced what Fay—and Perles and Flatow—hoped would be a key link in showing that Iran played a major role in Alisa's death. Clawson had not been able to show that Iran specifically ordered the bombing of Alisa's bus. Nor had he shown that Iranian money paid for the bomb that killed her. But Clawson's message was undeniably strong: Without Iran's money, Palestinian militants might never have been able to build the bombs that killed Alisa and others in terrorist attacks. What's more, the Iranian financial contributions to Palestinian terrorist activities were so high that they demanded some sort of response, even if Iranian operatives played no direct role in Alisa's death.

In citing those dollar figures, however, Clawson had also provided Judge Lamberth with a general framework for awarding damages to the Flatow family—if, of course, Lamberth concluded that the case for Iranian complicity was clear.

Fay then turned to another line of questions: Would Iran change its terrorist activities in the face of economic pressure?

Fay's implication was clear. A major goal of the Flatow lawsuit was not just to punish Iran for one bombing but to impose a large enough financial penalty that Iran would change its ways and stop funding other terrorist activities, not just among the Palestinians but elsewhere, too.

Clawson cited two examples of how Iran changed its policies in the face of financial pressure. The first was the seizure of American hostages at the Iranian embassy in 1979 and diplomatic discussions of how they would be released. "The issue which quickly became the centerpiece of negotiations was money and exactly how much money would Iran get back that the United States had frozen," Clawson said. The second example was the seizure of US hostages during the 1980s in Lebanon. "What quickly became the centerpiece of Iranian demands was US action on frozen assets," Clawson said.

In return for gaining the release of the embassy hostages, Clawson said, the US government paid Iran "on the order of $8 billion" in Iranian assets that had been frozen after the hostages were seized. In return for the release of the US hostages who had been seized in Lebanon, Clawson said that Iran received "several hundred million dollars." But he noted that the payment was not the amount that the Iranians had hoped for.

Fay paused again, then turned to Clawson.

"In your opinion, and again within a reasonable degree of certainty, is it valid to take this experience as a starting point from which this court, or anyone considering the question, may consider the appropriate amount which would deter Iran from further actions such as the action at Kfar Darom in which Alisa Flatow was killed?"

"Well, certainly," Clawson said. "I would say that these two episodes illustrate a pattern of behavior in which Iran has been responsive to monetary concerns."

Clawson's message was undeniable: For Iran, money talks. But how much would it take for Iran to pay attention?

Perles and Fay knew that they not only had to show how much money Iran contributes to terrorist activities, or, at least, to put forth a believable estimate, they also had to offer a framework that Judge Lamberth could use in determining how large Iran's financial penalty should be.

Fay returned to Clawson's earlier estimate that Iran contributes an average of $75 million each year to Palestinian terror. It was a critical moment, a not-so-subtle turning point. Fay knew that in any personal injury trial, especially one involving a negligent death, that he had to offer the judge an idea of what that financial penalty might be, not only as a proper punishment but as a potential deterrent. If the monetary figure was too high, a judge might disregard it—and reject other key testimony as being too exaggerated. A low figure might open the door to a paltry ruling.

"Doctor, can you give us an opinion with regard to a multiple of $75 million you've estimated as the bill, the tab for terrorism by the Iranian government, which then might deter Iran from further action?" Fay asked Clawson.

"Well," said Clawson, "the higher the multiple, the more sure we can be that they will be deterred. In other words, if you tell me that the multiple is going to be ten, I can tell you that I'm going to be extremely confident that the Iranians are deterred. If you tell me that the multiple is only going to be one, I would say, well, I don't know. You're running a much higher risk."

Fay pressed on: "What, in your opinion as an expert, seems reasonable?"

Clawson delicately mentioned two scenarios. In doing so, he waved a nuanced flag of caution. Penalizing Iran "with a multiple that's more in a range of two to five" times the $75 million allocated for terrorism would be effective—in effect, a financial penalty of $150 million to $375 million for killing a US citizen. Such a penalty "would really change the debate in Iran about whether this is worthwhile doing—this being attacking Americans." Then, Clawson switched gears.

"If you ask me what it's going to take to deter Iran from engaging in any terrorist attacks, I'm going to tell you it's going to take a whole lot more," Clawson said. "Then you're going to have to have a much higher sum because then you're establishing a much more ambitious target. To get Iran to desist from all of its terrorist actions is going to require showing Iran that there's a very high price it's paying for these terrorist actions."

Fay pressed harder: "What are we talking about in terms of a multiple there?"

"Oh, I would think that a multiple of ten is much more likely necessary to deter Iran from carrying out all terrorist actions," Clawson responded.

Fay did not ask Clawson for a specific dollar figure; there was no need. The message that Fay delicately guided Clawson to deliver was clear: With Iran, as with so many other nations, money can be an effective way to send a message. But when it comes to terrorism, the size of a penalty matters too.

Fay announced that he had no further questions.

At this point in most trials, a defense lawyer would normally step forward to cross-examine Clawson and attempt to undermine or at least weaken the impact of his testimony. With no lawyer for Iran in the courtroom, however, Fay's acknowledgment that he had no other questions to ask was essentially a signal that Clawson's testimony was over.

Before Clawson could leave the witness stand, however, Judge Lamberth interrupted: "If the court were to enter a judgment in the multiples you're talking about in terms of punitive damages, how do you think that would be viewed by Iran?"

In some trials, judges send signals on what they are thinking about a case. Certainly, Lamberth was not afraid to interject himself into the trial's testimony with an occasional question, sometimes to merely clarify a point that a witness had made or perhaps to understand a lawyer's question more clearly. But Lamberth's question to Clawson was a clear indication of the critical issue he was weighing: Lamberth had the power to impose a heavy punishment on Iran, but would Iran pay attention and change its ways?

Clawson seemed ready for the question.

"I think the Iranians would view any judgment by this Court as being politically motivated," Clawson said.

Clawson's answer was not surprising. The Flatow trial may have been presented by Steve Perles and Tom Fay as the equivalent of an ordinary civil lawsuit involving the negligent death of a young woman who only wanted to take a bus to the beach. But, as Clawson and others noted, the implications of the Flatow case involved a complicated array of political issues, many of them framed by the long-standing mutual distrust between Iran and the United States.

Clawson was not finished.

The Iranians, he said, would likely view a ruling by Lamberth and a heavy financial penalty "as another bargaining chip that would be used by the United States in the discussions with the Iranians about the settlement of the mutual disputes between the two parties." In other words, Alisa Flatow and the lawsuit by her family might be just another political footnote in a more complicated diplomatic arena.

Clawson said that the Iranians had already filed complaints in the International Court of Justice against what they felt was improper behavior by the United States, including an attack by the US military on an offshore Iranian oil platform after a mine, planted by Iran in Persian Gulf shipping lanes, damaged a US oil tanker. Without addressing their responsibility for planting a mine in a crowded shipping lane, the Iranians nonetheless claimed in their case to the International Court of Justice that the attack on their oil platform violated a treaty signed years earlier.

Clawson said the Iranians would see any ruling by Lamberth as a shrewd attempt by the US government to create a bargaining chip that could be used by American lawyers to persuade the Iranians to drop their case before the International Court of Justice. Or as Clawson noted, "We'll drop that if you drop your" International Court of Justice case.

Clawson's message was both cautionary and factual. In mentioning the ICJ cases and the array of international legal disputes between the United States and Iran, he was pointing out that the Flatow lawsuit was not so simple. Then again, he said, a clear message in the form of a heavy financial punishment in a ruling from Judge Lamberth would not be ignored by the Iranians either.

"I think that this sort of punitive damages would cause the Iranian government to think twice about the advisability of targeting American citizens," Clawson said. Iran would probably not stop all terrorist activities, but it might stop attacks on US citizens. "To the extent that we have the very limited purpose of stopping attacks on American citizens, we might well be able to accomplish that through this kind of an action, without necessarily accomplishing the overall political goal, say, of the United States government deterring Iranian terrorism."

Lamberth still was not satisfied.

"But you think they would not just ignore this as a piece of paper?" The judge asked. Or would Iran take note of "the assumed threat" in any ruling "that there would be further judgments if they continued to kill other Americans?"

It was a logical and understandable question. Would a ruling by the judge force Iran to change its ways?

Once again, Clawson offered a nuanced prognosis: "The Iranian leadership is very much, by orientations, sensitive to bargaining techniques and bargaining chips that people can bring to bear."

Lamberth listened intently. When Clawson finished, the judge asked, "So if you were sitting here advising the court, do you think it's something I should do?"

The question was not inappropriate or flippant. As the Flatow trial progressed, Lamberth wondered whether he was presiding over a case that was more symbol than substance. Yes, judges' rulings are often interpreted as sending messages to the larger society about the impact of serious crimes. Certainly Lamberth knew that. But like many experienced judges, he also knew that his fundamental task was to reach a conclusion that was not empty of meaning or power.

Clawson shared Lamberth's concerns. On one hand, a strong decision by Lamberth, accompanied by a substantial penalty, could stop some attacks on US citizens. But it would probably not stop all terrorist attacks by Iran.

"I think we have to decide very specifically what it is we want to deter and have a clear concept of what it is that this law and that these punitive damages are designed to do," Clawson said.

Patrick Clawson's testimony was strong. But Fay and Perles felt it would be stronger if another expert could corroborate Clawson's central conclusions—that Iran not only contributed large sums of money to terrorist groups but that it was closely involved with Palestinian Islamic Jihad, which was responsible for killing Alisa Flatow. Clawson was knowledgeable but he was an academic and Perles and Fay believed they needed a witness with tangible experience in tracking terrorists. After Clawson left the witness stand, Fay called Harry Brandon, the former chief of counterterrorism and intelligence at the FBI.

Brandon retired from the FBI in 1993 after a twenty-three-year career. Unlike most FBI agents who spend their careers specializing in some of the bureau's more conventional crime-solving investigations, such as bank robberies and political corruption, Brandon developed an early expertise in counterterrorism and in particular the gathering of intelligence on foreign groups that might try to attack American targets overseas or inside the United States.

Within the tradition-bound FBI, where promotions were often awarded to agents who brought major cases to trial, gathering intelligence on potential terrorists was sometimes considered a dead-end career. Information was difficult to collect and was often so murky that it was useless if the government managed to bring a case to trial. But Brandon happened to enter the counterterrorism field just as Islamic terrorism was becoming a major geopolitical force.

Before he left the FBI in 1993 to form his own private security consulting firm, Brandon led the FBI's counterterrorism division for two years and was a key player in the bureau's investigation of the 1993 attack on the World Trade Center in New York City by Islamic militants who had worshipped at a mosque in Jersey City, New Jersey.

Stephen Flatow knew the mosque well. It was located only a few blocks from his Jersey City title search firm. And, the mere proximity of a mosque where jihadist theology had been openly discussed was deeply unsettling to Flatow and a reminder of how vulnerable he had come to feel.

Fay wasted little time addressing a critical element of Brandon's expertise. "Are you able to give us an estimate, within a reasonable degree of certainty, as to the amount spent upon terrorism by the government of Iran?" Fay asked.

"Specifics are difficult," Brandon cautioned before offering a figure that was remarkably similar to that given by Patrick Clawson.

"My estimate would be in the neighborhood of $100 million per year, supporting various terrorist movements," Brandon said.

Fay wanted Brandon to be more definitive. He asked about Palestinian Islamic Jihad—notably the so-called "Shaqaqi Faction" that had claimed responsibility for the bombing that killed Alisa Flatow.

"The leaders of the Shaqaqi faction were philosophically aligned with the politics of Iran. That was what I would characterize as a 'take no prisoners approach,' direct, open use of terrorism as state policy and the Shaqaqi faction was an arm of that," Brandon said. "The government of Iran supported them directly, as they did others, including Hezbollah, their nearby neighbors, supported them in terms of training, supported them in terms of equipment and certainly in terms of money."

Fay moved to another issue he had already explored with Clawson. Would a heavy financial penalty deter Iran from supporting terrorists such as the Shaqaqi faction?

"Yes, I think so," Brandon said. "When you take away resources, something has to give."

Fay had one more topic to examine, one that he had not raised with Patrick Clawson. The Flatow lawsuit not only targeted the Islamic Republic of Iran, but three of its most prominent leaders, in particular Iran's supreme leader, Ayatollah Ali Hosseini Khamenei.

"In a decision of this magnitude," Fay said, describing the Iranian support for terrorism against Israel that resulted in the death of Alisa Flatow, "would this, of necessity, have to be cleared by Mr. Khamenei?"

Harry Brandon did not offer a nuanced answer—or even one filled with complicated facts.

"Yes," he said. "Absolutely, without question. He approved this."

—~—

Eight days later, the Flatow family returned to Judge Lamberth's courtroom with their lawyers. Perles and Fay felt confident that Lamberth would rule in their favor. Their main concern was the size of the penalty against Iran. As he sat down, Perles whispered to Tom Fay: "I hope we get at least a million."

Judge Lamberth had prepared a sixty-page memorandum. But he reduced his ruling to only six pages. He needed only eight minutes to read it.

Lamberth summarized the case. He ruled that law which allowed Flatow to file his wrongful death lawsuit against Iran was constitutional. Then, he got to the crux—assigning responsibility for the death of Alisa Flatow.

"The death of the decedent was caused by the actions of the Islamic Republic of Iran," the judge said.

Next, Lamberth addressed an equally consequential question: How to punish Iran?

Lamberth began with the basic issues of any wrongful death case. He established that the "economic loss" resulting from Alisa Flatow's early death amounted to slightly more than $1.5 million. He also ordered Iran to pay another $1 million for the suffering and pain Alisa experienced before she died.

Lamberth then turned to Alisa's parents, her three sisters, and her brother. "The amount of pain and suffering of the decedent's parents and siblings is difficult to value," he conceded. Nonetheless, Lamberth found a case in Texas that set a benchmark of $5 million. So he ordered Iran to pay $5 million to Stephen Flatow and another $5 million to his wife, Rosalyn, along with $2.5 million to each of Alisa's three sisters and her brother.

While the damage amounted to more than $22 million so far, Lamberth was not through.

"The court also has determined that an award of punitive damages is appropriate," Lamberth said, noting his belief that a "monetary sanction against Iran will have some impact on their continuing to sponsor terrorist acts."

Without pausing, as perhaps an actor in a play or movie might do to allow the weight of his next statement to sink in, he continued matter of factly. "The court is determined to award $225,000,000 in punitive damages against the Islamic Republic of Iran."

Coupled with the $20 million in compensatory damages, the total was nearly a quarter of a billion dollars.

Lamberth complimented Perles and Fay for their presentation. Then he looked at Stephen Flatow.

"This is a tragic case," Lamberth began. "But you have made something of it. You've tried to do something. . . . The Court has been quite impressed with what you have been able to accomplish here."

Next, Lamberth turned to the absent party—Iran.

"At some point, maybe Iran will come forward and we will have Iran here in the courtroom and we can deal with any legal arguments they want to make," Lamberth said. "I certainly will listen."

Lamberth again praised Flatow for doing "exactly what Congress has empowered him to do."

Lamberth noted that "this court has followed its duty" but he finished with a final thought about the unpredictable and violent world he had found himself and his courtroom suddenly drawn into.

"I hope that the rule of law can contribute ultimately to the solution of the problems presented in this case, where an innocent girl was needlessly killed, for no reason, in a way that doesn't support anything," Lamberth said. "It doesn't contribute to the Mideast peace process to kill an innocent girl like this and the court can not be stronger in condemning this kind of action. It has no place in a civilized society."

Steven Flatow listened quietly. He had taken a seat with Perles and Fay at the attorneys' table in front of Judge Lamberth. As the judge finished reading his ruling, Flatow clenched his fists and gently tapped the table. Then he looked heavenward.

He could feel Alisa's presence in the room. He smiled and whispered: "Yes, Alisa."

# CHAPTER 11

THE NEWS OF STEPHEN FLATOW'S LEGAL VICTORY—IN PARTICULAR, the penalty of nearly a quarter-billion dollars imposed by Judge Royce Lamberth against the Islamic Republic of Iran—galvanized Washington's legal community, especially the city's small cadre of attorneys who represented victims of terrorism. Suddenly, here was a potential gold mine for civil litigators. Or so it seemed.

If Flatow could successfully sue Iran for playing a role in the death of his daughter and win such a large judgment, who knew what might be possible? Of course, it still remained to be seen whether Flatow and his lawyers could actually collect money from Iran, either by submitting a direct claim to the Iranian government or gaining control of Iranian properties and financial assets within the United States.

For now, those details hardly seemed to matter. Dozens of US citizens who had been victimized by terrorism in various corners of the world suddenly felt empowered by what Flatow accomplished with Perles and Fay. Several Americans who had been taken hostage in Lebanon during the 1980s were planning imminent lawsuits, along with the families of other US citizens who had been killed in Israel, the West Bank, or the Gaza Strip in Palestinian attacks, including Arline Duker and Vicki and Len Eisenfeld.

Arline, Vicki, and Len had not only come to admire Flatow but saw him as just the sort of emotional and legal trailblazer they needed to propel them to seek justice in the deaths of their children. After Sara and Matthew were killed, the prospect of pushing ahead with a lawsuit—with all the unknown expenses—seemed overwhelming to Arline, Vicki, and Len, especially as they were coping with their own grief and anger. They devoted much of the previous two years to collecting research on Iran's connection to Palestinian terrorism. They also interviewed a variety of lawyers. But after watching Flatow's seemingly tireless crusade, they decided it was time to go to court, too. Two months after Judge Lamberth's ruling, Arline, Vicki, and Len hired Flatow's lawyers.

Another notable Washington lawyer, however, was not so impressed with the Flatow case or the impact it might have on other potential lawsuits, including one by Arline, Vicki, and Len. From his office at the US State Department, just over a mile from Judge Lamberth's courtroom, Stuart Eizenstat saw trouble in the Flatow decision—trouble for the White House, for his own State Department and its diplomats, for America's courts, even for the Flatow family and for others such as Arline Duker and Len and Vicki Eisenfeld who were considering similar lawsuits.

To Eizenstat, any attempt by Flatow and his lawyers—or even by Arline, Vicki, and Len—to take money from Iran could imperil US diplomacy overseas that extended far beyond Iran. If Flatow's lawyers managed to seize Iranian property within the United States, Eizenstat believed that would set off a chain reaction across the world, with all manner of nations, who had been suspected of supporting terrorism, grabbing control of American properties and essentially holding them as financial hostages in case US courts imposed heavy financial penalties on them.

On a personal level, Eizenstat felt torn. He knew that Iran and the United States had already agreed to work together with an international court to settle various claims that each nation had filed against the other. Yet Eizenstat, who was Jewish, sympathized greatly with Flatow and even admired his dogged efforts to hold Iran accountable for the death of Alisa.

To many Jews, the bus bombings that killed Alisa, Matthew, and Sara were nothing less than horrific acts of anti-Semitism. Eizenstat fully understood the legal and emotional arguments that Flatow's attorneys put forth. But as a lawyer and a State Department official, Eizenstat felt larger issues were at stake for the United States. He came to view the Flatow case and others as the equivalent of legal end-runs that could ultimately disrupt future negotiations between Iran and the United States and possibly with other nations. Instead of US diplomats using various financial claims against Iran as potential bargaining chips in negotiations on a variety of issues, from trade to Iran's support for international terrorism, American citizens like Stephen Flatow now entered into the already complicated situation. To Eizenstat, this was not good.

Oddly enough, Eizenstat's concerns mirrored to some degree those of Judge Royce Lamberth. Even though he had delivered a precedent-setting ruling in the Flatow case, Lamberth made no secret that he still worried that the law he applied had drawn America's federal courts into the arena of foreign policy in ways that could erode the constitutional power of the president.

Eizenstat felt he needed to stop Flatow and his lawyers before they went too far and before other lawyers followed with other cases on behalf of other victims such as Sara Duker and Matthew Eisenfeld.

But how?

Stephen Flatow's lawyers were not wasting time. Days after Judge Lamberth's ruling, Steve Perles and Tom Fay went back to court to begin the next step in their lawsuit—to collect the financial penalties or "damages" that had been imposed on the Islamic Republic of Iran.

On any day in the hundreds of federal, state, and municipal courthouses across America, lawyers on the winning side of lawsuits simply send a letter to the losers asking them to pay up. In this case, Perles and Fay faced an unusual opponent. They knew they could not simply send a bill of nearly $250 million to the Iranian government and expect to get a check in the mail. Iran had never responded to any aspect of the lawsuit. Certainly, Perles and Fay did not expect Iran to respond now. They concluded that their only option was to file a claim against Iran's financial and real estate holdings in the United States. Most of those assets had been seized, or "frozen," by the US government just after the 1979 Iranian revolution. To collect the damages that Judge Lamberth had ordered Iran to pay, Perles and Fay figured they would start with those frozen bank accounts and pieces of property, which included Iran's former embassy and other diplomatic buildings in Washington.

Looking for political leverage, they turned first to Senator Frank Lautenberg, the New Jersey democrat who had championed the legislation that allowed Flatow to file his lawsuit. Five weeks after Lambert's ruling, Lautenberg wrote to President Clinton, Secretary of State Madeleine Albright, and to Treasury Secretary Robert Rubin, asking for help in tracking down Iran's assets in the United States. Meanwhile, when Perles and Fay contacted the US Treasury Department on their own, and requested a list of Iranian holdings, Treasury officials told Perles and Fay that compiling such a list was too burdensome.

Lautenberg waited more than a month to hear from Clinton, Albright, and Rubin. When he did not get an answer, Lautenberg asked to talk with Vice President Al Gore. On June 10, as Lautenberg prepared to meet with Gore, a letter written by a mid-level official at the State Department arrived at Lautenberg's Washington office. The letter was respectful, but amid its bureaucratically polite and imprecise phrasing it foreshadowed the rhetorical battles that Flatow and others, including Arline Duker and Len and Vicki Eisenfeld, would encounter. While the letter was not written by Stuart Eizenstat, it reflected his concerns that the claim on Iranian assets that Flatow wanted to impose would circumvent a process before an international tribunal in which the United States and Iran were negotiating a large number of other claims dating back decades.

The letter noted that most Iranian bank assets and properties in America that had been frozen by the US government were already under litigation by other US citizens or businesses that had filed claims long before Flatow's. But, confusing the issue even more, the letter added that the government has "consistently advised that there are currently no Iranian assets held by or under the control of the United States government which could be used to pay claims against Iran."

After studying the letter, Lautenberg's staff drafted a two-page memo that included "talking points" for him to use in his discussion with Gore. The memo pointed out that President Clinton had the authority to personally intervene in Flatow's efforts to claim Iranian assets and noted that, in particular, Clinton had already said that frozen Cuban assets could be used to compensate the families of the Brothers to the Rescue pilots.

"They also won a court judgment under the antiterrorism statute," the memo said of the pilots who had been killed the day before Sara and Matt died in Jerusalem. "President Clinton should do the same for the Flatow family."

Lautenberg's memo next raised an issue that had nothing to do with terrorism but everything to do with the political wars between the

Clinton White House and Republicans in Congress. "This issue is going to become a hot political potato and the Republicans will soon be very critical of the administration," the memo said.

Lautenberg was in a political and personal bind. As a Democrat, he wanted to support Clinton as much as possible. But he also felt passionately that Flatow deserved to be compensated for the murder of his daughter. The senator understood the arguments on both sides of the issue, in particular the view by some officials in the White House and the State Department who believed that the frozen Iranian assets could be used as leverage in the ongoing, yet quiet, efforts to improve diplomatic relations between the US and Iran. But he was perplexed by the White House and wondered exactly what Clinton meant by his earlier promise to help American families pursue justice against terrorists. Was Clinton serious about his promise? If so, why was his administration pushing back so hard against Flatow?

Lautenberg's staff was aware of the potential political problems that could arise from the administration's reaction to Flatow's lawsuit. Already some Republicans were saying that the White House was flip-flopping, first supporting the lawsuits and now blocking efforts to collect damages In its internal memo, Lautenberg's staff pointed out that "the press is beginning to question whether the Administration is more interested in pursuing a dialogue with the Iranians than compensating victims of Iranian terrorism."

Lautenberg told Gore that he wanted to work with the president to find a solution to the Flatow lawsuit and avoid a confrontation with Republicans. But Lautenberg made it clear that if the White House would not cooperate with him and Flatow that he would not hold back his criticism of the president.

Perles and Fay, meanwhile, pursued a separate strategy. A month after Lautenberg met with Gore, they returned to Judge Lamberth's courtroom to formally ask for an order to enforce the ruling so they could file claims against Iran's financial and real estate holdings in the United States. It was July 7, 1998. Judge Lamberth signed the order. Two days later, a battery of US government attorneys walked into Lamberth's courtroom with a request for the judge to postpone his order. The government lawyers argued that seizing Iran's embassy would violate diplomatic protocols and wanted time to present their case.

Lamberth agreed to temporarily delay his order until the government's attorneys could formulate legal arguments to back up their side of the case. Iran's attorneys had still not come to Lamberth's courtroom. But lawyers working for the US government had achieved, perhaps inadvertently, what Iran wanted. For now, Flatow's mission to hold Iran accountable for Alisa's death had been shelved.

After the meeting between Gore and Lautenberg, Clinton wrote to Lautenberg, stating his desire to assist the Flatow family in obtaining justice. But Clinton was not specific. The president had not promised to release the Iranian assets that Flatow wanted. Nor had Clinton's Treasury Department bothered to answer Lautenberg's letter asking for help.

Lautenberg was frustrated. Since meeting Gore, he had decided to take a tougher stance with the White House on the Flatow issue. Lautenberg did not want to unnecessarily pressure the president because he knew Clinton was facing increased criticism from Republicans over revelations of his sexual affair with White House intern Monica Lewinsky. And while other Democrats, especially those in the Senate and House were trying to build a wall of unified support for Clinton amid the growing political maelstrom surrounding the Lewinsky controversy, Lautenberg knew that even the smallest criticism from him would not be taken well.

He didn't care. Throughout the spring of 1998, Lautenberg and his staff had grown frustrated with the foot-dragging and mixed messages from the White House and throughout the Clinton administration. Why would the president sign a bill in 1996 allowing US citizens to file lawsuits against terrorist nations and two years later try to hinder one of the most passionate and articulate of those citizens from trying to collect financial damages? Lautenberg considered himself a loyal Democrat. But he considered Stephen Flatow a victim who also was his constituent in New Jersey. Lautenberg had achieved great wealth in private business as the owner of a data processing firm, yet he often approached difficult issues such as this with the basic values and street smarts that he learned while growing up during the Great Depression in

Paterson, New Jersey, tenements. To Lautenberg, White House behavior on the Flatow matter made little sense. Even worse, he believed it was fundamentally unjust.

The day before Lamberth ordered a temporary halt to Flatow's efforts to retrieve financial penalties from Iran, Lautenberg sat down with one of President Clinton's closest aides, Sandy Berger. Samuel Richard "Sandy" Berger had known Bill Clinton since 1972, when the two met as operatives on the ill-fated Democratic presidential campaign of George McGovern to unseat incumbent Republican Richard Nixon. Berger, now fifty-two, had become a foreign policy expert within the Clinton administration. During Clinton's first term, he served as a deputy national security advisor. Now, in Clinton's second term, Berger had been promoted to the president's top national security advisor.

After reminding Berger that Clinton had ordered the Treasury Department to release frozen Cuban assets to each of the families of the Brothers to the Rescue pilots, Lautenberg proposed a solution. If the president does not feel he has the specific authority to grant permission for Flatow to claim some portion of Iranian assets in the United States, Lautenberg could draft generalized legislation that would give the president the power to remove government protections from blocked or "frozen" assets of countries designated as state sponsors of terrorism, but only to make them available to US citizens who had been victimized by terrorism. As part of a memorandum to help Lautenberg prepare for the meeting with Berger, the senator's staff wrote, "if the United States government can come to the aid of the American families of Cuban-American victims who were killed by the military and not killed in a terrorist attack, it should come to the aid of an American family of the innocent victim of an Iranian terrorist attack."

The memo concluded with a suggestion that Lautenberg wanted to stress to Berger: "I really am hoping that the Administration can be more responsive. This is very important to me. If the President lacks authority to release these funds, then I'd like to have your support if I seek to give him that authority."

Nine days later, Lautenberg met again with Sandy Berger at the White House. This time, he brought Stephen Flatow and Steve Perles. The meeting lasted only thirty minutes, and, to Flatow, Lautenberg seemed frustrated.

Lautenberg again mentioned what he felt was the discrepancy in how the Cuban-American families of the pilots had been compensated with previously frozen Cuban assets while Flatow had been blocked from putting a claim on Iranian properties in the United States or frozen Iranian bank accounts. Lautenberg also explained that two days earlier he had proposed an amendment to the annual Treasury appropriations bill that would give families of terrorist victims the right to seize blocked assets of state sponsors of terrorism. But Lautenberg's amendment contained a loophole that gave the president the right to decline to release frozen assets if he felt America's national security might be placed in jeopardy. As with his previous meeting with Berger, Lautenberg had asked his senate staff to prepare a memo containing proposed "talking points." Like the memo Lautenberg's staff assembled for that first meeting, the memo for the second meeting with Berger concluded ominously: "I hope that the administration will not allow this issue to become a political tool for the Republicans."

Within the tight-knit world of the Clinton administration, where politics was inevitably part of almost every discussion about policy, it became the job of Stuart Eizenstat to negotiate a solution that would satisfy Flatow's desire to hold Iran accountable, yet not create a legal and diplomatic precedent that would derail America's ability to conduct foreign affairs. To be sure, it was a delicate strategy. Eizenstat had to deter Flatow without making it seem that the Clinton administration was opposing Flatow's efforts to hold terrorists accountable for murdering his daughter. The political stakes were enormous and potentially embarrassing for the White House.

By the summer of 1998, as the legal and political ramifications of Lamberth's ruling rippled through the White House, Congress, and throughout the sprawling federal bureaucracy, Eizenstat held the title of Under Secretary of State for Economic, Business and Agricultural Affairs. But his reputation for tackling some of the federal government's thorniest problems and navigating Washington's political tempests extended far beyond his work at the State Department.

Raised in Atlanta, where he was educated in the city's public schools, Eizenstat went on to the University of North Carolina and then earned a law degree from Harvard University. After finishing law school and a clerkship for a federal judge, Eizenstat headed for Washington where he landed a job as a research director for Vice President Hubert Humphrey. He quickly moved into the White House as part of President Lyndon Johnson's staff where he became known for his meticulous analysis of complicated political and policy issues—and, perhaps most notably, his ability to foresee future problems from a variety of perspectives.

By the mid-1970s, Eizenstat, still in his early thirties, had caught the attention of a fellow Georgian with presidential aspirations, Governor Jimmy Carter. As Carter formally launched his presidential campaign, he looked to Eizenstat to become the policy director. After Carter's victory in 1976 over incumbent president Gerald Ford, Eizenstat served four years as the White House chief domestic policy advisor. It was a difficult and unpredictable time for anyone to take on that job, but Eizenstat gained respect for his insight and thoroughness, especially his analysis of how the nation's economic downturn affected women. He was one of the first government officials to draw attention to what he described as the "feminization of poverty."

By the 1990s, Eizenstat had turned his focus to international issues. For him, it was the kind of switch that underscored his ability to quickly gain expertise—and respect—in a variety of subjects. Called back to government service with the election of Bill Clinton, Eizenstat became adept at handling trade agreements, climate change debates and even negotiations for reparations on behalf of Holocaust victims.

During the first three years of Clinton's presidency, Eizenstat served as the US ambassador to the European Union. In 1996, he returned to Washington as Under Secretary of Commerce for International Trade and moved a year later to his post at the State Department, specializing in US sanctions against foreign governments and the worldwide impact of American economic policy. Beginning with his job as the American ambassador to the European Union, Eizenstat found himself in the middle of a fifty-year-old question that no other American official, or international figure, had been able to resolve: how to justly compensate victims of the Nazi Holocaust.

Eizenstat came to refer to the lingering Holocaust issue as "the unfinished business of the twentieth century." He had lost relatives in the Holocaust, so he had a personal link to the issue. But as he had done with other policy issues earlier in his career, Eizenstat set aside his personal passion and approached the problem with a researcher's meticulousness. He assembled a vast amount of information that not only defined the size and depth of the problem but helped point him toward a wide-ranging series of settlements to help compensate victims.

Eizenstat discovered, for instance, long-dormant Swiss bank accounts of Jews who had been murdered by the Nazis. He tracked down millions of dollars worth of property that had been wrongly confiscated from Jewish families across Europe and never returned to them. He found paintings, once owned by Jews, among the estimated six hundred thousand works of art stolen by the Nazis that had been hanging in art museums, with no one bothering to ask where they came from. He even lent support to efforts—including one by Hugo Princz—to hold German businesses accountable for their profits from slave labor by Jewish workers during World War II. Eizenstat's work was so extensive and relentless that an editorial in the *New York Times* praised his attempts to "explore the dark corners of history."

With the Flatow case, Eizenstat was not probing inaccessible corners as much as trying to find his way down a path that was filled with numerous political, legal, and emotional pitfalls. With lawyers planning to file other cases, Eizenstat knew he had to act swiftly. "There was a steamroller here," Eizenstat said. "Congress had created a right without a remedy. Congress had said you could file a lawsuit for terrorism against a foreign country, but it did not say how you could collect. Instead Congress cast the burden back on the executive branch. It really raised expectations and put the executive branch in an extremely awkward position."

But Eizenstat soon faced another nettlesome, unforeseen dilemma in President Bill Clinton's own words and deeds. Eizenstat knew that Clinton had already voiced support for cases like Flatow's when he signed the law allowing antiterror lawsuits. Separately, Clinton had also raised the possibility that the compensation for victims could come from bank accounts and other terrorist nation assets that had been frozen by the US government. But now, it seemed as if Clinton's own State Department was siding with Iran against American citizens. Legally and politically, the strategy appeared confusing, even ridiculous. To Eizenstat, this was just the sort of conflicting message that inevitably embarrassed political leaders. The timing was bad, too. Adding to the dilemma, Bill Clinton was in the midst of battling allegations about his sexual affair with a White House intern. Republicans in Congress had already launched an impeachment investigation.

But with the Flatow case, the political and legal dilemma for Eizenstat was even more complicated. Clinton and Flatow seemed to have established a positive and personal rapport. The president not only consoled Flatow for his loss but never hinted that his lawsuit was troubling.

Besides Clinton's telephone call to Flatow in Israel after Alisa's death, the two had spoken several times afterwards. In one instance, Flatow asked Clinton for help in determining which terrorist group was responsible for Alisa's death. Shortly afterward, Flatow and his lawyers were invited to the State Department, where they said officials told them that Iran had provided money to Palestinian Islamic Jihad, which carried out the bombing. While Flatow was never entirely sure that Clinton helped to arrange the State Department meeting (Clinton never said one way or the other), Flatow had come to believe the president was on his side and had opened an important door for his legal team to assemble important evidence against Iran.

Just before he filed his lawsuit, Flatow happened to meet Clinton again. Flatow told the president of his plans to take Iran to court. Clinton did not seem surprised, Flatow recalled. "I know what you're doing," Flatow remembers the president telling him. "You're brave and courageous."

Clinton and Flatow had not spoken since Lamberth's ruling. But now, as he began to feel the full weight of the State Department's challenge to his claim against Iran, Flatow decided to publicly criticize Clinton. In an interview on the CBS newsmagazine *60 Minutes*, Flatow was asked what he would say to the president if he had another chance to speak to him. Flatow said he would ask Clinton a question:

"What are you doing to me?"

⌒

Several months after Judge Lamberth's decision, and as criticism against President Clinton continued to build, Stuart Eizenstat asked to meet with Flatow.

Eizenstat's office at the State Department was located in a section of Washington known as "Foggy Bottom." But the neighborhood's nickname had little to do with the occasionally obscure messages that emanated from the State's legions of diplomatic experts. Long before Washington had become lined with elegant buildings, statues, and museums, "Foggy Bottom" was known mostly for the persistent mist that drifted off the Potomac River and shrouded the area's streets.

Flatow was accompanied by his lawyers, Steve Perles and Tom Fay, as well as a staffer from Senator Lautenberg's office. Eisenstat ushered the group into a conference room with a large horseshoe-shaped table. Flatow sat down on one side with Perles and Fay; Eizenstat and his staff took seats on the other side.

As he prepared himself to meet Eizenstat, Flatow decided to try to set a friendly tone. Flatow had made no secret of his disappointment that the Clinton administration had dispatched its lawyers to Judge Lamberth's courtroom to stall his legal judgment against Iran. But as a lawyer familiar with the give-and-take of negotiations, Flatow figured that Eizenstat might be willing to help find a compromise that would penalize Iran and also protect US diplomatic interests. And so, Flatow hoped the meeting would not be confrontational. "You catch more flies with honey than with vinegar," he thought as he thanked Eizenstat for inviting him to the State Department.

Eizenstat, however, seemed in no mood to compromise. He began by reiterating his belief that Flatow's lawsuit could damage the ability of the State Department to conduct diplomatic relations overseas.

Flatow understood the argument. He reminded Eizenstat that his daughter, Alisa, had been murdered in an act of terrorism—and that a US

District Court judge had ruled that a country officially labeled by the US government as a "state sponsor of terrorism" was complicit.

Eizenstat did not try to disagree. "If I was the father of a daughter who was blown up, I would want compensation," Eizenstat said years later as he reflected on the meeting. "He lost his daughter. It's impossible not to be sympathetic. But when you are in office, you have to look at broader issues."

As the two men faced each other across the horseshoe, it was almost as if they were speaking about two different worlds. Flatow wanted assurances that his government was on his side. Eizenstat, representing that government, made no secret of his belief that larger political, diplomatic, and legal issues were at stake.

Eizenstat knew, for instance, that Flatow was merely the first of a long list of victims who would want to tap into Iran's frozen assets—or into the assets of other nations, such as Cuba and Libya, that had also been designated as sponsors of terrorism. Not only did Eizenstat fear the backlash against American-owned properties in other nations if the victims' families gained control of the frozen assets, but he felt he was playing a difficult game of arithmetic that neither he nor President Clinton could win. "Politically, there was tremendous support for paying the families," Eizenstat said. "They had won court judgments. But the problem was we didn't have enough frozen assets to be able to satisfy the judgments."

As the discussion volleyed back and forth, Steve Perles, who had been listening quietly, found himself becoming angry. He felt that the tone set by Eizenstat was not that of a negotiation. To Perles, it seemed more akin to a lecture and a subtle defense of President Clinton's mixed messages on the issue of compensating victims of terrorism. "I knew what this was about," Perles thought. "This was about a Jewish guy from the administration delivering a message to another Jewish guy."

Perles felt the urge to interject, but held back. So what, he thought, if Flatow displeased Bill Clinton? The news was awash with stories about Clinton's sexual dalliances with Monica Lewinsky, and a rising call on Capitol Hill for impeachment.

"It's only Bill Clinton," Perles remembered thinking. "He has his Lewinsky problems. He's going to be impeached in a couple of months anyway."

Finally, Perles spoke. He mentioned Judge Lamberth's ruling and said that he and Fay planned to pursue their quest to compensate Flatow with Iranian assets.

"I have a duty to the Flatow family," Perles said.

Eizenstat, the veteran negotiator, understood. As the meeting ended, Eizenstat asked his staff to give two cardboard boxes of files to Flatow. The files contained listings of Iranian government properties that had not been frozen by the US government. Perhaps Flatow could file claims against these Iranian-owned assets and collect a portion of his judgment.

Flatow was elated. Perles was cautious, as was Tom Fay.

As Perles left, one of the congressional staffers who watched the meeting, said, "Feel better now?"

The meeting with Eizenstat had been testy. But perhaps a partial solution to their troubles might be found in the boxes from Eizenstat.

As they rode back across Washington in a taxi, Perles and Fay began looking through the files.

"They were useless," Perles said.

---

Along with Vicki and Len Eisenfeld, Arline Duker had been following Flatow's battles with the Clinton administration. In the two years since Sara and Matthew had been killed, the families had grown closer, and the prospect of mounting a legal case had been cathartic in some ways, yet also distressing.

"You're always thinking about it," said Vicki.

Even as they watched Flatow confront the legal and political road-blocks that emerged after Judge Lamberth's ruling, Arline, Vicki, and Len felt energized. On August 10, 1998, they formally filed their lawsuit against the Islamic Republic of Iran for the wrongful deaths of Sara and Matt. Their legal strategy was similar to Flatow's in many respects. Iran was cited as the primary financier and some of the witnesses who testified in Flatow's case, including Patrick Clawson, had agreed to appear on their behalf.

Thirteen days later, however, Arline, Vicki, and Len received an unexpected gift that would strengthen their case in ways they never expected.

Hassan Salameh, whose name had only seemed like a brief footnote in the letter more than a year earlier from State Department counter-terrorism director Kenneth McKune, had decided to speak publicly. In an interview from prison, broadcast on the CBS newsmagazine *60 Minutes* for a segment entitled "Suicide Bomber," Salameh described how he orchestrated the bombing of the Number 18 bus on Jaffa Road.

Salameh drew a diagram of the bomb he assembled. He described why he chose the Number 18 bus and how he recruited the bomber, Majdi Abu Wardeh, from the al-Fawwar refugee camp. Much of what Salameh said mirrored his confession to Israeli authorities and the evidence presented at his trial before the military court in Beit El.

But until that point, Arline, Vicki and Len knew nothing about Salameh's confession or his trial. No one had ever told them.

Vicki happened to be watching *60 Minutes*.

"Oh, my God," she said. "That's the guy who did it."

# CHAPTER 12

SEVERAL MONTHS AFTER THE DUKER AND EISENFELD FAMILIES FILED
their lawsuit against the Islamic Republic of Iran, two FBI agents arrived
in Jerusalem, accompanied by two prosecutors from the US Department
of Justice. The group had come from Washington with the permission
of the Israeli government but otherwise took great pains not to attract
attention.

There was no press conference, no entourage of guards. The FBI agents
did not even bring their guns. The four-man team quietly checked into
the American Colony Hotel, a former pasha's villa on Jerusalem's north-
east side that became a Christian pilgrims' hostel in the late 1880s and
was now a favorite hangout for visiting diplomats, academics, journalists,
entertainers, and Israeli and Palestinian officials who needed a quiet spot
to talk. To many in Jerusalem, the Colony, with its thick walls surrounding a quiet courtyard of olive and palm trees, was considered one of the
city's few neutral meeting spots—so neutral that it hosted secret prelimi-
nary sessions of the Oslo peace negotiations. But the mission assigned to
the American agents and prosecutors who arrived there had nothing to
do with diplomacy or resolving the Israeli-Palestinian conflict. They were
in Jerusalem to collect evidence for a murder case.

By the fall of 1998, the hopeful aura of the Oslo accords had been
nearly eviscerated by the series of attacks by Hamas and Palestinian
Islamic Jihad. Besides Alisa Flatow, Matthew Eisenfeld and Sara Duker,
eight other Americans had perished in various attacks across Israel, the
West Bank, and the Gaza Strip since the Oslo accords had been signed
in 1993. Several dozen others had been injured, along with hundreds of
Israelis.

The carnage did not go unnoticed in America. Stephen Flatow's dramatic court ruling drew attention to the increasing number of attacks and
the number of Americans killed or wounded. But in addition to a growing interest by victims' families in filing civil lawsuits similar to those by

the Flatows, the Dukers, and the Eisenfelds, a parallel effort was building to deal with terrorists in a more conventional manner—by arresting them in the Middle East, extraditing them to the US, and putting them on trial for murder, with possible punishments that included lengthy prison sentences and even the death penalty. In essence, these criminal prosecutions of terrorists would extend US laws far beyond the civil lawsuits of the Flatow, Duker, and Eisenfeld families and their uncertain struggle over collecting financial rewards.

Israeli authorities had been conducting trials of alleged terrorists for decades. They filled prisons with hundreds of Palestinians convicted in bombing plots and others detained under controversial security laws that had been harshly criticized by some Israeli legal scholars as violating due process and human rights. Hassan Salameh was already beginning his sentence of forty-six consecutive life terms in an Israeli prison. But as the toll of Americans killed in terrorist attacks rose during the mid-1990s, several Congressional leaders and others pushed for the FBI and Justice Department to examine whether they could prosecute terrorists in criminal trials on US soil.

The Antiterrorism and Effective Death Penalty Act not only gave US citizens the right to file lawsuits against nations that sponsored terrorism but also contained provisions that made it easier for federal prosecutors to file criminal charges against terrorists and even to seek the death penalty. But the legal issues in these types of criminal cases seemed daunting amid the Israeli-Palestinian conflict. How would US investigators collect evidence? Would the Israelis cooperate with the FBI or other US law enforcement agencies in tracking down alleged terrorists, especially if the investigations touched on issues of Israel's classified military intelligence? Would the Palestinians cooperate? And how would America's long-standing constitutional standards of due process be applied to alleged acts of terrorism in that part of the world?

Also troubling were the inherent diplomatic issues posed by these cases. With the US government actively trying to salvage the Oslo accords and pursuing a settlement to the Israeli-Palestinian conflict, the prospect of teams of American investigators arriving in that troubled land and charging Palestinian operatives with murder might have seemed counterproductive, especially now that some of these cases could result in a death sentence. US State Department officials worried that future negotiations with Palestinian officials over various pieces of the Oslo accords would collapse. Adding to the complexity was the fact that some Palestinian officials were uncomfortably close to terrorist operatives. As more Americans were killed or injured, such links could not easily be overlooked or forgotten.

For decades, Yasser Arafat was considered a terrorist by many in Israel and throughout the world, including diplomats who were trying to negotiate with him to complete the Oslo accords. America's special Middle East envoy, Dennis Ross, said he harbored deep suspicions about Arafat's links to ongoing terrorist attacks. And in light of Arafat's warning to stay away from Jerusalem on the February 1996 Sunday when Hassan Salameh's bomb destroyed the Number 18 bus on Jaffa Road, Norway's Terje Roed-Larsen also came to share Ross's misgivings about Arafat. Meanwhile, among many Israeli officials, Arafat remained a largely mistrusted figure, but one they nevertheless had to deal with, for now.

Arafat was not the only concern for diplomats. Palestinian security chief, Jibril Rajoub, had also been linked to attacks against Israel years before. His new title within Arafat's fledgling government initially brought Rajoub some respect with Israelis. But questions about Rajoub were again raised after his cousin Rizzek Rajoub was arrested driving the car that carried Hassan Salameh on the night Salameh was arrested in Hebron. Before capturing Salameh, Israel's Shin Bet had turned to Rajoub for help in tracking down Salameh. But Rajoub's security apparatus offered few leads on Salameh's whereabouts. Now, knowing that Salameh was hiding with one of Rajoub's cousins—a distant cousin, but nevertheless related—only added to the suspicion about the links of Palestinian leaders to terrorist attacks that were slowly eroding the trust that many felt was critical to the survival of the Oslo peace process.

For US diplomats such as Ross who worked feverishly to save the Oslo process, the implications of the continued attacks on American citizens and the possibility that US authorities would launch criminal investigations were daunting. How could the US credibly cast itself as a neutral player in the Israeli-Palestinian conflict if it was also trying to arrest Palestinians and bring them back to the US to stand trial?

As the Duker and Eisenfeld families still weighed the pros and cons of filing a civil lawsuit against Iran—and months before Flatow's case went to trial before Judge Lamberth—the Zionist Organization of America, a pro-Israel advocacy group based in New York City, called on the US government to mount criminal cases against Palestinian operatives involved in attacks that killed Americans. In a letter, the group's president, Morton Klein, specifically requested that US law enforcement authorities consider arresting a Palestinian activist, Nafez Mahmoud Sabih, who was suspected as playing a role in the attack on the Number 18 bus on Jaffa Road and the killing of Matt Eisenfeld and Sara Duker.

But as US and Israelis law enforcement officials would learn—far too late and after far too many expectations had been raised for the Dukers and Eisenfelds—Sabih was not involved in the Jaffa Road bombing. The story of the brief but occasionally heated campaign to bring him to America for a criminal trial illustrated the complexity in setting up an extradition process with Israel and the Palestinians. It also revealed an even more fundamental problem: How to identify who was a suspect in an attack and who was not.

Soon after the Jaffa Road bombing, Israeli authorities listed Sabih as a suspect. His name also surfaced in several media reports. But the lack of firm evidence of his connection to the bombing should have been a warning.

Israel discovered that Sabih had not only gone into hiding but had escaped to an undisclosed location in either the West Bank or the Gaza Strip—all areas controlled by Arafat. Israeli authorities formally requested that Palestinian police track down Sabih and send him back to Israel for trial. Soon, a variety of American political figures and others raised the question of whether Sabih could also be brought to the US for trial after the Israelis were finished with him in their courts.

Rather than assessing the evidence against Sabih—if there was any—and determining whether it provided a credible link to the Jaffa Road bombings, US and Israeli officials quickly became caught up in another controversy about Sabih. Arafat's security forces declined to cooperate with Israel in tracking down Sabih. With Sabih still hiding as a fugitive—and Arafat not helping to find him—Israeli and US officials again questioned whether Arafat could be trusted.

Back in the US the pressure to capture and extradite Sabih even emerged when Dennis Ross received an honorary degree in May 1997 from the Jewish Theological Seminary. "This community has been devastated by the loss of our students and we particularly felt the loss of Sara and Matt here," said the seminary's vice chancellor and dean, Rabbi William Lebeau, in a statement about Sabih's status as a fugitive in either the West Bank or in the Gaza Strip. "My own personal message to Mr. Ross will be that [Mr. Sabih] will be extradited to Israel and brought to trial there."

Morton Klein showed up at the seminary to hand out leaflets demanding Sabih's arrest and extradition. Attorney Nathan Lewin, who was representing the family of another American victim, David Boim, also called for Sabih's capture. Asked by seminary students in a question-and-answer session how he felt about Sabih, Ross said: "The Palestinians are required to act if they haven't imprisoned these people. Our concern is that they be arrested and prosecuted to the fullest extent."

The issue soon caught the attention of the US Justice Department. Two months after Ross visited the seminary in New York and six months after Morton Klein wrote a letter requesting Sabih's extradition, Deputy Assistant Attorney General Mark Richard addressed the issue. In a letter of July 31, 1997, Richard, who oversaw the Justice Department's Terrorism and Violent Crime section, noted that Sabih "is suspected of helping plan" the Jaffa Road bus bombing. "I share your outrage about this cowardly act of violence," Richard wrote. "The United States is committed to seeing that the perpetrators of these and similar acts are brought to justice, whether in the United States or in another country that has criminal jurisdiction."

Richard went on to explain that the FBI and federal prosecutors "have been working on this case with Israeli law enforcement authorities," but that "since this is an open case, I hope you will understand that I am not in a position to provide additional information."

But what case was Richard actually referring to? If the FBI and Justice Department had done any basic research at that point, they would have discovered that Sabih was no longer considered a major suspect in the Jaffa Road bombing. By late 1996—and certainly by July 1997 when Hassan Salameh had been convicted and sentenced to forty-six life terms in prison—Israeli investigators had begun to doubt whether Sabih was involved in the Jaffa Road attacks at all.

It's still unclear why Mark Richard did not know that. Nor is it clear why Richard did not mention in his letter that Salameh, the bomb-maker and prime planner of the Jaffa Road bombing had been convicted and sent to prison in Israel. Richard has since died. Decades later, the FBI and Justice Department refused to discuss the investigation into the Jaffa Road bombing, claiming that it is still an open case.

In hindsight, it seems entirely likely that the FBI and Justice Department, despite promising only days after the Jaffa Road bombing to mount an investigation, had done almost no work on the case in 1996 and 1997, preferring to leave the investigation and collection of evidence in the hands of Israeli police and Shin Bet agents. Richard's letter says as much: "Because the attack occurred in Israel and involved a great many Israeli casualties, we understand that Israeli authorities have brought criminal charges and are seeking the extradition of the alleged perpetrator."

But a clue to Richard's erroneous assumption about Sabih might be found in the January 21, 1997, letter from the State Department's counterterrorism chief Kenneth McKune to Len Eisenfeld, listing the Palestinian operatives who were considered to be suspects in the Jaffa Road bombing. Salameh was mentioned—and his role described in a minimal way. Sabih was also listed, and McKune wrote that he "has been connected" to the Jaffa Road bombing.

In his letter, McKune noted that "Israel requested" Sabih's "transfer" from the Palestinian Authority in July 1996, but that Sabih "is believed to be at large" in the West Bank or Gaza. "We do not know," McKune wrote, "if he is considered a fugitive by the PA."

It's not clear how McKune assembled the list or his information on Sabih—or Salameh, for that matter. (McKune declined to be interviewed.) Nor is it clear whether he tried to obtain updated information about Sabih from Israeli authorities when he wrote his letter to Len Eisenfeld. If he had, perhaps the campaign to extradite Sabih would have evolved differently—or not at all. But McKune's assessment of Sabih reflected the belief by US officials at that time that he was involved in the Jaffa Road attack. Unfortunately, it seems to be based on old and incorrect information.

For US authorities, the strategy of looking to Israeli law enforcement officials to take the lead in investigating Palestinian attacks in which Americans had been killed or wounded changed in October 1998 when the team of FBI agents and federal prosecutors moved into the American Colony Hotel. The team was part of the Justice Department's Terrorism and Violent Crime section, which had been formed five years earlier and had already become involved in several notable investigations, including the Oklahoma City bombing and the growth of the Branch Davidian cult. Before leaving Washington for Jerusalem, the group began assembling case files on each American death in Israel, all under the same heading of "AmCits"—an abbreviation for American citizens. While each case differed, all were linked in the minds of the Justice Department's team by a singular question: Could the Palestinian operatives involved in these killings be tracked down, arrested, and extradited to the United States to face criminal trials and, if convicted, be given long prison sentences or perhaps the death penalty?

That question yielded no easy answers. The investigative process in Israel sometimes appeared to be as complicated as negotiations for the Oslo accords. Counterterror agents from Israel's Shin Bet, for example, generally were assigned to collect evidence and interview Palestinian suspects. But Shin Bet agents, who preferred to keep their identities secret so they could retain their undercover status, rarely testified in court. Or if Shin Bet agents took the witness stand, they used false names and spoke from behind a screen to protect their identity. In most cases, Shin Bet investigators passed their evidence to Israeli police who took the witness stand for them. While that process may have suited the Israeli court system, to the FBI and federal prosecutors it was not only cumbersome, but the use of police officers to pass on evidence collected by Shin Bet agents might be considered hearsay in an American court and probably challenged by a judge or a defense lawyer.

Justice Department officials had spent months negotiating with their Israeli counterparts on gaining permission to review case files on the attacks in which Americans had been killed. But even those files could be confusing. Simply finding correct spellings of names of Palestinian suspects or sorting out aliases became an arduous task, along with determining the whereabouts of those suspects or whether they were even connected to a particular attack at all.

Finally, there was the matter of assessing the forensic evidence from crime scenes, which had been collected by Israeli investigators under standards that were far less exacting than those followed by the FBI or the Justice Department. Israeli police, for example, took great pride in how fast they cleared away rubble from a terrorist bombing and reopened a road or an intersection. For the FBI, however, a quickly cleaned site of any crime—especially a bombing—was the hallmark of a flawed case that could be easily challenged and eventually discredited by a skilled defense lawyer. "The kind of crime scene that we would take six or seven days to examine, they would clean in six or seven hours," said Tom Graney, one of the FBI agents who came to Jerusalem.

Despite those obstacles, Graney and the others from the Justice Department team had already focused much of their attention on one case and one suspect—the bombing of the Number 18 bus by Hassan Salameh.

Of all the possible crimes assessed by the Americans, Salameh's role in the Jaffa Road bombing seemed to have the most definitive evidence that could lead to a clear conviction in a US court. The FBI agents and Justice Department prosecutors were primarily drawn to the fact that Salameh had already confessed in detail about how he built the bomb, recruited the suicide bomber, and directed the overall plot. They also knew he had asked to be executed. Could the agents and prosecutors collect enough evidence in Israel to convict Salameh of murder and grant his wish?

⟶ ⟬ ⟵

By the fall of 1998, Steve Perles and Tom Fay also wanted Salameh in a US court—at least, they wanted his testimony.

Salameh's interview on *60 Minutes* in August was one of those potentially transformative moments that every lawyer dreams about after filing a lawsuit. As in the lawsuit by Stephen Flatow against Iran, Perles and Fay initially planned to follow a similar strategy with the Duker-Eisenfeld case by turning to Patrick Clawson and his analysis of terrorist funding that linked Iran to Hamas. The emergence of Hassan Salameh changed that strategy, though. With Salameh, Perles and Fay had a potential witness who not only described how he built the bomb that killed Sara and Matt, but admitted that he had learned bomb-making in Iran. Perles and Fay still planned to call Clawson to the witness stand. But as powerful as his testimony had been in the Flatow case, Perles and Fay believed that Salameh's detailed description of his Iranian training would carry even more weight before Judge Lamberth.

Salameh had already admitted his Iranian connection to Israeli interrogators—in far greater detail than his *60 Minutes* segment. During those interrogations he had even drawn a diagram for them of the bomb he designed for the Number 18 bus. Salameh's own words had been introduced as evidence in his trial in Israel more than a year before. But neither Perles nor Fay knew anything about Salameh's confessions to the Israelis—or his public trial in the military court in Beit El. Until the *60 Minutes* broadcast in August 1998, Perles and Fay did not even know that Hassan Salameh existed, much less that he was the leader of the team of Hamas operatives in the Jaffa Road bombing. Even though Salameh's arrest had been major news in Israel and his trial and conviction were also widely covered by the Israeli media, no police officials in Israel—or in the US—notified the Duker and Eisenfeld families that their children's killer had been brought to justice.

Adding to the confusion was the fact that Salameh's appearance on *60 Minutes* in August 1998 was actually a rebroadcast of a segment on his suicide bombing operations that first aired in October 1997. So his name and his story had been in the public domain in America for almost a year before Perles and Fay learned of him and what he had done. Len Eisenfeld, of course, had already received the State Department letter with Salameh's name. But the description of Salameh had been so brief that Len did not consider him a major suspect either. But after the *60 Minutes* story was rebroadcast in August 1998, Perles and Fay were determined to learn more about Salameh, and from the man himself if possible.

They asked for more footage from *60 Minutes*, but were turned down. Perles and Fay then turned to another source. From their contacts in Israel, they learned that Salameh confessed extensively to Israeli authorities. Perles and Fay asked for a transcript, but Israeli law enforcement authorities balked, claiming that Salameh's revelations were classified as top secret.

Perles did not expect much help from the US government, so he decided to try something different. He remembered an old contact of his in Israel—a former spy in the Mossad. Could he help? Perles figured he would take a chance.

Meanwhile, Flatow turned again to Senator Frank Lautenberg for assistance. Lautenberg had already alerted Clinton's staffers that he planned to champion Flatow's efforts to collect on his court judgment against Iran. If those efforts ran counter to White House policies, so be it.

Lautenberg moved forward with his threat to insert an amendment in an annual Treasury Department appropriations bill that would allow US citizens like Flatow who won court judgments against terrorist-sponsoring nations to seize embassies or other diplomatic properties of those nations. It was a bold step to draw attention to the issue. At the same time, Lautenberg was careful not to embarrass Clinton. So Lautenberg also inserted the clause that allowed Clinton to cancel or waive the amendment "in the interest of national security."

It was the political equivalent of an escape hatch for the president. On October 21, 1998, Clinton used it. As the team of Justice Department prosecutors and FBI agents were hard at work in Jerusalem, Clinton exercised that waiver. Stephen Flatow would have to wait still longer to collect on his judgment.

"The United States has been unrelenting in the fight against terrorism," the White House said in a statement, noting, "we have also supported efforts to obtain justice on behalf of victims of terrorism, including Alisa Flatow." But "the struggle to defeat terrorism would be weakened, not strengthened" if the Flatow family was allowed to seize the Iranian Embassy or other properties. "Other countries could retaliate, placing our embassies and citizens overseas at grave risk," the statement continued. "Our ability to use foreign properties as leverage in foreign policy disputes would also be undermined."

The statement ended by noting "the administration stands ready to work with the Flatow family" and "will work to achieve justice for Alisa Flatow."

Stephen Flatow did not believe it. He no longer trusted Bill Clinton.

In Jerusalem, the FBI agents and prosecutors drew up a list of what they needed from their Israeli counterparts. The document ran on for three single-spaced pages and included photographs, police files, names of aliases of Palestinian suspects, video tapes, and requests to interview Israeli investigators. At the top of the list was Hassan Salameh's name. The US agents and prosecutors wanted records of his "indictment, verdict, and sentence." They also asked for what they described as the "Hassan Salameh statement,"—the transcripts of Salameh's four interrogations during a six-month period in 1996.

The American team already had obtained but could not read copies of statements from five other Hamas operatives who helped Salameh in the Jaffa Road bombing; the statements were written in Hebrew and the team was still waiting for Justice Department translators to convert them to English. The Salemeh confessions were more elusive. In reading Salameh's indictment, which they had translated into English, FBI agents and prosecutors knew that Salemeh had confessed to the Jaffa Road bombing and other attacks. But Israeli authorities had still not handed over any of the transcripts of Salameh's interrogations.

Meanwhile, other problems loomed. In Washington, the chief of the Terrorism and Violent Crime Section, Jim Reynolds, worried that his team was being forced to develop a case merely for symbolic reasons and to soothe politically charged requests from Congress and advocacy groups such as the Zionist Organization of America. Reynolds was concerned that his team's efforts to collect evidence might be so bogged down and limited that the Justice Department could not mount a strong criminal case in a US court. The last thing Reynolds wanted was to indict and extradite a high-profile terrorist such as Hassan Salameh and then lose the case on American soil—with US politicians and the media watching. "We only indicted if we felt we could successfully prosecute the case," Reynolds said years later. "We did not indict for show reasons."

One of Reynolds's prosecutors on the ground in Jerualem, Jeffrey Breinholt, harbored similar concerns. Breinholt had spent weeks assembling files on each of the Americans who had been killed. Now, Breinholt realized that most of the cases were seriously flawed—not necessarily because there was any doubt that a murder had occurred but because the Israeli system of collecting evidence did not come close to matching Justice Department standards.

"The question was always whether we had admissible evidence," Breinholt said. "The admissible evidence came from a certainty that what we had could be introduced in an American court."

In assessing all the possible prosecutions, however, Breinholt came to believe that the case against Hassan Salameh was the strongest, in part because Salameh had confessed. But even if Breinholt was able to obtain a copy of Salameh's confession, another question haunted him and the other US prosecutors: How did they know Salameh had spoken freely and that his confession was not coerced in some way by police?

Breinholt and the others from the Justice Department Team at the American Colony had no idea. Israeli law enforcement officials—and Salameh's court records, for that matter—did not shed much light on the matter either.

At that time, Israeli law enforcement authorities occasionally were given permission by judges to use physical force to prod prisoners to divulge information, especially in terrorism cases. In December 1996, after Salemeh had been interrogated four times and admitted carrying out the Jaffa Road bombing and other attacks, the Israel Supreme Court issued a special ruling, granting Shin Bet permission to use force in additional interrogations of Salameh to gain information on future attacks by Hamas. But the Court ordered Shin Bet officials to explain within forty-five days why they felt it was "necessary" to now use physical force against Salameh.

It was never clear to Breinholt and the others on the US team whether Salameh had been roughed up or forced to talk in those later interrogation sessions—or whether those sessions even took place. No records of additional interrogations of Salameh were introduced in his trial in 1997. (In an interview with this author, Salameh never spoke of being tortured. In later years, Israeli courts also invoked severe restrictions on the use of physical force in police interrogations.)

The Americans eventually were given only a declassified version of Salameh's four interrogations that took place before the Israeli Supreme Court granted Shin Bet permission to use physical force against Salameh. There was no mention in the documents about additional interrogations or any use of force.

But Breinholt foresaw major problems if Salameh was brought to the United States to stand trial. Although the declassified transcripts of Salameh's four interrogation sessions contained a wealth of information, including detailed descriptions of how Salameh was trained in Iran, how he smuggled explosives into Israel, recruited the suicide bomber, and assembled the explosives that destroyed the Number 18 bus and other buses in two other attacks, Breinholt never was able to obtain a convincing answer to his question of whether any of Salameh's statements were coerced during any part of his captivity.

That lack of a clear explanation bothered Breinholt and the other US prosecutors deeply. If there was any hint that Salameh had been subjected to physical coercion—and certainly a ruling by Israel's Supreme Court granting Shin Bet permission to use force might be viewed as evidence enough—Breinholt feared that an American defense lawyer would pounce and attempt to discredit all of his testimony in a US trial.

Breinholt eventually surmised that Salameh's confessions were not coerced, though he couldn't prove it. It was just a gut feeling he had. But gut feelings do not satisfy the Justice Department's demanding standards of evidence. If the American team was going to use Salameh's words against him, they concluded that they could not rely on Salameh's confession to Israeli police.

They had to interview Salameh themselves. But when? After three weeks, the team left Jerusalem and returned to Washington.

Their goal to build a murder case was a long way off.

———

When prosecutors collect evidence in a criminal case, they periodically assess what they have and what they still need. The team of prosecutors and FBI agents who went to Jerusalem in October 1998 were no different. The team returned to their offices—a portion of a floor of an otherwise nondescript Washington office building named after Revolutionary War patriot Patrick Henry and just a short walk from the courthouse where Judge Lamberth presided. With other members of the Justice Department's section on Terrorism and Violent Crime, they began the meticulous process of sorting through the reports and other pieces of evidence they were able to obtain from Israelis.

On November 18, Jeff Breinholt wrote a twelve-page, single-spaced memo to his section chief, James Reynolds, in which he summarized each potential case the team was trying to build. He described the separate shooting deaths of Americans David Ungar and David Boim in Israeli communities on the West Bank in May and June 1996. He detailed the kidnapping and murder in October 1994 of an Israeli soldier, Nachshon Wachsman, who had dual US and Israeli citizenship. He examined the killing of a visiting Connecticut teacher, Joan Davenny, in August 1995 in a bus bombing in Jerusalem, the killing of Leah Stern in a July 1997 bombing at a market near Jaffa Road and and the death of Yael Botwin in a similar bombing two months later.

In assessing Alisa Flatow's case, Breinholt noted that of the nine Palestinian operatives who participated in the bombing of her bus, two had been killed and two more were imprisoned in Israeli jails. Breinholt could not determine the status of five others—including Adnan al-Ghoul, who had previously been linked to Hassan Salameh. Breinholt noted they were "either in PA (Palestinian Authority) custody or at large in Palestinian-controlled areas."

It was not a good sign. Breinholt's brief notation of the status of the five operatives illustrated one of the fundamental obstacles that the team of FBI agents and prosecutors faced in Israel. With the Israeli-Palestinian conflict still in dispute, the already arduous process of tracking down suspected murderers was even more difficult because of the lack of credible police record keeping by Yasser Arafat's Palestinian government. At the same time, the American team found it could not even conduct basic interviews with the Israeli police detectives who investigated Alisa Flatow's murder. "We were not able to speak to any of the police officers assigned to these cases," Breinholt wrote.

Breinholt's assessment of the Duker-Eisenfeld case was slightly more hopeful, though he cited nagging problems. For instance, basic Israeli police reports of the bombing had still not been translated into English. And while Israeli authorities gave the Americans the autopsy reports for Matthew Eisenfeld and Sara Duker, crime scene photos of the bombing, a summary of the chemical analysis of the explosives, and allowed the team to speak with eight police officers assigned to the bombing—including Detective Koby Zrihen—the FBI agents and US prosecutors had not been able to review any statements from an eyewitness.

Breinholt also pointed out the mystery involving Nafez Mahmoud Sabih. "His role in the attack is not obvious," he wrote.

Breinholt then turned his attention to Hassan Salameh. Breinholt felt that federal prosecutors could build a solid criminal case against Salameh if they could convince him to cooperate as the Israelis had done. But Breinholt was concerned about whether Salameh would talk as extensively to FBI agents or a team of federal prosecutors. So Breinhold recommended that Salameh's interview on *60 Minutes* be analyzed by an FBI behavioral scientist who could develop a strategy "on how best to approach him."

As for Salameh, Breinholt was not hopeful that he would cooperate. "The Israeli prosecutors are not optimistic about Salameh's willingness, his braggadocio notwithstanding," Breinholt noted.

—◦—

Four months later, Jeff Breinholt walked into a hearing room in the Dirksen Senate Office Building on Capitol Hill for a Foreign Relations subcommittee meeting. By his side was Mark Richard, the deputy assistant attorney general from the Justice Department's criminal division. In the world of Washington politics, the hearing was another opportunity for competing political agendas to rub up against the reality of government. In this case, that friction was about whether the Justice Department and FBI would bring Palestinian operatives to America for a trial. Besides

Breinholt and Richard from the Justice Department, the former US Ambassador to Israel, Martin Indyk, who was now the assistant Secretary of State for Near Eastern Affairs, was also there. So were Stephen Flatow and Len and Vicki Eisenfeld.

At issue before the subcommittee was a proposal to send $400 million in aid to the Palestinian Authority to build roads, improve health-care programs, and hire additional police officers. The financial aid package was viewed by the Clinton administration as a necessary ingredient to help Yasser Arafat build a Palestinian government and, eventually, a nation.

Indyk urged Senators to approve the $400 million package, noting that future negotiations of the multiple steps in the Oslo peace process depended on Palestinians receiving substantial funds to strengthen their government. But several senators—notably Arlen Specter, the Pennsylvania Republican, and New Jersey's Frank Lautenberg—wanted to use the $400 million as leverage to gain more cooperation from the Palestinian Authority to prevent terrorist attacks and to track down Hamas and Islamic Jihad operatives who had planned them.

Unlike Martin Indyk, Jeff Breinholt was not a diplomat. But as he sat in the hearing room that morning on Capitol Hill, he grew uncomfortable as he sensed that the Justice Department had been drawn into the complicated web of Middle East and American politics. Breinholt had concluded privately that most of the so-called "AmCit" cases—the murders of Americans by Palestinian terrorists—were difficult to prosecute. But if the Justice Department wanted to take a shot at prosecuting one of them as a test case, Breinholt felt that indicting Hassan Salameh for murder was a good place to start.

"I felt we should bring one of the cases to a trial," Breinholt said years later. "Salameh's case was the strongest."

Having a strong case did not guarantee conviction, though. And that was the basic message that Richard had come to the committee to deliver as he read a statement that Breinholt helped to write.

Richard told the committee how he had traveled to Israel and to the Palestinian territories a year earlier, asking for cooperation from Israeli and Palestinian law enforcement officials. He described how FBI agents and federal prosecutors followed up during their three weeks at the American Colony in Jerusalem. Richard then cited the many problems: That most police reports were written in Hebrew, that evidence was collected under "evidentiary standards that are different from our own," and that while Israeli investigators were willing to give the FBI access to nonclassified information, they were "not prepared to allow joint US-Israeli investigations into terrorist attacks."

Richard did not mention Salemeh, and he deftly sidestepped the question of whether any case would be prosecuted, although he left little hope. His said the prosecutors on his team would seek an indictment "only when sufficient admissible evidence is developed and available for use at trial, such that we could obtain a conviction." He added: "Until that point is reached in these cases, there is not a basis for our seeking the transfer of suspects being held in Israeli or Palestinian custody."

Lautenberg tried to interject a question, but Specter, who chaired the hearing and made no secret of his impatience with the Justice Department's investigation of the AmCit cases, cut him off.

"Let me move on to the question as to the cooperation which we have had from both Israel and the Palestinians," said Specter, a former district attorney in Philadelphia. "I am informed that the FBI has encountered difficulties in obtaining Palestinian cooperation."

He did not wait for an answer but pointed out that at least ten Hamas and Islamic Jihad operatives were believed to be hiding in Palestinian-controlled areas. Then he asked about whether confessions by Palestinians could be used in US courts.

"We have to judge the desirability by our standards," Richard said. "The question about the voluntariness, the corroboration of that confession . . ."

Voluntariness?" Specter asked.

Richard was using "voluntariness" as a Justice Department code word for possible coercion. He did not elaborate in detail, but his team was concerned that the Palestinians who confessed had been subjected to some sort of physical force. Richard also mentioned "prior treatment" of the Palestinian suspects—another coded phrase that implied the use of force during interrogations.

"Well, what was the prior treatment?" Specter shot back.

Again, Richard did not offer specifics but noted that the issue of prior treatment—or physical force—"becomes relevant" to US prosecutors in weighing whether to use a confession from Israel authorities as evidence.

Lautenberg finally got his chance to speak. Instead of the criminal indictments that Specter asked about, Lautenberg brought up the civil lawsuits—specifically the judgment that Stephen Flatow was trying to collect from Iran. He turned to Martin Indyk, who was still sitting at the witness table with Mark Richard.

"I want to ask Ambassador Indyk, do you think that the civil penalties that we were able to have awarded to Mr. Flatow serve as a deterrent to terrorist groups, for state-sponsored terrorism?"

"Well, I think we have to look at the record since the judgment was made," Indyk said. "We do not see a direct connection between the judgment and the change in behavior. In this case, we are talking about Iran."

Lautenberg then raised the issue of whether the Clinton administration was helping Flatow track down Iranian assets.

"The biggest problem seems to be access," Lautenberg said, adding: "I would ask, please, that you see to the extent you can that the Flatows and their representatives and the Eisenfelds have as much access as possible to records we have. That is the only way we are going to be able to see whether or not we can deter these acts before they occur."

Indyk said he would help. A few minutes later, he asked if he could interject a comment about the larger concern of the US response to terrorism. "I want to make clear that the issue of bringing to justice terrorist suspects accused of involvement in killing Americans citizens is a high priority for the administration," he said. "It has been a subject on President Clinton's agenda."

As Indyk finished, Specter turned to Mark Richard, who indicated his desire to speak again.

Richard said that "a variety of reasons" had prevented US authorities from extraditing suspected Palestinian terrorists for trial in the US. He even blamed Israel for not turning over terrorists they had imprisoned. "In terms of being able to get them out of custody, Israeli custody, there is no easy mechanism," Richard said.

—◆—

Stephen Flatow and Vicki Eisenfeld watched from the back of the hearing room as Indyk and Richard verbally sparred with Specter and Lautenberg. The more they listened, the more their frustrations grew. Just before noon, Specter invited them forward to speak from a witness table with two others—Diana Campuzano, who had survived a Hamas attack, and Nathan Lewin, the noted Washington attorney who had become a major advocate for the extradition of Palestinian operatives after he took on the case of the family of David Boim.

Flatow thanked the committee and Congress for supporting his quest to hold Iran accountable then turned to Indyk's statement that financial penalties—notably Flatow's $247 million judgment against Iran—would deter Iran from supporting terrorism.

"Our experts will tell you, senator, quite clearly that recovery on that judgment will be a deterrent to future terrorist attacks and the funding of such terrorist attacks. It is a well-known fact in academic circles and in practical circles in the field," Flatow said.

He continued, "I now understand what the phrase means that ignorance is bliss." He said he assumed that his daughter's killers would be tracked down. But Flatow said he had come to believe that his own government is not interested in pressuring the Palestinian Authority to arrest suspected terrorists and turn them over for trial in America.

"I must then ask what kind of partnership is the United States going to have with the Palestinian Authority," Flatow said. "Will it continue to turn a blind eye to this cancer?"

Vicki Eisenfeld spoke next. In recent months her admiration of Flatow had grown enormously, especially his unbridled forcefulness in speaking to government officials. He seemed unafraid. She did not want to confront the senators—or even Indyk and Richard—the way Flatow had. That was not her style. But she wanted to leave a clear message with all of them.

"Testifying in front of a Senate subcommittee on foreign operations is not something I would have chosen to have on my 'list of things to do'" before Matthew and Sara were killed, Vicki began. "The events of February 25, 1996 changed my life forever.

"Three years have passed now and with the great love of family and friends, my heart, my husband's heart and our daughter's heart, have begun to heal. We were blessed with the gift of Matthew and the example of his life. We were blessed with knowing he was loved, and in love with a wonderful young woman, Sara Duker."

Vicki told the committee of Matt's goal to become a rabbi, of Sara's dedication to environmental biology and how "their dreams were to participate actively and consciously in healing the wounds of the world physically and spiritually." But "there are forces that create havoc, chaos, and evil in this world, and they are very strong. Murderous, terrorist attacks strike at the soul and core of humanity and can erase the sanity that rests there . . .

"I have stated that my family has been healing," Vicki said. "Yet there is no closure."

Vicki continued as Specter and Lautenberg and other senators listened. Unlike Flatow, she had been careful to restrain her anger and feelings of bitterness. She mentioned the lawsuit against Iran that she and Len had filed along with Arline and asked the senators to pressure the Palestinian Authority to supply evidence of its links to Iranian funding.

"I am not a lawyer or a diplomat or a politician. I am just a mother," she said. "Terrorists try to force us to their will by threatening all Americans with what happened to Matt and Sara . . ."

Specter cut in. "Could you summarize the balance?" he asked. "I know this is very difficult for you. We are just about out of time."

Vicki nodded.

"I would just like to say that while I am Jewish and I support and love Israel, I am an American," she said. "I was born here and raised here, as was my son, and I would just like to ask you to help all of the people here in addressing these issues."

"Mrs. Eisenfeld," said Specter, "we will do our very best to get to the bottom of it and bring the murderers to justice."

—◦—

Several months later, during the summer of 1999, FBI Special Agent Tom Graney looked into the eyes of Hassan Salameh in a prison in Israel.

It was almost two years since Salameh's trial and sentencing to forty-six consecutive life terms—more than three years since the Jaffa Road bombing.

Graney, who had been part of the team of agents and prosecutors who stayed at the American Colony in October 1998, had returned to Israel to reexamine evidence in the "AmCit" cases and to interview captured terrorists.

He was curious about Salameh, though. The Israelis had finally turned over transcripts of Salameh's confessions to the Justice Department team. To the FBI agents and federal prosecutors of the Terrorism and Violent Crime section who studied the transcripts, Salameh provided a remarkable window into a terrorist operation. If Salameh confirmed the details about his training in Iran, his smuggling of explosives into Jerusalem and his recruiting of the suicide bomber, it would be explosive evidence in a trial on US soil. If Salameh pleaded guilty, as he had done in his murder trial in Israel, he could be sentenced to life in prison or perhaps given the death penalty.

Graney did not merely want to interview Salameh; he wanted to assess how Salameh might behave in a US trial.

Salameh was unafraid to speak. To Graney, he was not the braggart that Israeli authorities had said he would be. "He looked at himself as a combatant, more or less as a prisoner of war," Graney said afterwards. "He didn't have any problems discussing the facts of the case."

Graney asked Salameh how he felt about killing innocent civilians like Matt Eisenfeld and Sara Duker.

The answer would bother Graney for years afterward.

"They were just in the wrong place at the wrong time," Salameh said.

# CHAPTER 13

COURTROOMS INVARIABLY RAISE OUR HOPES. WHEN A TRIAL BEGINS, we expect justice of some sort—that the guilty will be punished and the innocent protected, or perhaps that a complicated legal dilemma can be unraveled and made clear.

Many trials don't live up to such high-minded standards. And, certainly, Arline Duker and Len and Vicki Eisenfeld harbored many misgivings when they walked into Judge Royce Lamberth's courtroom at the US District Courthouse in Washington, DC, for the trial of their lawsuit against the Islamic Republic of Iran. They dutifully carried their hopes for justice. They also brought a healthy dose of self-protective skepticism.

It was May 1, 2000. Six months earlier, while visiting Washington, Vicki met with Tom Fay, who was again joining Steve Perles to present the Duker-Eisenfeld lawsuit before Judge Lamberth as they had done in Stephen Flatow's case. Like any seasoned litigator preparing for a trial, Fay wanted to gauge Vicki's state of mind.

"This isn't going to be an easy thing," he said, deliberately trying to needle her. "Are you sure you want to go ahead with this?"

Vicki wondered what prompted Fay to ask such a question. She knew, as he did, that their lawsuit was risky, with no guarantee of receiving compensation even if they won. After all, it had been more than two years since Flatow's victory, yet he was still waiting for the money Lamberth ordered Iran to pay him. But Vicki felt angry at the thought of giving up.

"You're not going to hear me back off," she shot back.

Fay was pleased. He had shepherded hundreds of lawsuits into courtrooms like Lamberth's and he knew the importance of having clients who were not merely going through the motions of a case—especially one that involved international terrorism and an Iranian government that had not even bothered to respond to accusations raised in the lawsuit. Along with her husband and Arline Duker, Vicki wanted to win the case, of course. But she also hoped to send a message.

"We want to let it be known that American citizens will not let this be ignored without some actions being taken," Vicki told a reporter for the Associated Press a day before the trial. "You want these settlements to make it uncomfortable for Iran to sponsor terrorism."

Yet as the trial began, Vicki harbored an uneasy feeling, along with Len and Arline, about the aftermath. Would her family and the Dukers face the same fate as Stephen Flatow: Awarded a substantial financial penalty by Lamberth, but stymied by the White House and other branches of the administration from collecting even a penny?

The thought was maddening to Vicki. One branch of her government blocking the action of another branch to protect a foreign government that did not even have the courtesy to show up in court. What kind of message was that?

It was no secret, as media commentators had increasingly noticed, that the Clinton administration was sending mixed, often confusing signals over the terrorism lawsuits. The president had not tried to rescind or amend the law he signed four years earlier that permitted the lawsuits. But one of Clinton's key advisors on the lawsuits, Stuart Eizenstat, had now taken an even more public and forthright role in arguing that Flatow and others who won their lawsuits should not be allowed to draw on Iranian assets. Eizenstat's belief that those assets could be used as bargaining chips in future diplomatic negotiations took on greater importance now as the Clinton administration had stepped up efforts to improve diplomatic relations with Iran. The administration had already publicly apologized in March to Iran for the CIA's attempts to meddle in Iranian affairs years before.

More than four years had passed since Hassan Salameh's bomb tore through the Number 18 bus on Jaffa Road. While Arline, Vicki, and Len found themselves still very much emotionally frozen by that Sunday morning in February 1996 when Matt and Sara were killed, they were also keenly aware of how much had changed in America and elsewhere.

Bill Clinton had survived an impeachment trial over his sexual affair with a White House intern. His wife, Hillary Rodham Clinton, was running for the US senate seat in New York. Texas Governor George W. Bush, the son of the incumbent president who was defeated by Bill Clinton in

1992, was leading the race for the Republican presidential nomination and the chance to succeed Clinton. Meanwhile, Clinton's vice president, Al Gore, had nearly sewn up the Democratic presidential nomination and was preparing for the fall campaign.

In Israel, Prime Minister Benjamin Netanyahu had been ousted ten months earlier in an election and replaced by the former defense minister and military chief of staff, Ehud Barak. Elsewhere in the Middle East, Terje Roed-Larsen, still in his role as the United Nations special envoy to the Palestinian Authority, was trying to save the Oslo accords he had worked so hard to shape a decade earlier. Larsen never directly confronted Yasser Arafat about his cryptic warning to stay away from Jerusalem on the morning the Number 18 bus was blown up. He had slowly come to believe that Arafat would never tell him the truth about that day.

"He was a very secretive guy," Larsen said years later of Arafat. "He would never have told me that he knew the bombing was going to happen. He would never discuss things like that."

In the years following the Jaffa Road bombing, Larsen pushed Arafat to crack down on Hamas and Palestinian Islamic Jihad. But Arafat never followed through. By 2000, Larsen gave up hope on Arafat and rarely spoke to him.

Nevertheless Arafat's message to stay away from Jerusalem on the day the Number 18 bus was attacked bothered Larsen greatly. He eventually told US Middle East special envoy Dennis Ross about it. But Ross was also mystified—and hamstrung.

By the summer of 2000 and with Bill Clinton in the final months of his presidency, Ross, was assembling plans for a meeting at Camp David between Arafat and Ehud Barak to finally settle the Israeli-Palestinian conflict. To Ross, Arafat was still seen as a key to making the Oslo accords work. At the same time, Ross had begun to lose trust in Arafat too, especially when it came to the Palestinian leader's promise to stop terrorist attacks.

Stephen Flatow continued his pursuit of Iranian assets. So far, he had not collected a penny. And while he was still in contact with Stuart Eizenstat, who had been promoted by Clinton a year earlier to be deputy secretary of the Treasury, Flatow increasingly wondered if his legal victory would be merely symbolic.

On Capitol Hill, Senator Frank Lautenberg had not given up on the notion of prying loose some of those protected Iranian assets. In October 1999, a month before Vicki Eisenfeld told Tom Fay she was not backing off her lawsuit, Lautenberg co-sponsored a new piece of legislation. Called the "Justice for Victims of Terrorism Act," the bill would allow Flatow, the Dukers and Eisenfelds, and others, if they won their lawsuits, to have access to Iran's blocked assets in US banks or its embassy in Washington and other diplomatic property that had been seized by the federal government. The bill would also restrict the president from stopping US citizens from laying claim to foreign assets by citing national security concerns, as Clinton had done in 1998. Perhaps most notably for Lautenberg—and for Flatow and the other families—was the addition of another senator's name to the sponsorship of the legislation.

In writing the new bill, Lautenberg enlisted the help of a Republican senator from Florida, Connie Mack, the grandson of the legendary baseball manager. Like Lautenberg, Mack had taken up the cause of a group of constituents from his state—the families of the Brothers to the Rescue pilots—in their case against Cuba. And like Flatow in his effort to gain control of some of Iran's holdings, the families of the Brothers pilots were still waiting for permission to lay claim to some of Cuba's frozen assets in the US. Like Lautenberg, Mack had become convinced that, outside of an unlikely US military strike, the most effective punishment against Castro was a financial penalty.

Meanwhile, other Americans who had been victimized in some way by Iran had won lawsuits, thus increasing pressure on the Clinton administration to find a way to settle the financial issues with Iran. One of the most vocal victims turned out to be Terry Anderson, the former chief Middle East correspondent for the Associated Press who had been held hostage for more than six years by Iranian-backed militants in Lebanon. A month before Arline, Vicki, and Len began their trial, Anderson won a $341 million damage claim against Iran. "Terrorism is a cheap way for them to wage war against their enemies," Anderson said of Iran's strategy. "We have to take away their money and punish them for it."

Such was the political, diplomatic, and legal landscape that Arline, Vicki, and Len faced as they took their seats in Judge Lamberth's courtroom. They had become somewhat resigned, as had Stephen Flatow, that they might never collect on that judgment—if they won.

"I felt like we had to do it," said Vicki years later of her decision to go ahead with the trial. "We had to respond. I had to fight for Matt. I had to fight for all of us who were involved in this way."

Flatow did not come to the trial to watch the testimony. But both families could feel his presence. Besides Flatow's lawyers, Steve Perles and Tom Fay, the Dukers and Eisenfelds also summoned several of the same witnesses who testified at the Flatow case. But they also faced the same problem as Flatow: the absence of any representatives from the Iranian government to fight the lawsuit.

For the Duker-Eisenfeld trial, however, Perles and Fay developed a slightly different strategy than the one that was so successful with the Flatow case. Instead of scheduling testimony about Iran's links to the Jaffa Road bombing in the trial's final hours, they devoted most of the first day to it.

Once again, the star witness was Patrick Clawson, meticulously guiding everyone through his analysis of the Iranian government budget and its appropriations for Palestinian militant attacks against Israel. This time Clawson's conclusions were bolstered by Hassan Salameh's own words in which he explained how he had learned his bomb-making skills in Iran and then how he sneaked into Israel from the Gaza Strip and recruited a suicide bomber. Salameh did not testify in person, but Perles, with the help of his contacts in Israel's Mossad spy service, obtained a declassified copy of Salameh's statement to Israeli authorities and introduced it as evidence. Perles and Fay also brought in the Israeli terrorism expert Reuven Paz to analyze the transcript of Salameh's statement and to explain the significance of his Iranian training.

Perles and Fay needed to show that Iran played a direct role in the Jaffa Road bombing. Certainly, the testimony of the first day offered ample proof. But in a case that involves a charge of wrongful death, experienced trial lawyers say it's also important to hear from the victims.

After Clawson and Paz testified on the first day, Matt's younger sister, Amy, rose from her seat and took the witness stand. She spoke of how, as a little girl, she would call her brother "Bubba" and constantly repeat what he said. She also described hearing of Matt's death while finishing the final semester of her senior year of college and of the gaping emotional hole that had suddenly appeared in her close-knit family.

"Our family was not what it was," Amy said. She said her brother's murder "changed completely who I am" and that she feels a "deep loss that I carry with me wherever I go. It's a loss that ripples outward from me."

Sara Duker's youngest sister, Ariella, followed Amy. It was now the second day of the trial. Ariella was fourteen when Sara was killed. Now nineteen and a college freshman at the State University of New York in Binghamton, she noted—as Amy had done the previous day—how still deeply painful was the loss of her sister.

"Tell me a little bit about what you remember first when you think of Sara," Fay asked.

"The thing I think of first is a Monopoly board," Ariella said. "Because she taught me how to play Monopoly, and we'd always play that every week when I was growing up."

Fay's strategy was to humanize Sara and Matt—to portray them as more than just names on a list of victims of a bombing in Jerusalem. At the same time, Fay wanted to show that Sara's death—and Matt's, too—had left a void in their family's lives and in the extended family that would have been shaped by their probable marriage.

Ariella spoke of how she occasionally asked Sara for help in explaining Jewish customs. She described how she and Sara sometimes made "noodle necklaces." She mentioned how she told Matt once how much she loved old T-shirts, and that he immediately reached into a drawer and handed her a stack from the various wrestling camps he attended.

"Do you still have them?" Fay asked.

"Yep," said Ariella.

Fay then gently guided Ariella through her memories of the day Sara died.

"How did you feel then?" Fay asked.

"I pictured her flawless in this coffin," Ariella said. "But I knew that it wasn't like that and I knew that it was really violent."

Fay paused.

"Okay. What do you think Sara would want to have come out of this litigation?"

"I like to think that she's looking down on this and she's thinking that if this can somehow make a few less bombings happen, then it's worth it," Ariella said. "Because it's not just the people who die in these things. It's the people who have to live with this every day that have to suffer the most."

Ariella then turned her thoughts to the testimony earlier in the trial by an economist, called by Fay to explain what the deaths of Matt and Sara meant in terms of lost income. For both families, it was emotionally distressing to hear two lives reduced to a dollar figure. But in most wrongful death lawsuits, such testimony is a necessary ingredient and a guide for a judge in arriving at how much financial compensation should be awarded to the victims' families.

Economist Jerome Paige described how he had calculated the potential financial worth of Matt and Sara, based on their life expectancies, their education, and the professions they were likely to enter—Matt as a rabbi and Sara as a scientist. Paige estimated that Sara would have earned more than $3.2 million over her lifetime and Matt's gross income would have been $2.6 million.

"There are things that I don't think other nineteen-year-olds need to know," Ariella said. "I don't think anyone should have to know how to calculate somebody's life—like how much they're worth. I think that's awful, and I don't want anyone else to have to do that."

Amy Eisenfeid and Ariella Duker each testified for less than thirty minutes. But in their comments both managed to drive home a key point that Fay and Perles wanted to make, namely, that the Jaffa Road bombing, was not an act of war between two armies. Innocent people had been killed—and their relatives were still wounded.

It was a theme that continued throughout the afternoon.

Ariella stepped down from the witness stand, and Fay called Sara's other sister, twenty-four-year-old Tamara, who had graduated from Duke University two years earlier and was finishing up a master's degree at Georgetown University's School of Foreign Service.

Tamara remembered how she and Sara often watched TV cartoon shows on Saturday mornings as little girls. She described Sara's quirky style of dressing in high school and in college. She talked of how Sara had grown closer to Matt. Then, Fay asked "If Sara—and Matt, for that matter—if both of them were here, what do you think they would want to see come out of litigation like this?"

"You know," said Tamara, "they read a lot and they had a sense of literary irony. And so, I think some sort of poetic justice in which, when decision-makers in Iran choose to spend their dollars to subsidize terrorist activity, that it would be imposed on them that for every dollar they spend, two dollars goes toward a cause that's completely inimical to their views of hatred and violence. So for every dollar they spend to sponsor a terrorist, two dollars would go toward charities or organizations that sponsor peaceful types of coexistence activities, and so maybe they'd think twice about subsidizing the activities that they have chosen to subsidize."

Next Fay called Vicki Eisenfeld. Fay began with several basic questions such as the names of her children.

The question was not meant to reveal any unusual information. It was merely Fay's attempt to set a calm tone.

Vicki mentioned Matthew first, but as she said Amy's name, she started to choke up.

"Do you want a moment?" Fay interjected.

"I'll be okay," Vicki said.

She went on to describe Matt's birth and how the family moved to Alabama and then New Orleans because her husband served as a physician in the US Army after he graduated from Yale Medical School. She talked of Matt's allergies, his love of learning, his "tremendous curiosity" and how he "learned very quickly how to make friends and bring friends into the house" because the family moved so often in those early years. She mentioned how he captained three high school teams—wrestling, cross country, and track—and how he loved taking classes in humanities and in languages, including Chinese, and, finally, how he had grown intensely interested in exploring his Jewish faith and pursuing a career as a rabbi.

"I think it was a natural progression," Vicki said of Matt's focus on Judaism. "The more he studied, the more he wanted to know."

Fay asked how Matt and Sara got along.

"It was—it seemed—like a perfect match," Vicki said.

Then Fay turned his attention to February 25, 1996.

Vicki described the early morning telephone call from Kathleen Riley at the US Consulate in Jerusalem.

"Could you tell the court what this has done to you?" Fay said. "What Matthew's death has done to you—this whole event, Matthew's death and Sara's, for that matter? What this event has done to you personally, and to your husband and your daughter."

"Well," Vicki began. "It changes everything. You are not the same. Everything changes. You're not the same person you were before. You're just not. So you basically have to—you start to rebuild a whole person all over again."

She paused.

"The relationships to people change," she continued. "It breaks your heart when you have to listen to your daughter go through all this pain and watch her on the stand having to talk about this. And you never wanted her to be an only child and there she is, and she's trying to take care of you and you're supposed to be taking care of her."

She paused again. Fay did not interrupt. He wanted Vicki to keep talking.

"You wish you weren't breathing," she said. "And then at the same time, you know, Matthew will come back in my head and it's like—you make a choice every single day. You have a choice to be miserable every single day or you have a choice to get up and find joy again and make that be a part of your life. You have to learn that when it comes, that it's okay to feel it."

"Ms. Eisenfeld," Fay interjected. "If Matt could be here and tell us what he would want to come out of this litigation, what do you think he would say?"

"I think don't give up," Vicki said. "That each one of us has a piece in this. Take it one step at a time. Find a way to find the peace. Find a way. Don't ever believe you can't change things. Every time there's an act of terror—every time there's some evil piece, answer it. Do it one person at a time. That each of us has a responsibility. And don't give up."

Fay had one more question.

"Would you want to see something done to stop this type of attack?" he asked.

"That's why I'm here," Vicki said. "Because at the moment, it's the only way I know to at least begin to address it."

She then thought of what her daughter, Amy, had said once when the two spoke about Matt's death and whether the family should pursue a lawsuit.

"I remember saying to Amy, 'Do you think we're doing the right thing?' And she said, 'Mom, if we don't do anything, it's like we said, well, it's okay to kill our kid. You can do whatever you want.'"

Vicki paused a last time.

"I think this is the best means we have right now to respond in some civil, peaceful, responsible way," she said.

"Thank you," Fay said, turning to Judge Lamberth.

"Your honor, do you have any questions?" Fay asked.

"No," Lamberth said.

Fay then summoned Len Eisenfeld to the stand.

As the afternoon wore on, Fay's goal was to craft a verbal portrait of Matt and Sara through the words of their siblings and parents while also demonstrating how their deaths had left deep emotional scars too. As Vicki had done moments earlier, Len spoke of how Matt had many diverse interests as a boy, from games such as Dungeons and Dragons to sports, even football in a father-son league.

"We had T-shirts," Len said. "We developed a name of the team. We were called the Scorpions. And we played against other father and son teams, and sometimes we won and a lot of times we lost."

Len described Matt's budding interest in Judaism, how he studied the Hebrew language, and eventually how he began to consider becoming a rabbi.

"What was your impression of Sara when you met her?" Fay asked.

"I remember that very vividly," Len said. "I had known about her and his feeling about her and what kind of person she was, and within a second of meeting her my arms were around her and we were giving each other hugs. She was somebody I connected to instantaneously."

Fay asked about the last time he spoke to Matt on the telephone—the Sunday before the bombing.

"We talked every Sunday," Len said.

Fay wondered if Matt mentioned that he planned to take a trip with Sara to explore the archaeological site at Petra in Jordan.

"It sounded like a great opportunity," Len said. But at the same time, he worried whether his son and Sara would be safe.

"I was afraid," Len said. "I thought he should take his *kippah*—his yarmulke—and put it in his pocket and not be identified as Jewish in Jordan and that he would be a target. And I said to him—there were two last things I said to him. I didn't want anybody doing anything wonderful for Allah. And the last thing I told him was I loved him."

Fay decided to raise an issue he had not discussed before: Was Len aware that other victims, such as Stephen Flatow, faced "difficulties" in "collecting damages" even though they had won favorable judgments in their lawsuits?

"Yes. I am aware," Len said.

Fay pressed on. "Could you tell us a little bit what you would like to see come out of this and why you went ahead with it, knowing that there is no guarantee of ever getting any kind of compensation for all the pain you've gone through and are going through with this litigation?"

Len began by mentioning how his father had been a lawyer and had instilled in him a "tremendous respect for United States jurisprudence" as a "civilized way" to address grievances. He said he would like to use some of the money his family might collect from Iran "to do good in the world rather than doing harm."

"I hope to God that we will be able to help people," he added.

Then Len turned his attention to the target of his family's lawsuit—Iran.

"I would like to see the Islamic Republic of Iran stop doing terrorism, and that we could have that republic, that country, rejoin civilized humanity and that there would be understanding and peace," Len said. "That's the only way to go."

Len left the witness stand and Arline Duker rose from her seat and came forward. Fay wanted hers to be the last voice.

Arline talked of Sara's budding interest in science, "a natural born scientist," she said. But at the same time, Sara loved writing and Judaism and had developed an intellectual desire to approach old topics with a new flair—so much so that, for her senior Centennial Scholars' thesis on a first-century rabbi's writings, she sought guidance from a Roman Catholic nun, Sister Celia Deutsch, who was an expert in Jewish scriptures.

Fay interjected that "Sister Celia Deutsch said that Sara wanted to be a part of history, not just read history, a doer; in other words, not just an intellectual."

Arline responded by mentioning a quote Sara had selected to appear with her photo in her high school yearbook: "Keep both feet planted firmly in the clouds."

"I've not found this anywhere else," Arline said, "so she may have actually made this up. And I think that it really captures both sides of her."

As with Vicki and Len, Fay guided Arline through a recounting of the day she learned of Sara's death. Then, Fay asked: "Could you tell us the effect that this has had on you and your family?"

Arline began with a general answer. "I think we've all struggled to maintain our lives or to rebuild," she said. Then she corrected herself slightly.

"It's not even maintaining," she said. "Your life falls apart. I've spent four years trying to live what appears to be somewhat of a normal life. I work and I do okay at work. I have some friends and I go out and I try to be with people because I don't want to throw my life away or my children's lives. But I have to tell you that every day it's like walking uphill . . . Every morning when I wake up, or at some time during the day, there is some part of something that reminds me that there's this hole, that there is this child of mine who isn't here and never will be."

As he had done with other witnesses, Fay concluded by asking what Arline would like to see happen with her lawsuit as "the end result."

"This is not something I came to right away," Arline said. "It took months and months to really decide to do this."

But she said she harbored a fundamental hope: "that the killing of innocent people" could stop.

"If some people's lives are saved," Arline said, "if some of the terrorism can stop, if somebody has to pay such a high price for this that it's just not worth it, then that's fine. That's good enough."

Three weeks later, the families gathered again in Judge Lamberth's courtroom. Tom Fay stepped forward. For days after the testimony of Arline, Vicki, and Len and their children, along with the other testimony— including Hassan Salameh's own words in his confession—Fay struggled to summarize what had been said during the trial and how best to convey the pain of the families he represented and the obstacles they faced in merely coming to Lamberth's courtroom.

He began by mentioning the Declaration of Independence and how Thomas Jefferson "spoke of unalienable rights, among which he listed first, the right to life itself."

"Two hundred and twenty years after Jefferson wrote those words," said Fay, "the Congress enacted the anti-terrorism" law that was the basis of the Duker-Eisenfeld lawsuit.

Fay mentioned that the new law was "an attempt by Congress to discharge its duty to secure those rights against international terrorism" and "a response to the failure" of the White House "to exercise its vast powers against a growing tide of international terrorism."

Then he turned his attention to Matt and Sara and how their personal stories—and dreams of a life together—were at the heart of the lawsuit before Judge Lamberth.

Matt and Sara, said Fay, "are the classical victims of terrorism. Terrorism is distinguished by the selection of innocent victims, instead of opponents in arms."

But he pointed out that "a common thread runs through" the lawsuits that he and Steve Perles had filed on behalf of Matt, Sara, and Alisa Flatow.

"All were distinguished by their sympathy for the very people that the national instigator of terrorism, Iran, was supposedly assisting," Fay said. "None was, in any way, a threat to the terrorist leaders, the Palestinian people, or Iran."

"While Sara Duker waded through bogs trying to unlock the mysteries of microorganisms to protect the environment, Hassan Salameh was being trained by the agents of the defendants and learning how to extract explosives from land mines," Fay said. "While Matt Eisenfeld reached out to a child lest the child feel left out, Hassan Salameh reached out to a child to spread the malignancy of hate without concern for the life of the young boy he enticed into suicide and murder."

A few days earlier, Palestinian authorities announced that they had arrested Mohammed Deif, the Hamas commander who ordered Hassan Salameh to carry out the Jaffa Road bombing—and who had also been linked to the plot that resulted in Alisa Flatow's death. But merely being arrested by Palestinians, said Fay, was no guarantee that Deif would be prosecuted. As Fay noted, US Justice Department officials had still not tried to extradite any suspected Palestinian terrorists for trial in America. He felt Deif's extradition was highly unlikely.

"There is no reason to think that he will be prosecuted by the Clinton administration," Fay told Judge Lamberth, adding that lawsuits like those by Flatow, Duker, and Eisenfeld "are the only remedy available to the victims of Iranian terrorism."

Fay then addressed the politics that had increasingly whirled around Stephen Flatow's lawsuit and his attempt to collect on the damages that Lamberth had ordered Iran to pay. If Lamberth had any thought about holding back on ruling in favor of the Duker and Eisenfeld families, Fay wanted to dissuade him.

"Our clients, counsel, and, of course, this court are fully aware that President Clinton has mounted an unprecedented effort intended to protect the assets of the defendant, the Islamic Republic of Iran, and essentially nullify any judgment of this court," Fay said. "I note for the record that on our last visit to this courtroom in the Flatow case, I counted fourteen lawyers, headed up by the deputy assistant attorney general of the United States, sent by the Clinton administration in defense of Iranian assets."

"We recognize that this court does not have unlimited power," Fay added, "but I say to the court for these families: Give us the tools in the form of a judgment, which, if enforced over the opposition of President Clinton, will deter Iran, and we will go up the hill or up through the courts or do whatever else is necessary, to the full extent of our resources and ability to get the job done and stop the killing."

Seven weeks later, Judge Lamberth ordered Iran to pay $327 million to the Duker and Eisenfeld families.

Reporting on Lamberth's ruling, the *New York Times* noted that it "may be largely symbolic" because of the Clinton administration's continued efforts to block any attempt by victims' families to place legal claims on Iran's financial and real estate assets in the US.

In the final lines of his 4,400-word ruling, Lamberth decided to send a message to the White House. He began by mentioning Steve Flatow and his fight with the Clinton administration to collect on his $247 million judgment.

"The court views with considerable dismay the fact that the rule of law is being frustrated in that case," Lamberth declared. "Nevertheless, the court can not shrink from its duty to declare the applicable law in this case and must express its conviction that ultimately this judgment will not be a mere Pyrrhic victory for the Eisenfeld and Duker families. Their courage and steadfastness in pursuing this litigation, and their efforts to do something to deter more tragic deaths and suffering of innocent Americans at the hands of these terrorists, are to be commended and admired."

Speaking to reporters afterwards, Arline Duker described Lamberth's ruling as "a $327 million weapon against Iran's use of terrorism to conduct foreign policy." She said "the issue is for Iran not to have the money, for Iran to be punished."

But would the Dukers and Eisenfelds ever collect that money?

Steve Perles said the Clinton administration had recently hinted that it wanted to find a way to compromise on the issue. But he was dubious just the same.

"Frankly, all they've done so far is stiff us," Perles said.

He did not expect the White House to change.

# CHAPTER 14

Even before the Duker-Eisenfeld trial ended and Judge Royce Lamberth delivered his less-than-subtle verbal slap at the Clinton administration, a compromise was being shaped for victims' families to claim Iran's assets.

There was no formal announcement by the White House or by anyone on Capitol Hill, no press releases, no ceremonial handshake between lawyers. The process began with a phone conversation. A prominent advocate of Jewish causes, Dr. Mandell Ganchrow, called and invited Stephen Flatow to a lunch in Manhattan with a group of Jewish leaders. The guest of honor would be Hillary Clinton.

By the summer of 1999, less than six months after her husband managed to avoid impeachment over his sexual dalliances with a White House intern and a year before the Duker-Eisenfeld trial, Hillary Clinton began her own political journey. In carefully parsed phrasing that withheld a firm commitment, she signaled that she wanted to enter the race for a US Senate seat in New York that would become vacant with the retirement of Daniel Patrick Moynihan.

No presidential wife had ever attempted what Hillary was setting out to do, and almost every step of her path seemed to be packed with social and political potholes. For starters, she did not live in New York and was not intimately familiar with the state's complex political map. Also, with her husband still in the White House for almost two more years, she had to find a comfortable way of staking out her own political positions without diverging too much from his—or from the overall agenda of the Clinton administration.

Mandell Ganchrow—known as "Mendy" to his friends—was in no mood to celebrate Hillary Clinton's new venture even though she had reached out to him to assist her in meeting Jewish leaders in New York. Ganchrow, a prominent surgeon in the New York City region and a well-known Jewish activist, had risen to the presidency of the Orthodox Union, which had become one of the nation's most powerful advocates for Jewish causes. He had become deeply distrustful of Hillary Clinton and made no secret of the fact that he hoped New York City Mayor Rudolph Giuliani, a Republican, would run for Moynihan's Senate seat.

Ganchrow's wife was even helping to raise money for Giuliani's possible campaign. As Hillary's campaign grew, Ganchrow felt it was time to put her on the spot with some pointed questions about hot-button issues that were important to Jewish voters. He scheduled a luncheon with her and Jewish leaders at the Orthodox Union's offices in New York City. Then he telephoned Flatow.

Ganchrow wanted to know if Flatow would be willing to raise a potentially explosive question during the luncheon's question-and-answer session: What did Hillary Clinton think about the efforts by her husband's administration to block Flatow and other victims' families from collecting on their lawsuits against Iran?

The question underscored a dilemma for Bill and Hillary Clinton. As a candidate, Hillary could not be expected to agree with every policy that her husband advocated. Yet, with Bill Clinton making no secret of his efforts to improve diplomatic relations with Iran before his presidency ended, how would it look if America's first lady publicly declared that she supported the efforts of Flatow and other victims' families to claim Iranian assets in the US? That kind of husband-wife disagreement on policy might be easily accepted within the wide-open realm of modern American politics, but not in the more hidebound world of Iran. There it would be potentially confusing, even insulting.

On the other hand, if Hillary agreed with efforts by the administration to block the families from gaining access to those assets, she risked losing support from New York's Jewish voters and severe criticism from leaders such as Ganchrow in her Senate campaign. No matter what Hillary said, she would make news.

"Of course, I wanted to be there," Flatow said.

It was now December 1999. Hillary and Bill Clinton had already purchased a home in New York City suburb. The formal announcement that she was running for the Senate was two months away but she was already in trouble with Jewish voters.

A month earlier, in her dual roles as first lady and prospective Senate candidate, Clinton toured Israel and portions of the Palestinian West Bank. It was the kind of ticket-punching visit that US politicians routinely make, especially if they wanted to woo Jewish voters back home and demonstrate some familiarity with one of the world's most contentious regions. For the most part, Clinton's trip went smoothly—until she visited with Yasser Arafat's wife, Suha, in the Palestinian city of Ramallah, about ten miles north of Jerusalem.

During a joint appearance, Suha Arafat delivered a rambling discourse on Palestinian concerns in which she accused the Israelis of spreading cancer by using poison gas. "It is important to point out the severe damage caused by the intensive daily use of poison gas by Israeli forces in the past years that led to an increase in cancer cases among Palestinian women and children," Arafat said in Arabic.

There was no factual basis in what Arafat said, nor did she offer any. It didn't matter. What mattered was Hillary Clinton's reaction. As Arafat spoke, Clinton appeared to be listening in silence, wearing headphones that supposedly carried an English translation of Arafat's remarks. When Arafat finished, Clinton rose and the two embraced, with Clinton kissing Arafat on the cheek and saying nothing to challenge what Arafat had just said.

Clinton's entourage had barely left Ramallah before Israeli political figures and others, including Jewish leaders in the US, unleashed a torrent of criticism. When questioned by reporters traveling with her, Clinton seemed uneasy and verbally flat-footed; she said she had not been able to clearly hear the translation of Arafat's remarks. It wasn't until the following day after receiving what her staff described as an accurate translation that Clinton denounced Arafat's statement. The delay, however, infuriated Clinton's critics, including Mendy Ganchrow.

As Ganchrow strategized about the upcoming lunch with Hillary Clinton, Flatow's lawyer, Steve Perles, received a phone call from a prominent Democrat who also happened to be a major supporter of the first lady's senate campaign. The caller was worried about the negative fallout over Hillary's trip to Israel, not to mention the continuing friction between the Clinton administration and Stephen Flatow. The conversation was brief, but the message was clear. Could Perles help make peace between Flatow and the Clinton administration? Flatow had not toned down his criticism of the president and in late November 1999, he joined a group of Jewish activists and others, including families of the Brothers to the Rescue pilots, for a rally and press conference outside the new headquarters of Hillary Clinton's exploratory senate campaign committee.

Perles listened intently to the Democratic leader on the phone. For more than a year Perles had tried without success to gain access to Iran's assets through the courts and by lobbying for special legislation from Congress. Now, maybe, here was an opportunity for progress. The Democrat on the phone had an intriguing offer. He wanted to know if Flatow would attend Hillary's upcoming lunch at the Orthodox Union. It was the same invitation that Mendy Ganchrow had offered. But instead of coming from a critic of Hillary, this offer came from a supporter. Perles viewed this as a good sign.

Two weeks later, Flatow took a seat inside a large room at the Orthodox Union headquarters in Manhattan. Around him were more than one hundred of the area's most prominent rabbis and Jewish community leaders. Hillary Clinton walked from table to table, escorted by US Senator Joseph Lieberman, the Connecticut Democrat and an Orthodox Jew who would end up running for vice president in 2000, the same year Hillary planned to run for the Senate. After greeting everyone, Clinton offered some general remarks, then opened the floor to questions. When it was his turn, Flatow was as blunt as possible.

"Do you support the Clinton administration's continued blocking of terror victims from receiving compensation?" he asked.

Flatow sensed that Hillary was not surprised by his question. But he expected a politically nuanced answer that offered sympathy for the killing of his daughter with no firm commitment on resolving the legal issues with Iran. Instead, Hillary offered a blunt response of her own that was unmistakably clear and devoid of nuance.

"No, I do not," she said.

Flatow was stunned. After hearing what Clinton had said, Perles was thrilled, too. Was this the opening he needed to pry loose some of Iran's assets?

A month later, in January 2000, Perles and Flatow received a new message from a highly placed staffer in the Clinton administration. An ad-hoc committee was being formed to try to work out a settlement to the legal dispute over Iran's assets. Stuart Eizenstat would play a key role. As Eizenstat noted years later: "We wanted to get it done before the president left office."

Actually, the process had already begun.

—◦—

Roughly a year before Hillary Clinton spoke to the Orthodox Union and Eizenstat's ad-hoc committee stepped up efforts to find a compromise, Stephen Flatow met privately with Bill Clinton.

By early 1999, Bill Clinton was desperately trying to save his presidency. The House of Representatives, with its majority of Republicans had already voted to impeach him on charges that he committed perjury and obstructed justice during the federal investigation of several matters, including his sexual affair with a White House intern. In January, the US Senate, with its Democratic majority, opened the impeachment trial itself.

Flatow wanted another chance to speak to the president. Senator Frank Lautenberg contacted the White House and Bill Clinton agreed. The meeting would not take place at the White House, however. Flatow was instructed to come to the Washington Hilton Hotel for the National Prayer Breakfast.

On the first Thursday in February, as prosecutors and defense lawyers prepared to offer final arguments in Bill Clinton's impeachment trial in the Senate chambers at the US Capitol, more than 2,600 religious leaders, politicians, lobbyists and others assembled across town in the cavernous Hilton ballroom.

With its collection of clerics from all major religions, mixing with politicians of all stripes, the National Prayer Breakfast was long considered one of the few events in Washington where the lines between church and state were blurred. For politicians, it was a chance to send a message that they value religion in public life and even their personal lives, too. For religious leaders and their advocates, it was an opportunity to push for the inclusion of religious values in government policy decisions. Evangelicals rubbed shoulders with Catholics, Jews with Muslims, Buddhists with Hindus, Mormons with Jehovah's Witnesses. Besides Clinton, two other guests attracted the most attention, though—Leah Rabin, the wife of the assassinated Israeli prime minister, and Palestinian leader Yasser Arafat.

Clinton's staff sent word to Flatow that the two could meet before the breakfast.

Flatow passed through a security checkpoint and waited in a hotel hallway that was filled with guards. Arafat passed by, flanked by his retinue of aides. For a moment, Flatow was tempted to tap Arafat on the shoulder and mention Alisa's death. But he kept silent.

Flatow glanced down the hall. Clinton walked toward him with his national seurity advisor, Sandy Berger.

"He looked terrible," Flatow said, figuring that the impeachment ordeal had taken toll on the president.

Clinton stopped.

"Mister Flatow. Good to see you again."

Flatow knew he had only a minute or so to speak so he got right to the point. He mentioned the law that Clinton had signed in 1996 allowing him to file a lawsuit against Iran, then summarized his lawsuit and Judge Lamberth's ruling and the problems of trying to lay claim to Iran's assets in the US.

Clinton looked Flatow in the eye and nodded.

Flatow reminded Clinton that the president had promised assistance in helping him locate Iranian commercial assets that might not be blocked by the US State and Treasury Departments, although no help had been forthcoming.

As Flatow finished, Clinton fell silent for a second or two. Flatow studied the president's face. "You could see his mind working," Flatow recalled.

Clinton turned to Sandy Berger.

"Let's get this done," Flatow remembers Clinton saying.

Clinton then shook Flatow's hand and walked down the hall.

Flatow was elated. Perles had not been allowed into the hallway by the Secret Service and was waiting outside. Flatow couldn't wait to tell him what happened with the president.

"We hit a home run," Flatow said as he approached Perles.

Eight days later, the US Senate voted to acquit Bill Clinton of the impeachment charges. Almost as soon as the votes had been counted, another effort began to find a legislative solution to what was rapidly become known as Stephen Flatow's dispute with Bill Clinton.

On Capitol Hill, Frank Lautenberg and Connie Mack opposed each other on Clinton's impeachment. Mack supported a guilty verdict that would have led to Clinton's removal from office; Lautenberg sided with the majority and voted not guilty. But after the impeachment crisis passed, both reinvigorated their efforts to gain compensation for terrorist victims. Lautenberg and Mack also announced they planned to retire after their terms expired in 2000; like President Clinton, both wanted to finally settle the issue of compensation for terrorist victims.

In many ways, Mack and Lautenberg had formed a perfect partnership to force the president to embrace some sort of plan to compensate the families. Mack's fellow Republicans in the Senate and in the House of Representatives—especially conservatives—eagerly lined up behind any effort to embarrass Clinton and punish Iran for its support of terrorism and Fidel Castro for the shooting down of the Brothers to the Rescue Planes. Lautenberg, in turn, rallied Democrats in the Senate and in the House. With Lautenberg, a liberal and longtime Clinton supporter, taking a firm stance against Palestinian terrorism and opposing the president's efforts to protect Iran's assets, other Democratic liberals, who might have favored a more nuanced approach, felt free to follow.

With the impeachment behind them, Clinton's aides believed that the unusual alliance of conservative Republicans and liberal Democrats, could pose a formidable obstacle to attempts by the White House, or any arm of the administration, to continue blocking families from being compensated. What's more, Lautenberg and Mack had proposed a new—and stronger—version of their bill, the Justice for Victims of Terrorism Act, which would remove White House and State Department roadblocks that had stopped the families from claiming the frozen assets and property of terrorist-sponsoring nations. For the White House, a key question was how to compromise without embarrassing the president. But as a Senate staffer involved in the negotiations, explained, "The White House knew we had all the votes in Congress. And if we voted, the president would lose ninety-nine to one." The staffer was exaggerating on the ninety-nine-to-one vote tally, of course. But not by much.

In October 1999, the Senate Judiciary Committee opened hearings on the Lautenberg-Mack bill. Flatow was invited to speak. So was Stuart Eizenstat.

Eizenstat had not retreated from his belief that a dangerous political game was being played on Capitol Hill with terrorist victims recruiting political figures such as Frank Lautenberg and Connie Mack who would champion their causes. As Eizenstat saw things, the system was entirely unfair. It meant that many other victims, especially those who did not have the connections to hire an aggressive lawyer such as Steve Perles or the knowledge or financial wherewithal to come to Washington and lobby Congressional figures, would be left behind in what Eizenstat saw as a "rush to the courthouse." Also, Eizenstat knew that the pool of potential assets was limited. Yes, millions of dollars were potentially available to victims. But, with the likelihood of another favorable ruling calling for a large payment in the Duker-Eisenfeld case, Eizenstat feared that only a small number of families would get their share, leaving little for others—including what Eizenstat said would surely be future terrorist victims.

"It's grossly unfair," Eizenstat said. "It's a bad way to do the public's business."

In particular Eizenstat was concerned about the family of Ira Weinstein, the dual Israeli-US citizen who was traveling on the same bus as Sara Duker and Matthew Eisenfeld and who died six weeks after the explosion of massive burns. Weinstein's relatives had just begun to explore the possibility of a lawsuit but were far behind the others. What if Weinstein's relatives gained a favorable ruling but all of Iran's assets had been taken already?

Another concern was Leah Stein Mousa, who had been badly burned in the blast on the Number 18 bus. Unlike Ira Weinstein, Leah Stein Mousa survived—and was even visited by the emergency medic, David

Sofer, weeks later in the hospital. But Mousa had spent so much time trying to regain her ability to walk, see, and hear correctly that she was behind by several years in filing a lawsuit. Her attorney, John Karr, wondered if she was already too late.

For months, Eizenstat had tried to shape the outlines of a compensation settlement that would allow the White House to save face and not set a legal precedent that might endanger US diplomats overseas. He fancied himself as a skillful negotiator of delicate policy and legal matters, not to mention an objective analyst of policy. But as Eizenstat pondered the issue—and its inherent dilemmas—he concluded that the fairest way to compensate the victims was to create a federal commission that would weigh claims and award money from the US Treasury, not from the frozen assets of Iran and other nations that had been labeled by the State Department as state sponsors of terrorism.

"If you are going to do something, let's be transparent, and say it's worthy of taxpayer support," Eizenstat said.

When Eizenstat took a seat before the Senate Judiciary Committee, he was ready to test his proposal. He also knew he was reentering a debate that had become deeply politicized. It was now October 27, 1999. Two days earlier, in an op-ed article in *USA Today*, Senator Connie Mack outlined how the Clinton administration had first encouraged families to file lawsuits, then blocked their efforts to claim assets of such nations as Iran and Cuba. "The president has betrayed these American families," Mack wrote. However, "the US government's embarrassment could be over tomorrow. The president has the authority—indeed, the obligation—to respect the rule of law and the power of the courts."

Before Eizenstat spoke to the committee, Mack testified. He praised Eizenstat as "a most competent and dedicated government official" but Mack added that he was frustrated with Eizenstat's negotiating style. "After waiting so long, I must say with due respect there must be action for me to believe his words," Mack said. "To be frank, all I have noticed to date is a lack of response on behalf of the administration, and I sense no sincerity on their part at all."

Mack turned his attention to Clinton: "He has chosen to protect terrorist assets over the rights of American citizens seeking justice. This is simply not what America stands for. Victims' families must know that the US government stands with them in actions as well as words."

Lautenberg was no stranger to Republican criticism of a Democratic president. But after listening to Mack, Lautenberg felt he had to come to Clinton's defense.

Calling Mack "my friend and colleague," Lautenberg said, "I do not think that one can say with impunity that the president of the United States, President Clinton, is willing to subordinate the victims' rights to a grander scheme."

Lautenberg agreed with Eizenstat that victims' families should not be allowed to claim ownership of foreign embassies. But then he turned to a key argument that Eizenstat had been making—that Flatow and others such as the Duker and Eisenfeld families could drain away the pool of available assets from Iran before other victims might have a chance to apply for them. "Unfortunately or not," said Lautenberg, "that is the way American civil law treats all assets that are part of a court judgment, and, frankly, I agree with that, because perhaps by satisfying those claims, we can deter terrorist acts in the future."

Lautenberg noted that Eizenstat had proposed that Congress set aside a pool of US money—a Crime Victims Fund—to compensate American families for the loss of relatives to foreign terrorists. "But that proposal misses the point," Lautenberg said. "Foreign countries that sponsor terrorist attacks should have to pay a price."

Finally, perhaps aware that he would soon announce his retirement, Lautenberg pointed out that time was slipping away. "Do we make the victims of terrorism like the Flatows and the others, wait years longer?" he asked. "Waiting is not the answer."

After Eizenstat spoke and answered questions, Flatow stepped forward. It had been almost ten months since his brief meeting with President Clinton at the Hilton Hotel. Flatow had heard nothing further from the White House, and, once again, he had reached a point where he doubted whether a settlement would ever be reached.

"Am I frustrated and discouraged?" Flatow told the committee. "Absolutely. Am I going to quit? No, Mr. Chairman, I am not. A father's responsibility to his child does not end with her murder."

Tom Fay sat in the audience in the room listening to Eizenstat and Flatow. During a break in the testimony, a man Fay had never met tapped him on the shoulder and asked him to step into the hall for a private conversation. Fay got up and followed the man into the hallway. The man said he'd listened to Eizenstat and Flatow but what surprised him were Eizenstat's conclusions about Iran's limited resources. Eizenstat did not mention a large pool of money left by Iran at the Pentagon decades before to buy warships, tanks, and other military weapons, the man said. The pool of money was more than $400 million.

Fay couldn't wait to tell Perles and Flatow. An Iranian account with $400 million was more than enough to cover Judge Lamberth's order that Flatow should receive $247 million. It might even be enough to cover what he expected to be a large award for the Duker and Eisenfeld families, too.

But how would this account be tapped? It would take another year to answer that question.

—————

The pathways of political deal-making are not always straight or obvious. In retrospect, participants in the compromise say that after Hillary Clinton formally announced in February 2000 that she was running for the US Senate in New York State, the obstacles that blocked Stephen Flatow and others from collecting the rewards for their lawsuits began to slowly vanish. Those legal and political barriers seemed to disappear even more quickly after the Dukers and Eisenfelds won their lawsuit in Judge Lamberth's court.

Hillary's political career was not the only factor. Key figures in the negotiations point to Bill Clinton's own desire to settle some unfinished business as he was winding down his presidency. Perles and Fay, meanwhile, believed they had a powerful trump card—the $400 million in Iranian funds in the Pentagon account with the obscure title of "Foreign Military Sales." For the first time in more than two years, they had a firm target for their claim that was not considered diplomatic property.

Then, Stuart Eizenstat intervened again.

By 2000, Eizenstat had embraced two roles. First, he felt he needed to find a way to compensate the families. He also felt duty-bound to protect

President Clinton—and future presidents—by setting a precedent that would automatically allow US citizens to take foreign assets if they won court judgments in terrorist cases. Eizenstat had a few trump cards of his own to play, however. "Politically there was tremendous support for paying the families," he said.

Eizenstat suggested that Flatow and the others could be paid with a specific funding appropriation's bill, passed by Congress. But Flatow rejected the proposal.

"I did not want any American taxpayers' money used," he said. "I want the Iranians to pay."

Eizenstat turned to Frank Lautenberg and Connie Mack for help.

Lautenberg and Mack were moving ahead with their own proposal—a rewritten version of their Justice for Victims of Terrorism Act that included a provision for terrorist victims to lay claim to the $400 million in the Pentagon's account as well as another $22 million in other properties owned by Iran in the US.

Not surprisingly, this new proposal set off a debate between the White House and Congress over whether the US would be liable to pay Iran for the missing funds if the $400 million was turned over to the victims' families along with the $22 million in diplomatic properties. No clear answer could be found. The White House offered one explanation; Congress offered another.

For instance, the White House's budgetary arm, the Office of Management and Budget, declared that the US would be liable if an international tribunal ruled in favor of an Iranian request for the US to return the money and diplomatic properties. Perhaps more ominously, OMB analysts pointed out in an internal memo that the amount of claims against Iran from the court judgments far exceeded the amount of money in the Pentagon account and the value of the Iranian diplomatic properties. Plus, other court judgments were likely to to come. "These subsequent judgments represent an unknown liability for the US," the OMB memo said.

In its own memo, entitled "Fallacies and Realities" of the Lautenberg-Mack legislation, Congress's own budgetary arm, the Government Accountability Office, offered an entirely different scenario. The GAO said the use of the Iranian assets to pay terror victims was permitted under US laws and would likely be approved by an international claims tribunal that handled US and Iranian disputes over frozen assets and other financial issues. "There is no likelihood that the United States would be liable to Iran for the amounts paid out to valid judgment creditors," the memo said.

Then came the July 11, 2000, ruling and $327 million award by Judge Lamberth in the Duker-Eisenfeld lawsuit—a confirmation that the size of the awards to terror victims far exceeded the pool of Iranian assets. Combined with the $247 million that Lamberth awarded to Flatow and additional rulings by federal judges in other cases such as one involving the journalist Terry Anderson, a hard reality began to frame the negotiations between the Eizenstat, Lautenberg, Mack and the Flatow, Duker and Eisenfeld families: There was not enough money to pay everyone.

It was now August 2000. The group was well aware that time was running out for a solution. President Clinton's last day in office was January 20, 2001, less than five months away. But the Congress would adjourn before then.

A variety of participants in the negotiations began to seriously examine a compromise proposal that had first been outlined months earlier in a letter from Eizenstat to Connie Mack. Under the plan, Eizenstat wanted to address Flatow's demand that no US funds would be used, and that the families involved in the lawsuits would be paid with the financial assets of Iran and Cuba. Eizenstat also hoped the families would take less money. As Eizenstat wrote, the families would "receive partial and advance payment for compensatory damages" from "blocked assets and other appropriated funds" from Iran and Cuba.

But Eisenstat also invoked a murky legal term—"subrogation"—that would become a center of dispute in years to come. Under the proposed plan, the US Treasury would issue checks to the families, then try to recoup "these payments directly from the country concerned as part of any normalization of relations." Left unsaid in the Eizenstat letter and in other negotiations was a basic question: How would the Flatows, Dukers, and Eisenfelds ever know that the US Treasury actually recouped the money from Iran?

Lautenberg and Mack, meanwhile, began to worry that the Eizenstat proposal was little more than an elaborate diversion to curtail criticism from the families and allow the White House to stall until the end of Clinton's term in office. The Justice for Victims of Terrorism Act had plenty of votes to pass both the Senate and the House of Representatives. But Lautenberg and Mack were concerned that, if the bill passed, Clinton would veto it before he left office and leave the families with no money. Their fears worsened when one of Mack's staffers discovered that Clinton had received an internal White House memo that said "the bill's passage is inevitable. Therefore we will continue with current tactics of running out the clock."

Mack's staff also learned that the White House had reached out to a prominent Jewish leader and asked him to "get Flatow to back off." In a follow-up memo to Mack recounting the incident, a staffer wrote: "I am skeptical as to whether we really have a negotiation ongoing. I think we are prepared to move forward and tell everyone we can that we have not been dealt with in good faith."

———

In the end, there was no dramatic reckoning, no meeting of adversaries, no handshakes. The deal was subtle and as deftly orchestrated as that phone call almost a year earlier inviting Stephen Flatow to the lunch with Hillary Clinton.

The families bowed to a key pragmatic wish from Eizenstat. They agreed to take less money and allow the US Treasury to "subrogate" a claim on the blocked assets. The Lautenberg-Mack bill was rewritten to give the families the compensatory portion of the rulings, with an additional 10 percent bonus if they promised not to pursue the larger punitive damage claims in the United States.

So, eventually, instead of $247 million, the Flatow family agreed to take approximately $25 million. Instead of more than $327 million, the Duker and Eisenfeld families would eventually collect about $27.4 million.

However, the families still worried that the rug could be pulled out from under them at the last minute. And they wanted some guarantee that the reduced payments would actually be made.

The memory of Bill Clinton signing a law giving them the power to file lawsuits, then watching the White House and other branches of the administration block their efforts to collect from Iran was all too vivid. Almost no one in the Flatow, Duker, and Eisenfeld camps trusted the Clintons, especially after they learned that some White House advisors had actively discussed a plan to keep the families waiting as the clock ran down in Clinton's presidency and Hillary Clinton pursued a seat in the US Senate.

Frank Lautenberg and Connie Mack came up with what amounted to a legislative end-run. Instead of a separate bill that President Clinton could ignore or veto again by citing national security concerns, the Justice for Victims of Terrorism Act and the provision for paying the Flatows, Dukers, and Eisenfelds were inserted into a much larger piece of legislation to prevent what had become a modern-day version of slavery, in which immigrants were forcibly brought to America for sexual exploitation, forced labor or, in the worst cases, for the extraction of organs or tissues.

It was a shrewd maneuver by Lautenberg and Mack. The Victims of Trafficking and Violence Prevention Act of 2000 was the first US law to address the growing worldwide problem of human trafficking. Feminists supported it, along with liberal human rights advocates and even conservatives who wanted tougher immigration standards. That the law also had a provision to pay victims of terrorism seemed like a footnote. And if Clinton wanted to block the terrorism clause, he would have to veto the entire trafficking bill.

Lautenberg and Mack knew—along with just about everyone else in American politics—that such a veto by Bill Clinton was unlikely, certainly not with Hillary Clinton in the final weeks of her US Senate campaign and his own presidency about to end. The last thing Bill Clinton wanted as he left the White House was the universal scorn of his liberal base and his conservative critics.

The Senate and House voted overwhelmingly for the bill in mid-October. On October 28, Bill Clinton signed the bill into law. Unlike the legislation he signed four years earlier on the south lawn of the White House to give families such as the Flatows, Dukers, and Eisenfelds the right to file lawsuits against terrorist-sponsoring nations, there was no ceremony. There was, however, a presidential statement released by the White House. It ran on for more than two thousand words.

"This landmark legislation," said Clinton, "accomplishes a number of important objectives and Administration priorities. It strengthens and improves upon the nation's efforts to fight violence against women. It also provides important new tools and resources to combat the worldwide scourge of trafficking in persons and provides vital assistance to victims of trafficking. And it helps American victims of terrorism abroad to collect court-awarded compensation."

As he had done so masterfully in previous political battles, Bill Clinton found a way to declare his own victory in the efforts by the Flatows, Dukers, and Eisenfelds to punish Iran even though his administration had worked so hard for almost four years to defeat them.

But signing a bill to clear the way for the Flatows, Dukers, and Eisenfelds to collect on their court rulings was one thing. Paying them was something else. The bill never specified that.

Bill Clinton did not call Stephen Flatow—or Arline Duker or Vicki and Len Eisenfeld. No one from the White House or the State and Treasury departments contacted them. But ten days after Clinton signed the anti-trafficking law, Hillary Clinton won a seat in the US Senate. She defeated her opponent, a little-known Republican congressman from Long Island, Rick Lazio, by more than 12 percentage points.

The calendar turned to a new year—2001. America prepared to welcome a new president, George W. Bush. Bill and Hillary Clinton busied themselves by packing books and other personal items and preparing to settle into a rambling white colonial home in the wooded hills of Chappaqua, New York. Bill planned to write and start a foundation; Hillary planned to settle into her new role as a US senator.

Several days before the Clintons left the White House, the telephone rang in the home of Arline Duker.

Steve Perles was on the line.

He explained that the the US Treasury Department had finally transferred the money that was meant to compensate Arline for Sara's murder. Perles said Flatows and the Eisenfelds would also be paid that day.

Arline hung up the phone. Neither she, nor Vicki and Len Eisenfeld or Stephen Flatow and his family would receive the hundreds of millions that Judge Lamberth ordered. But the amount was substantial nevertheless.

Arline thought about the bills she would pay and how she would give large portions to Ariella and Tamara to establish financial security as they moved into adulthood. She vowed also to set aside another chunk of the award to fund charities and scholarships. But she was in no mood to rejoice—or even feel a sense of relief.

She thought of Sara and Matt. If they lived, Matt would have celebrated his thirtieth birthday in a few days. Sara would have turned twenty-eight in August. There probably would have been a wedding. Matt would be a rabbi, Sara a successful scientist, perhaps even a professor at a prestigious university.

And, yes, Arline would have possibly been a grandmother.

But on this day, there would be no celebration. Arline was alone. She decided to spend the rest of the day at work.

"Having the money," she said, "doesn't make the sadness go away."

# EPILOGUE

# What Remains . . .

"WHY DID YOU KILL HER?"

The question hung in the stale prison air like an uninvited guest. Hassan Salameh stared into my eyes. He seemed momentarily confused.

"Why did you kill Sara Duker," I asked again.

" . . . And Matthew Eisenfeld?"

" . . . And the others on the bus?"

Salameh shook his head. He smiled faintly, then frowned as my questions were translated into Arabic.

"You don't understand," he said. "She wasn't the target. She was there."

"*She was there?*"

I repeated Salameh's words back to him.

"What do you mean by that?" I asked.

Salameh fell silent and stared at me again.

"We don't really think about who is being killed," he said, finally. "She was not the target. The target was Israeli occupation. That was her bad luck that she was on the bus."

And so we began. We sat in straight-backed chairs, facing each other in a windowless room at Eshel Prison on the edge of the Negev Desert. After removing Salameh's handcuffs, two guards settled into chairs behind him and two more sat behind me. A framed blue-and-white Israeli flag hung on the wall. It was a Sunday morning in late March 2006, and Salameh had been in jail for almost ten years. He was thirty-four. If she had lived, Sara would have been thirty-two. Matthew would have recently celebrated his thirty-fifth birthday.

I asked to speak to Salameh to assess whether he had any regrets. It was, to be sure, a naïve request. I knew that. But I also knew that, if peace could ever be forged between Israelis and Palestinians, then, as some observers on both sides point out, killers like Salameh might be released and that both sides would begin the long journey to finding some measure of reconciliation over all the blood that had been shed between them. Did Salameh want to reconcile?

Outside the prison walls, Israel faced yet another election that spring and what many felt could be a significant turning point in its history. The Oslo accords no longer seemed to be working. Israel was expanding its settlements in the West Bank and the Palestinian government seemed deeply divided by rival factions with Yasser Arafat's Fatah party ruling the West Bank while Hamas was now in control of the the Gaza Strip. There would, of course, be renewed efforts to revive the Oslo process in the coming years, but something clearly had broken down after more than a decade of suicide attacks. Even many Israelis who once favored a complete withdrawal from the West Bank felt they could no longer trust the peace process and, in particular, either side's ability to end the fighting. Whatever hope had blossomed in the early 1990s—a hope that prompted Sara and Matt to plan a trip to Jordan—had now given way to deep cynicism among ordinary Palestinians and Israelis.

Israeli authorities had become so frustrated with suicide attacks by Palestinian militants that they had constructed a series of concrete walls and other security barriers along the border of the West Bank and near various Palestinian towns. Some roads now were lined with high barriers to protect Israeli drivers from snipers' bullets. Ten months earlier, Israel evacuated its residents from the Gaza Strip and closed down a string of settlements, including the beach community where Alisa Flatow planned a short vacation in April 1995. The roadside memorial to Alisa's murder had been removed and placed in storage in Israel.

Before visiting Salameh, I passed through a border checkpoint separating Israel from the West Bank and drove into Ramallah. Yasser Arafat died several years earlier, but his tomb was still not finished and his former compound lay in ruins.

I walked down a hill to "Martyrs' Crossing," the causeway the led to an Israeli checkpoint at the Beit El community and military base where Salameh had been convicted. All was silent now. The gun battles I witnessed on the causeway years earlier between Israeli soldiers and Palestinian fighters were now rare and the burned out cars and tires had been removed. But most of the nearby buildings were still abandoned.

On the other side of Ramallah, I stopped at a government building and met with Dr. Mahmoud al-Ramahi, an Italian-trained physician and Hamas official who had recently become the secretary-general of the Palestinian Legislative Council. In years to come, al-Ramahi would be arrested and imprisoned on several occasions by Israel authorities because of his Hamas affiliation. When I spoke to him, he was in no mood to try to resurrect the Oslo accords or discuss any sort of compromise peace deal with Israel. He talked, instead, of more bloodshed.

I asked about Salameh and whether the kinds of attacks he orchestrated would ever end. "The suicide bombings were the reactions against what Israelis do," al-Ramahi said, sharply, almost as a rebuke to my question. "We are the victims," he added. "We have to continue the resistance. We said that until the occupation is over, the resistance is legitimate."

A few days later, I headed for the Gaza Strip, passing through another Israeli checkpoint and catching a ride into Gaza City.

"Welcome to Gaza Planet," said Osama, a twenty-seven-year-old Palestinian youth counselor who spoke fluent English and told me how he dreamed of leaving for another country.

Gaza was, indeed, a different planet—perhaps even a different universe—compared to other cities in the region. In an election three months earlier, Hamas had won control of Gaza's government. Cars competed with donkey carts on roads where few traffic lights worked. Potholes seemed as numerous as people, and piles of trash burned on almost every corner. Most homes and buildings seemed to have at least one broken window. Many had no windows.

We drove up to the city's main outdoor market, al-Saha Plaza and parked. I opened the car door and got out. The air was laced with wood smoke, dust and diesel exhaust. A breeze off the Mediterranean pushed an old Arabic newspaper along the sidewalk.

I looked up. The plaza was rimmed with billboards but not the kind that advertise soft drinks, clothes, or electronic devices. These billboards proclaimed the exploits of Palestinians who attacked Israelis. I looked for Salameh's picture. Nothing. Nor was there any mention of the bus bombing on Jaffa Road and how it had damaged the Oslo process and affected the Israeli elections a decade before. Among Gaza's Palestinians, Salameh's exploits had simply been folded into far larger violent tapestry. Salameh may have orchestrated one of the most dramatic and politically consequential bombing campaigns in the long struggle between Israelis and Palestinians. But he was not the last. After his arrest, other bomb-makers emerged, along with other suicide bombers, and a decade after Sara and Matt were killed, Salameh's mayhem was not considered all that unusual by either side. Bombing had become the new normal.

As I walked through the plaza, I met Nahed Abu Khair, who was trying to support his wife and eight children by selling Chinese-made baggy jeans.

"What is it like trying to live here?" I asked.

Khair wiped a sweaty film from his forehead. From a minivan parked at a nearby curb, a man with a bullhorn pleaded for donations to a mosque. Khair turned and listened for a few seconds, then looked at me again.

"I'm hoping for a better future for my kids," Khair said.

"How old are you?" I asked.

"Forty-three," said Khair, adding sadly: "My time is gone."

I left and headed for the narrow alleys of the old refugee camps whose tents had been replaced by concrete homes that seemed to fit together like children's blocks. Around noon, I ate a pita sandwich in a restaurant where the electricity kept shutting down. Later, I spoke with fishermen who cast lines into the Mediterranean by wrecks of ships and not far from the abandoned home where Yasser Arafat warned Terje Roed-Larsen to stay away from Jerusalem on the day the Number 18 bus blew up.

By evening, as a taxi drove a photographer and me back to the border checkpoint, Israeli artillery fired overhead toward positions near the Mediterranean where Palestinian militants fired rockets into Israeli towns. No one talked in our car as shells streaked across the sky and we navigated a two-lane road that crossed fields dotted with olive trees. I gazed out a window as the sun set into the Mediterranean and wondered what the future would be like for this troubled land.

In Eshel prison now, I asked Salameh about his own future. He shrugged his shoulders and said he was resigned to dying in prison, celibate and alone—as the Israeli prosecutor, Avinoam Sharon, predicted. Perhaps as solace or perhaps merely to survive in a place with few choices, Salameh said he awoke at 4:30 each morning. He ate all of his meals in his cell and left only for an hour of exercise, alone in a prison yard that was four meters square and surrounded on three sides by concrete walls and on the fourth side by a chain-link fence. He said he studied portions of the Koran each day. He also said he read Israeli and Arabic newspapers when he could get them. Later, I learned that he had been writing a short book about his exploits as a bomb-maker, entitled *The Revenge of the Sacred.*

I mentioned Sara and Matt again. Salameh's voice hardened, his phrasing became more clipped. He nodded and said he remembered the names from an interview years before with FBI agents.

Salameh described himself as a soldier. I moved my chair closer, and suggested that soldiers sometimes regret years later the enemies they had killed in battle, even when those wartime killings may have been justified. Did Salameh regret any of the lives he had taken?

He leaned back in his chair and rested his chin in his hand, sizing me up.

"I'm not happy when civilians are killed," he said.

For a moment, he seemed softer. I wondered if this was Salameh's way of expressing a small flicker of remorse. But just as suddenly, he caught himself. He took a breath, and quickly added: "It's not in my hands."

Our conversation continued like that for another hour. Salameh argued that the bombs he assembled were his way of defending his homeland. I countered by pointing out that every victim on the Jaffa Road commuter bus—and the other buses he targeted—was unarmed. He tried to avoid responsibility; I questioned why he would consider killing so many innocent civilians, no matter how justified he felt his cause was.

"How can you call yourself a soldier if you kill unarmed civilians?" I asked.

For every point I raised, however, Salameh seemed to have an answer. Finally, I fell silent. Salameh shook his head.

"You look at the picture in a different way than I do," he said. "You speak about emotions and feelings. The subject is a lot bigger and more complicated than you make it."

I mentioned Sara again.

"If Sara's mother was sitting here with me, what would you say to her?"

Salameh shifted in his chair.

"Her daughter was not the target. The target was the Israeli occupation," he said.

"Sometimes when you make a suicide attack, mistakes can be made."

"So was this a mistake?" I asked, wondering if he was offering another hint of remorse.

Salameh paused.

"I can't say that it was a mistake," he said. He stopped himself, then returned to a phrase he uttered earlier: "It was her bad luck."

Our time was winding down. The guards explained that Salameh should return to his cell. I said I only had a few more question. Could we talk just a few more minutes? Salameh nodded and looked at me, waiting.

"Does the Koran allow you to kill innocent civilians?" I asked.

"No," Salameh said.

"Then how do you justify killing all those people on the bus?"

"I didn't kill civilians," he said. "It was the situation. It is written in the Koran that we are allowed to defend ourselves."

"And what will God say?" I asked.

It was a clumsy question—a final attempt to shake Salameh out of his scripted rhetoric and jaded theology that advocates suicide bombing as a path to spiritual paradise. He didn't flinch.

"I did what was allowed by God."

———

I returned to Israel six years later. It was early January 2012—more than a decade since the 9/11 attacks and almost sixteen years since the bus bombing by Salameh on Jaffa Road. Benjamin Netanyahu was again the prime minister. Christmas lights flickered atop the stone buildings in Jerusalem's Old City. Jaffa Road was no longer a bus route but now home to a gleaming light rail line. A memorial plaque listing Sara's and Matthew's names and all the others who died on the Number 18 bus hung on a wall of a building near the intersection of Jaffa Road and Sarei Yisrael Street. Nearby, a memorial of twisted and charred steel from the Number 18 bus had been fashioned by a local sculptor, with an inscription in Hebrew: "Fear shall not win. In good and bad, all of us together."

I asked to visit Salameh again, but Israeli prison authorities declined, saying he had been plotting protests inside his prison and was considered too dangerous. So I hired a driver at the American Colony Hotel and set out to find the family of the suicide bomber, Majdi Abu Wardeh.

On another Sunday, we headed southward, over the Jerusalem hills and past Bethlehem. Just before we reached the outskirts of Hebron, we turned onto a two-lane road. We passed olive groves and small meadows where sheep grazed, then drove to the top of a hill. In the valley below lay al-Fawwar refugee camp.

Along the camp's main thoroughfare, posters of Palestinians who were being held in Israeli prisons hung from walls of stores and homes. I approached a teenage boy and asked where the Wardeh family lived.

He led me through a series of narrow streets, then pointed to a vacant lot once occupied by Majdi's family home and introduced me to another boy, sixteen-year-old Mussab Wardeh—Majdi's cousin.

Mussab said he was born after the Jaffa Road bombing and did not know his cousin. But Mussab knew the story of how Majdi became a *shaheed*—a martyr—by carrying a black bag aboard a bus and calling out "Allahu Akbar" before pushing a detonator button. As we talked, Mussab pointed to a wall and two graffiti messages in Arabic about Majdi's death. FEBRUARY 25, 1996—THE DAY HE WAS MARTYRED, said one. Another said: THE 25TH OF FEBRUARY IS A BLESSED MEMORY.

Beneath both messages, in Arabic, was a signature—the tag of the graffiti artist.

"Hamas," it said.

I turned to Mussab. What did he think of Majdi's suicide?

"God will take care of this," he said. "God will bring us justice eventually."

"Where is Majdi's family now?" I asked.

Mussab motioned me to follow him. We got in the car and rolled down the hill and back along camp's main thoroughfare. After passing stores that sold fruit and vegetables and the stares from a cluster of elderly men who sat in plastic chairs, we turned onto another street and drove up another hill.

I got out and walked up to a middle-aged man in a wrinkled jacket—Majdi's father, Muhammed Abu Wardeh.

"Welcome," he said, when I explained why I was there. "Come inside."

Muhammed led me up the stairs and into a room with no furniture and only one photo on the wall—the eight-by-ten martyrdom poster of his son. He motioned me to sit on a floor cushion. One of Muhammed's five remaining sons brought tea.

I turned the conversation to February 25, 1996. Why did Majdi become a suicide bomber?

Muhammed repeated the story he told Israeli police—that he thought his son left on a Friday to find work and that he was shocked to discovered Majdi was a suicide bomber.

"If I had known I would have stopped him," he said.

He took a sip of tea, then continued.

"I was sad," he said. "Because I lost my son. You are talking about a father's feelings after losing his son."

Muhammed explained that he understands why some young men decide to become suicide bombers and listed a common litany of reasons, ranging from the Israeli occupation to the lack of jobs and the feeling that they have no future for themselves.

Then he fell silent.

"As a father I couldn't bear dealing with this issue," he said. "As a father . . ."

His voice trailed off.

I pointed to Majdi's photo on the wall.

"Why do you keep his photo there?" I asked.

"Because he is my son," Muhammed said.

Beyond the door, children laughed as they frolicked on the stairwell to the apartment building where Muhammed lived with his wife, Intesar.

Muhammed smiled, nodded toward the door and said the laughter came from his grandchildren. He had recently turned sixty-one and still worked as a principal of a local school. His wife was fifty-nine. Most of their ten remaining children had moved out, he said.

I asked about Majdi again. How old would he be?

"Thirty-five," said Muhammed.

"Do people in al-Fawwar still talk about him?" I asked.

Muhammed shook his head from side to side.

"Not very much," he said. "Things like that go into oblivion."

━ ⁀

A year later, I drove into the Connecticut hills, west of Hartford. It was now August 2013. If she had lived, Sara would be preparing for her fortieth birthday party.

I knocked on the door of Len and Vicki Eisenfeld's house. Arline Duker arrived a few minutes later with her youngest daughter, Ariella, and a new puppy.

Len, Vicki, and Arline were grandparents now. The Eisenfelds still lived in West Hartford, and Arline had stayed in Teaneck and had remarried. But the two families—as Len predicted in the days after Sara and Matt had been killed—had become one. Both purchased vacation homes in the same Rhode Island beach community and often celebrated holidays together.

They had not given up on their pursuit of Iran, however. After agreeing to take only a fraction of what Judge Lamberth awarded them, the Dukers and Eisenfelds, along with the Flatow family decided to take their case to courts in other nations where Iran had substantial investments. Their first test was an Italian court. But no settlement—or final judgment—had been rendered. In June 2014 the US Justice Department, along with the Manhattan district attorney, credited Flatow's research into Iranian holdings with helping them expose illegal money transfers by Iran through several large banks, including France's BNP Paribas, which pleaded guilty and paid an $8.9 billion penalty.

Steve Perles and Tom Fay were now pursuing other terrorism cases, most notably a lawsuit on behalf of some of the families of the 220 Marines, eighteen sailors, and three Army soldiers killed in the 1983 bombing of their compound in Beirut by Iranian-supported Hezbollah militants. Perles and Fay had already won their case before Judge Royce Lamberth in Washington. But as with the other cases involving the Flatows, Dukers, and Eisenfelds, the major concern was how to collect money from Iran.

A few weeks before I met with Len, Vicki, and Arline, I sat in a courtroom in Manhattan's federal court, as Perles, Fay, and other attorneys argued with a judge about possibly collecting a substantial portion of the judgment from an Iranian investment account they had recently discovered. But with the case already almost ten years old, no ruling was expected soon.

Officially, the Department of Justice still maintains that it is weighing a possible criminal indictment—and extradition—of Hassan Salameh for killing US citizens. But internal memos circulated within the Justice Department told a different story. From almost the day FBI agents and prosecutors checked into the American Colony Hotel, they harbored major doubts that they could gain a conviction of Salameh in a US court, under American rules of evidence. The Justice Department team eventually decided not to prosecute Salameh. Among other concerns, they worried that Salameh's confession to his Israeli handlers had been coerced. And while no evidence existed that Salameh was, in fact, forced to confess, the US prosecutors feared that they would not be able to successfully deflect challenges from defense lawyers that Salameh was subjected to harsh treatment. The only legal recourse for American families was the civil lawsuits similar to those filed by the Flatows, Dukers, and Eisenfelds.

In Washington, Judge Lamberth, who had been promoted to the chief judge of the US District Court, decided to retire to senior status, handling a far lighter caseload. But when I visited with him at his office one afternoon, he conceded that he still worried about the ultimate effectiveness of the rulings he made in cases with the Flatows, Dukers, Eisenfelds, and other families. Lamberth said he was surprised that the families received any money—even the smaller amounts they agreed to take. "I'm not comfortable that the courts are the best place to do this kind of thing," he told me. "I'm still saying that twenty years later."

As for Iran, Lamberth wondered if any amount of money would cause it to renounce terrorism. He mentioned the Beirut Marines case and his decision in 2012, ordering Iran to pay more than $2 billion in damages to victims. "A billion dollars to Iran is a drop in the bucket," Lamberth said. "What is that, two days' oil? It's not going to deter their conduct."

He shook his head.

"I'm still as frustrated at that as I was at the time of the Flatow case," he said. "How do you actually deter their conduct?"

Like Judge Lamberth, Stuart Eizenstat also worried about the legacy of the terrorism cases. After the Flatows, Dukers, and Eisenfelds had been compensated, other US families who had lost relatives to terrorism complained. Why had they been left out of a piece of legislation that had been narrowly defined to compensate the Flatows, Dukers, Eisenfelds, and several others, including journalist Terry Anderson, who had been held hostage in Lebanon?

The question still seemed to haunt Eizenstat when we spoke. Even the family of Ira Weinstein, a dual Israel-US citizen who later died of burns suffered in the same bus bombing that killed Sara and Matt, had been left out. The Weinsteins filed their lawsuit too late to be included in the original compensation legislation sponsored by Senators Frank Lautenberg and Connie Mack. Lautenberg left the Senate, but returned after another New Jersey senator, Robert Torricelli, was forced to resign amid an ethics investigation. One of Lautenberg's first efforts was to introduce legislation to broaden the compensation for terrorist victims. But in spite of a compensation plan for relatives of those killed in the 9/11 attacks, the federal government was not able to agree on an all-encompassing strategy to compensate all other victims of terrorism.

Like Lautenberg, Eizenstat also decided to take up the issue again. After he left his last post at the Treasury Department and joined a law firm, he offered to help find compensation for the Weinstein family after Judge Lamberth ruled in 2002 that Iran should pay $160 million in damages. To date, the Weinsteins have collected only a fraction of the award.

The same was true of Leah Stein Mousa. Another federal judge ruled in 2001 that Iran owed her $132 million in pain and suffering for her injuries. She collected several hundred thousand, her attorney said.

When I visited with her at her Jerusalem apartment in 2012, Mousa still suffered from damage to her eyes and hearing and had trouble walking. She died a year later. Her friend Phyllis Rosenbaum told me that Leah had never recovered from the emotional and physical pain of the bombing of the Number 18 bus on Jaffa Road.

The Flatows, Dukers, and Eisenfelds, meanwhile, were led to believe that they had been paid with Iranian funds. But that does not seem to be the case. Even though they had received checks from the US Treasury, the Flatows, Dukers, and Eisenfelds had been told that an equivalent amount of money would be taken from the frozen Iranian account for military sales and used to repay the US Treasury.

The $400 million Iranian fund had not been tapped, however. A spokesman for the US Treasury told me that the equivalent of a lien had been placed on the Iranian fund—to be negotiated at some point in the future. As this book is published, those negotiations had not taken place.

For many families, however, no amount of compensation could ever erase the pain of their losses. To them, terrorism was still as personal as a funeral. And on a breezy evening in August 2013, Arline, Len, and Vicki decided to take another step in that personal journey. They paid a visit to the side-by-side graves of Sara and Matt.

Arline still worked as a psychologist in Teaneck. Len continued to practice medicine and care for sick children. Vicki still designed jewelry. To see them without knowing their backstory, you might think they were just three friends who had reached a satisfying and successful place in their lives. They laughed easily at their jokes and mentioned grandchildren and trips they planned to take. But the deaths of Sara and Matt—and the long fight through the courts and with the various political figures in Washington—had clearly changed them.

Several years earlier, after I had spoken to Hassan Salameh at Eshel Prison, I contacted each of them. I wanted them to know that I had met the man who murdered their children.

"What did you make of him?" Arline asked, as we sat in her therapist's office one afternoon.

I paused and drew a breath.

"I'm sorry, but he has no regrets," I said.

Arline leaned forward in her chair. She gazed at the floor for a few seconds, then looked up.

"The most disturbing thing is not about Hassan Salameh," she said. "It's this belief system that is tied to religious fanaticism."

Before calling Len and Vicki, I telephoned Stephen Flatow. He said he was not surprised by Salameh's lack of remorse. Alisa's killers had also never said they felt any sorrow. "If he gives up on that belief, if he weakens, he has to confront what he did," Flatow said.

On the phone with me, Len echoed Stephen Flatow's feelings. "We're not surprised," Len said. "This is a long-term effort on how we address terror and this different mindset. Hassan Salameh symbolized that."

Vicki listened to Len on another telephone extension at their home. After several minutes, she joined in.

Salameh's intransigence was upsetting, she said. "It's difficult to think that we can't reason or debate."

In the car now, on the ride to the cemetery, no one mentioned Salameh. There was no need. Len had offered to drive. Vicki, Arline, and Ariella sat in the back.

Len turned at a light and steered the car on to a narrow road that led through a grove of oaks and maples. Everyone fell silent. It was after 6 p.m. The August sun, already starting to sink into the western Connecticut hills, left wide pools of shadows under the leafy trees.

Len parked and we got out and walked up a gentle slope to a headstone that simply said: DUKER EISENFELD.

Arline laid a rock atop the headstone—a traditional Jewish custom. Len and Vicki followed suit.

Someone mentioned that Sara would have turned forty in a few days. Everyone nodded. A breeze kicked up and brushed the leaves in a nearby maple.

Arline, Len, and Vicki stood for a moment in front of the headstone and the side-by-side resting places of the daughter and son they once thought would marry.

"I wonder what they would have become," said Arline.

Her voice fell off, then she added:

"We'll never know."

—❧—

Several weeks later, just after Labor Day 2013, a man from Israel walked into the Jewish Theological Seminary in Manhattan. It had been several decades since he had ventured onto the Columbia University campus as an undergraduate student and explored the nearby Morningside Heights neighborhoods. But Avinoam Sharon, the Israeli military officer who prosecuted Hassan Salameh, felt he had finally come home to a calling he had been following for years.

Salameh's trial had been Sharon's last as a military prosecutor. He had no regrets, he said. Indeed, he felt gladdened that the judges had sentenced Salameh to prison rather than giving him the death penalty and, in Salameh's view, a martyr's death.

But after years of working as a military prosecutor, Sharon decided to change careers. After Salameh went to prison, Sharon retired from the Israeli army and enrolled in a program to become a rabbi. After his ordination, he became affiliated with a synagogue. But over time, Sharon felt he wanted to delve deeper into Jewish scriptures and, by 2013, had been awarded a fellowship to pursue a doctorate at Jewish Theological Seminary.

As he entered through the main doors of the seminary, Sharon was told that new doctoral students would be meeting in a downstairs study hall—a *beit midrash*—for an orientation to the campus and to the neighborhood. Sharon walked down a flight of stairs, then opened a door. He stepped into a foyer, looked up and noticed a large plaque on the wall.

The plaque said the study hall had been dedicated to the memory of Sara and Matt and carried this inscription: STUDY IS GREAT FOR IT LEADS TO ACTION.

Sharon stopped. He remembered the names all too well—especially the story of how Sara and Matt planned to marry and were merely taking a short vacation to the ruins of Petra when the bus exploded on Jaffa Road.

After a few seconds, he turned and walked into the study hall and took a seat.

A seminary administrator gave a short talk about the school and what the students could expect in the years ahead. When he finished, the administrator asked the students to introduce themselves to the group.

"Then it hit me," Sharon said.

Not only was he sitting in a room dedicated to the memory of Sara and Matt, but it was the same room where Sara and Matt had studied the Jewish scriptures and attended prayer meetings when they were alive and young students. Now, Sharon thought, he was studying Talmud—the same course of study that Matt intended to pursue.

When it was his turn, Sharon explained that he had served in the Israeli army as a criminal prosecutor for many years. Then he mentioned the names of Sara and Matt, and how he noticed as he walked through the door that the room had been dedicated to their memory. Most of the students knew that Sara and Matt died in a terrorist attack in Israel years before. But few knew all the details.

Sharon looked around the room. Many of the students were far younger. They were probably small children when Sara and Matt were killed. Finally, he said: "I was the military prosecutor who prosecuted the murderer of Sara and Matt."

The room fell silent. But Sharon did not feel out of place or uneasy about the piece of his past he had revealed. He had tried to leave his previous identity behind when he left the army. But now he understood that his previous career had led him to his new life as a rabbi. Equally important, it had led him to this new place to study the Talmud.

Months later, I met Avinoam Sharon at the seminary. It was March 2014, and Sharon was well into his doctoral studies.

"I just came from a Greek class," he said, as he walked up Broadway and shook my hand by the seminary entrance, not far from where the homeless woman, Annie, was befriended by Sara and Matt and encouraged to knit yarmulkes for the students. Sharon showed me to a doorway and we descended the stairs to the study hall dedicated to Sara and Matt.

We walked past the plaque with Matt's and Sara's names and opened a door to a room lined with bookshelves filled with volumes of the Talmud and a wide variety of other scriptural texts. Students chatted amiably at several tables as they discussed various Talmud passages. A young man with a beard perused a stack of books. Across the room, a large binder of writings by Sara and Matt sat on a shelf.

Sharon sat down at an empty table. His eyes darted from the tables with the students, then to the shelves of books, then back to the tables. He told me he had recently decided on a topic in the Talmud for his doctoral dissertation.

He smiled. Suddenly, a thought came to him. Death prevented Matt Eisenfeld from becoming a Talmud scholar. And death prevented Sara Duker from pursing her faith as a Jewish woman. But, here, was Avinoam Sharon, studying the Talmud in the room dedicated to Sara and Matt—the former prosecutor-turned-rabbi who argued all those years before in a military courtroom for some measure of imperfect justice and punishment for their killer who felt no remorse.

Sharon felt proud to be a rabbi—proud to be sitting in the same room where Sara and Matt had once studied and prayed. When he left his military career years ago to become a rabbi, he said he had no idea he would again connect with his most famous case in such a personal way.

Sharon stood up. He led me into the hallway and stopped again by the plaque with Sara's and Matt's names.

We studied the names for a second or two. Then Sharon turned to me.

"It's come full circle," he said.

# NOTE ON SOURCES

A BOMB EXPLODES IN ANOTHER PART OF THE WORLD AND FAMILIES ARE changed forever. But the ripples do not stop there. Others are changed too.

I began this journey as a newspaper columnist, when I knocked on the door of Sara Duker's home in Teaneck, New Jersey, the town I call home. It was February 1996. The news was filled with the sorrowful story that Sara had been killed with her boyfriend, Matthew Eisenfeld, and twenty-four others in a suicide bombing aboard a bus in Jerusalem. Amid the omnipresent pressure of a newspaper deadline, I stumbled through a conversation with Sara's broken-hearted family that day, then returned to the newsroom and my computer keyboard, hoping to offer some insight into what the loss of Sara meant. Ten years passed and I returned to the story. On assignment for my newspaper in Israel, I looked into the eyes of the man who built the bomb that took Sara's life and also recruited the young man who killed himself while detonating it in the hope of finding spiritual paradise. Five more years passed, and I decided to return to these events again—this time to explore, with this book, how such a horrific act took place and how a group of brave families tried to find some measure of justice amid the complicated landscape of politics, international diplomacy, and the numbing reality of continuing terrorism in so many corners of the world. As my research deepened, however, I found myself returning to that moment when I first knocked on the door to Sara's home. This story drew me back to Israel several more times, to the West Bank and to the Gaza Strip and, on numerous occasions, to Washington, DC. In the end, though, I found that terrorism is always personal. Bombs are detonated in the name of God or politics—or both. But innocent people inevitably suffer. And the hole left in the lives of their families, friends, and colleagues is deep, eternal, and unfathomable. As Arline Duker told Judge Lamberth when she took the witness stand, "There is this child of mine who isn't here and never will be." On every step of this journey, I tried to remember that.

I could have selected any number of terrorist attacks to study, not just in Israel but elsewhere. I chose this story and the search by these families for accountability because I found it to be remarkably emblematic of what terrorism has done to the world and to the lives of ordinary people.

To tell this story, I decided to chronicle the journeys of three American families—the Dukers, the Eisenfelds, and the Flatows. Their specific experiences do not mirror every victim's—and not even every victim of Middle East terrorism. But the pain they endured and their desire for answers embraces a basic desire—indeed, a fundamental need—that is universal. Why did this happen? Who did it?

Research included more than two hundred interviews in the United States, Israel, the West Bank, and the Gaza Strip. Additional research included the transcripts of three trials—two in the United States and another in Israel—as well as more than two thousand pages of documents, memos, and staff reports from the US Congress, the White House and the US Departments of State, Justice, and the Treasury. In addition, the account of the White House's role in efforts to provide compensation to victims of terrorism—and the internal debates within the Clinton administration on this issue—was gleaned from a variety of White House statements and documents, personal accounts of some of the participants, and interviews with a variety of officials and staffers, some of whom asked not to be named.

The portraits of Sara Duker, Matthew Eisenfeld, and Alisa Flatow were drawn from multiple conversations with their families, court transcripts, video depositions by their parents and siblings, letters, diaries, various academic papers that they produced, and interviews with a variety of friends and colleagues in the United States and in Israel. Descriptions of the thoughts of Arline Duker, Vicki and Len Eisenfeld, and Stephen Flatow and their reactions to various events at different times in this story were drawn from extensive interviews with each of them as well as letters they shared with me that expressed some of their sentiments at the time and copies of their speeches, press conferences and transcripts of their testimony in their trials and before several committees of the US Congress.

The description of the bombings on Jaffa Road was based on first-hand accounts by members of Israel's ambulance service, Magen David Adom, and investigators for Israeli's National Police and the Shin Bet counterterrorism agency. My descriptions were enhanced by my review of news video from Israeli television, photographs by police and news agencies, and by a variety of news articles by Israeli, American, British, French, German, Austrailian, and Palestinian media. For documentation of injuries to victims, I relied on records and accounts by Dr. Avi Rivkind, the chief trauma surgeon at Hadassah Ein Kerem Medical Center in Jerusalem, and from autopsy reports complied by Israeli's National Institute of Forensic Medicine and its chief pathologist at the time, Dr. Yehuda Hiss. The description of the bombing in Kfar Darom in which Alisa Flatow was killed was based on court transcripts and police reports. News video on Israeli and US TV, along with newspaper accounts, also provided extensive background on each bombing.

Research on Hassan Salameh's role in the Jaffa Road bombing—and his wider affiliation with other Palestinian militants, including his connection with some of those involved in the Kfar Darom bombing—is based on the transcripts of his declassified interrogations by Israeli authorities, as well as the transcript of his trial, his own interviews with me and with CBS, his writings (which were published by Hamas and obtained and translated by me), and my interviews with the chief judge and prosecutor of Salameh's military trial in Israel, a variety of officials from Israel's counterterror and police agencies, and with the Palestinian Authority's Jibril Rajoub. I also obtained additional information on the suicide bomber of the Jaffa Road bus, Majdi Abu Wardeh, in conversations with his family at the al-Fawwar refugee camp as well as from the transcripts of Hassan Salameh's interrogations and conversations with Israel's National Police and the Shin Bet.

Research on the wider acceptance of suicide bombing among Sunni Muslims was based on a variety of documents from the Islamic Resistance Movement (Hamas) and, in particular, the writings of Sheik Ahmed Yassin, the now-deceased spiritual leader of Hamas. For background on the theology and politics of suicide bombers, I drew on a variety of books that were based on original research, in particular: *The Path to Paradise:*

*The Inner World of Suicide Bombers and their Dispatchers* by Anat Berko; *Manufacturing Human Bombs: The Making of Palestinian Suicide Bombers* by Mohammed M. Hafez; and *Hamas: Politics, Charity and Terrorism in the Service of Jihad* by Matthew Levitt.

Research about the efforts by the Federal Bureau of Investigation and the Department of Justice to seek a criminal indictment against Hassan Salameh and other Palestinians was based on interviews with federal prosecutors and with FBI agents, as well as from internal memos and reports obtained by me.

————

*"It is the scientist's job to deal with the rational. The writer is privileged to go beyond, and prod the mystical elements that God has left beyond our understanding."*

I found those lines by Sara Duker, scrawled on a piece of paper and tucked into the back of one of her diaries. I copied the passage and tacked it to the bulletin board above my desk as I researched and wrote this book, often looking to those words for inspiration and as a stark reminder of the difficulty in fully understanding the impact of terrorism on the lives of ordinary people. As I came to discover, murder in the name of God is not rational. Yet, as I also learned, it is not mystical either. It is born in one of life's darkest places. My guiding wish throughout this project was that the hope-filled lives of Sara, Matthew, and Alisa will shine light into that dark place.

Mike Kelly
April 2014

# Acknowledgments

My wife, Judy, has been the steady guide to me as I researched and wrote this book. She not only offered love, kindness, and a patient ear as I recounted almost every step of this story, but she also volunteered her sharp and graceful eye in reviewing each page. I could not have written this book without her by my side. Likewise, my daughters, Michelle and Anne, always were there with advice, encouragement, and good humor.

Tim Hays was not merely a literary agent; he was a source of inspiration. Every writer should be as lucky as I am to have such an agent. I am deeply grateful for his friendship.

At Globe Pequot Press, Steve Culpepper spotted the significance of this story early on and kept me on track as I told it. He is an editor of exceptional ability, not just in his care of the language and the craft of writing, but in nurturing a writer's ideas. I am also grateful to Globe Pequot's project editor, Meredith Dias, for shepherding this book through its final stages.

Early in the process, Samuel S. Vaughan, the legendary publishing executive and editor of my first book, pushed me to explore more deeply the impact of terrorism on people. Sam died before this book was finished. But his voice still rings true to me as a writer who was briefly blessed by his guiding hand. To know him was one of the great gifts of my life.

The newspaper that I have called home for most of my career, *The (Bergen) Record*, allowed me the freedom to cover terrorism, not only in northern New Jersey but across the world after the 9/11 attacks. I am especially grateful to the Borg family, which has owned *The Record* for almost a century. In a world where many newspapers are retreating, the Borgs are charging ahead with a commitment to first-rate journalism. They represent the best of American journalism.

At *The Record*, I have been blessed to work side by side with a variety of immensely talented colleagues who were always there to inspire me and offer advice. These include: Martin Gottlieb, Diedre Sykes, Tim Nostrand, Dan Sforza, Will Lamb, Lindy Washburn, Peter Grad, Tom Franklin, Jim Wright, Carmine Galasso, Frank Scandale, and Vivian Waixel.

*The Record*'s Jon Naso, James Anness, and Youssef Amre helped to track down photos, as did Nancy Glowinski of Reuters and Mike Piskorski, Stephen Dunn, and Mark Mirko of the *Hartford Courant*.

Steven Perles and Thomas Fortune Fay offered hours of insight into the court cases they shepherded through the US federal courts on behalf of the Flatow, Duker, and Eisenfeld families. Other attorneys who offered observations on these landmark cases and background of the laws on which they were based, include: John Karr, Stuart Newberger, Allan Gerson, and Mark Zaid.

US District Court Judge Royce Lamberth generously offered background on the decisions he wrote in the Flatow and Duker-Eisenfeld cases, as well as others terrorism cases he handled. Judge Lamberth's chief of staff, Sheldon Snook, was a much-needed guidepost as I tracked down court records at the National Archives with the help of Bryant Johnson and Michael Darby.

Stuart Eizenstat scrupulously explained his role in sculpting a compromise between the US Congress and the Clinton Administration. Former US Ambassador to Israel Martin Indyk, brought his sharp eye to history, as did former Middle East envoy Dennis Ross and former Norwegian ambassador and United Nations Middle East specialist, Terje Roed-Larsen, who was one of the chief architects of the Oslo Accords.

At the Department of State, Lisa Grosh, Ron Kleinman, and Ron Bettauer were especially helpful in detailing the legal issues that the Flatow and Duker-Eisenfeld cases posed for US diplomacy. Also, at the State Department, retired foreign service officer Kathleen Riley guided me through her efforts to notify the Duker and Eisenfeld families about the bombing on Jaffa Road.

At the Department of Justice, Jeff Breinholt and Jim Reynolds supplied background on the ill-fated efforts by federal prosecutors to build a criminal prosecution of Hassan Salameh and other Palestinian militants who had been linked to terrorist bombings. Retired FBI counterterrorism chief Harry Brandon and retired FBI special agent Thomas Graney also provided details on Palestinian terrorism and, in particular, the role of Hassan Salameh.

Former National Security Council official Richard Nuccio was among a number of former White House staffers who guided me through the series of political, legal, and military dilemmas facing the Clinton administration after the Jaffa Road bombing and the downing of the Brothers to the Rescue planes by the Cuban Air Force in February 1996.

Former staffers for US Senators Frank Lautenberg, Connie Mack, and Arlen Specter generously offered time and documents in explaining the passage of a variety of laws that led to the Flatow and Duker-Eisenfeld cases. Senator Lautenberg's chief of staff, Dan Katz, was especially helpful, as were Sharon Waxman and Frederic Baron. Senator Mack also contributed his personal insight, along with his former staffer, Gary Shiffman, who provided thousands of pages of documents. The former chief counsel to Senator Specter's subcommittee on terrorism, Richard Hertling, steered me through the difficult clauses of various laws that allowed US families to file lawsuits against foreign terrorists.

In Israel, Major Koby Zrihen of the Israeli National Police walked me through the crime scene of the Jaffa Road bombing. Dr. Yehuda Hiss of the National Institute of Forensic Medicine supplied autopsy records and background on the effect that explosions have on the human body. Dr. Avi Rivkind, the chief trauma surgeon of Hadassah Ein Karem Medical Center also explained the numerous medical issues from terrorist bombings and described in detail how he treated the dead and the wounded after the Jaffa Road bombings and later surgically repaired Hassan Salameh's wounds. Several staffers with Israel's national ambulance service, Madan David Adom, also guided me through the bomb scene. These include Yonatan Yagodovsky, Dr. Eli Jaffe, and David Sofer. Others who generously offered accounts of the bombing and its aftermath include Leah Stein Mousa, Phyllis Rosenbaum, Jeffrey Sosland, and journalists Roni Shaked and Nahum Barnea, whose son, Yonatan, was killed on the same bus with Sara Duker and Matthew Eisenfeld.

Israel's Shin Bet counterterrorism agency steered me through their investigation of the Jaffa Road bombing and their hunt for Hassan

Salameh. Among the former officials who spoke on the record were Ami Ayalon, Avi Dichter, Yisrael Hasson, Reuven Paz, and Barak Ben Zur.

Retired military judge Ilan Katz reviewed the transcripts of the Salameh trial, as did retired prosecutor Avinoam Sharon. Also, in Israel, Avi Gill offered insight into the issues facing Prime Minister Shimon Peres in the wake of the Jaffa Road bombings, as did David Baker and Mark Regev of the staff of Prime Minister Benjamin Netanyahu. Also helpful were staff members of the Israeli consulate in New York City, notably Shani Rozanes and Shahar Azani, as well as the former consul general, Colette Avital. Sivan Weitzman of Israel's prison service patiently answered my questions about Hassan Salameh, as did Emi Palmor of the Ministry of Justice. Lt. Col. Peter Lerner of the Israeli Defence Force helped track down transcripts from Salameh's military trial.

From the Palestinian side, a number of officials, including Jibril Rajoub, offered background on the influence of Hamas, the multiple dilemmas created by Yasser Arafat, and the problems in dealing with the rise in suicide bombings. Others declined to be named because of the volatile nature of Palestinian politics in both the West Bank and in the Gaza Strip.

In writing about Sara, Matthew, and Alisa, I relied heavily on their friends and former colleagues for insight into their personalities and dreams. I am especially grateful to Matthew Berkowitz, Shlomo Tucker, Joyce Raynor, Moshe Benovitz, Abby Sosland, Joshua Cahan, Menachem Schrader, David Hoffman, William Lebeau, Peter Beinart, Nora Selengut Brooke, Elli Saks, Tal Winberger, Devorah Schoenfeld, Avigayl Young, Edward Bernstein, Shai Held, Aharon Oren, Peter Bower, Stephanie Pfirman, Celia Deutsch, Ted Scott, Xiao-Guang Sun, Oshrat Carmiel, Charles Sheer, Ross Felix, Rivkah and Joel Fishman, Ayala Levin-Kruss, Aliza Berger-Cooper, Rahel Jaskow, James Ponet, Francine Sears, Michael Bernstein, Linda Gissen, Chana Henkin, and Simi Peters.

Finally, I owe my deepest gratitude to the Duker, Eisenfeld, and Flatow families—especially to Arline Duker, Leonard and Vicki Eisenfeld, and to Stephen Flatow. Recounting the stories of the deaths of their children was sometimes not easy for them, but each was invariably available to answer the smallest of questions or to supply personal documents and photographs. This book is a tribute to their courage and humanity.

# Index

# About the Author

MIKE KELLY IS AN AWARD-WINNING COLUMNIST AT *The (Bergen) Record* in New Jersey and the author of two previous books: *Color Lines*, a critically acclaimed account of race relations in a small town and *Fresh Jersey*, a collection of his columns. In the wake of the 9/11 attacks, Kelly embarked on a variety of reporting projects to chronicle the impact of terrorism on the lives of ordinary people. His travels have taken him to Iraq, Malaysia, Northern Ireland, Kenya, and Israel, the West Bank, and the Gaza Strip. He is married, the father of two daughters, and lives in Teaneck, New Jersey.